Fifth Edition

NorthStar 4

Reading & Writing

Authors: Andrew K. English
             Laura Monahon English

Series Editors: Frances Boyd
                    Carol Numrich

Dedication

To Connie, Woody, Joan, and Phil

NorthStar: Reading & Writing Level 4, Fifth Edition

Copyright © 2020, 2015, 2009, 2004 by Pearson Education, Inc.
All rights reserved.

No part of this publication may be reproduced, stored in a retrieval system, or transmitted in any form or by any means, electronic, mechanical, photocopying, recording, or otherwise, without the prior permission of the publisher.

Pearson Education, 221 River St, Hoboken, NJ 07030

Staff credits: The people who made up the *NorthStar: Reading & Writing Level 4, Fifth Edition* team, representing content creation, design, manufacturing, marketing, multimedia, project management, publishing, rights management, and testing, are Pietro Alongi, Stephanie Callahan, Gina DiLillo, Tracey Cataldo, Dave Dickey, Warren Fishbach, Sarah Hand, Lucy Hart, Gosia Jaros-White, Stefan Machura, Linda Moser, Dana Pinter, Karen Quinn, Katarzyna Starzynska-Kosciuszko, Paula Van Ells, Claire Van Poperin, Joseph Vella, Peter West, Autumn Westphal, Natalia Zaremba, and Marcin Zimny.

Project consultant: Debbie Sistino
Text composition: ElectraGraphics, Inc.
Development editing: Andrea Bryant
Cover design: Studio Montage

Library of Congress Cataloging-in-Publication Data

A Catalog record for the print edition is available from the Library of Congress.

Printed in the United States of America

ISBN-13: 978-0-13-523264-4 (Student Book with Digital Resources)
ISBN-10: 0-13-523264-3 (Student Book with Digital Resources)

1 2019

ISBN-13: 978-0-13-522698-8 (Student Book with MyEnglishLab Online Workbook and Resources)
ISBN-10: 0-13-522698-8 (Student Book with MyEnglishLab Online Workbook and Resources)

CONTENTS

WELCOME TO NORTHSTAR

A Letter from the Series Editors

We welcome you to the 5th edition of *NorthStar Reading & Writing Level 4*.

Engaging content, integrated skills, and critical thinking continue to be the touchstones of the series. For more than 20 years *NorthStar* has engaged and motivated students through contemporary, authentic topics. Our online component builds on the last edition by offering new and updated activities.

Since its first edition, *NorthStar* has been rigorous in its approach to critical thinking by systematically engaging students in tasks and activities that prepare them to move into high-level academic courses. The cognitive domains of Bloom's taxonomy provide the foundation for the critical thinking activities. Students develop the skills of analysis and evaluation and the ability to synthesize and summarize information from multiple sources. The capstone of each unit, the final writing or speaking task, supports students in the application of all academic, critical thinking, and language skills that are the focus of unit.

The new edition introduces additional academic skills for 21st century success: note-taking and presentation skills. There is also a focus on learning outcomes based on the Global Scale of English (GSE), an emphasis on the application of skills, and a new visual design. These refinements are our response to research in the field of language learning in addition to feedback from educators who have taught from our previous editions.

NorthStar has pioneered and perfected the blending of academic content and academic skills in an English Language series. Read on for a comprehensive overview of this new edition. As you and your students explore *NorthStar*, we wish you a great journey.

Carol Numrich and Frances Boyd, the editors

New for the FIFTH EDITION

New and Updated Themes

The new edition features one new theme per level (i.e., one new unit per book), with updated content and skills throughout the series. Current and thought-provoking topics presented in a variety of genres promote intellectual stimulation. The real-world-inspired content engages students, links them to language use outside the classroom, and encourages personal expression and critical thinking.

Learning Outcomes and Assessments

All unit skills, vocabulary, and grammar points are connected to GSE objectives to ensure effective progression of learning throughout the series. Learning outcomes are present at the opening and closing of each unit to clearly mark what is covered in the unit and encourage both pre- and post-unit self-reflection. A variety of assessment tools, including online diagnostic, formative, and summative assessments and a flexible gradebook aligned with clearly identified unit learning outcomes, allow teachers to individualize instruction and track student progress.

Note-Taking as a Skill in Every Unit

Grounded in the foundations of the Cornell Method of note-taking, the new note-taking practice is structured to allow students to reflect on and organize their notes, focusing on the most important points. Students are instructed, throughout the unit, on the most effective way to apply their notes to a classroom task, as well as encouraged to analyze and reflect on their growing note-taking skills.

Explicit Skill Instruction and Fully-Integrated Practice

Concise presentations and targeted practice in print and online prepare students for academic success. Language skills are highlighted in each unit, providing students with multiple, systematic exposures to language forms and structures in a variety of contexts. Academic and language skills in each unit are applied clearly and deliberately in the culminating writing or presentation task.

Scaffolded Critical Thinking

Activities within the unit are structured to follow the stages of Bloom's taxonomy from *remember* to *create*. The use of APPLY throughout the unit highlights culminating activities that allow students to use the skills being practiced in a free and authentic manner. Sections that are focused on developing critical thinking are marked with 🔍 to highlight their critical focus.

Explicit Focus on the Academic Word List

AWL words are highlighted at the end of the unit and in a master list at the end of the book.

The Pearson Practice English App

The **Pearson Practice English App** allows students on the go to complete vocabulary and grammar activities, listen to audio, and watch video.

ExamView

ExamView Test Generator allows teachers to customize assessments by reordering or editing existing questions, selecting test items from a bank, or writing new questions.

MyEnglishLab

New and revised online supplementary practice maps to the updates in the student book for this edition.

THE NORTHSTAR UNIT

1 FOCUS ON THE TOPIC

Each unit begins with an eye-catching unit opener spread that draws students into the topic. The learning outcomes are written in simple, student-friendly language to allow for self-assessment. Focus on the Topic questions connect to the unit theme and get students to think critically by making inferences and predicting the content of the unit.

Genius: Nature or Nurture?

UNIT 1

LEARNING OUTCOMES

> Understand assumptions
> Take notes by marking important information
> Distinguish voice in quotations

> Use past perfect
> Identify and correct sentence fragments
> Write a summary paragraph

Go to **MyEnglishLab** to check what you know.

1 FOCUS ON THE TOPIC

1. Why are some people geniuses and others are not? Does the environment a person is raised in create a genius (nurture), or was the person simply born that way (nature)?

2. What would it be like to be a genius? Describe the advantages and disadvantages.

2   UNIT 1

Genius: Nature or Nurture?   3

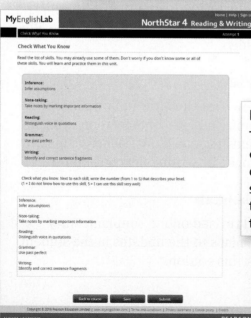

MyEnglishLab
The "Check What You Know" pre-unit diagnostic checklist provides a short self-assessment based on each unit's GSE-aligned learning outcomes to support the students in building an awareness of their own skill levels and to enable teachers to target instruction to their students' specific needs.

2 FOCUS ON READING

A vocabulary exercise introduces words that appear in the readings, encourages students to guess the meanings of the words from context, and connects to the theme presented in the final writing task.

Go to MyEnglishLab lines indicate when additional practice is available online.

Note-taking practice on main ideas and details appears in every unit.

Two contrasting readings on a contemporary topic are presented in every unit and represent a wide range of writing styles.

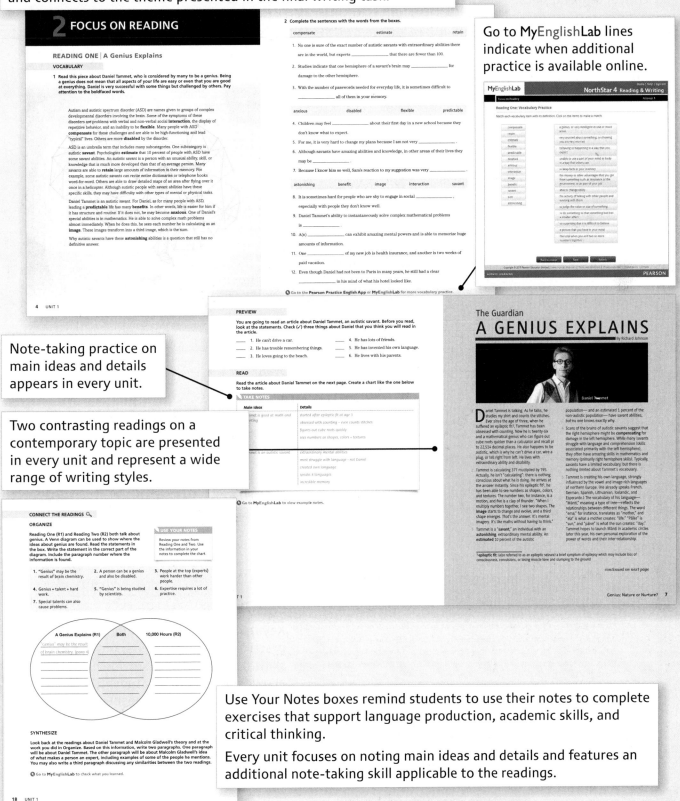

Use Your Notes boxes remind students to use their notes to complete exercises that support language production, academic skills, and critical thinking.

Every unit focuses on noting main ideas and details and features an additional note-taking skill applicable to the readings.

EXPLICIT SKILL INSTRUCTION AND PRACTICE

Step-by-step instructions and practice guide students to move beyond the literal meaning of the text. 🔍 highlights activities that help build critical thinking skills.

MAKE INFERENCES 🔍

Understanding Assumptions

An **inference** is an **educated guess** about something that is **not directly stated** in a text. *A Genius Explains* includes quotes from Daniel Tammet and Kim Peek that show what others might assume about the two men's disabilities. What assumptions can you infer from these quotations?

Look at the example and read the assumption and the explanation.

> "I just wanted to show people that disability needn't get in the way." (*paragraph 6*)

Assumption: People think that someone with a disability cannot do as much as someone without a disability.

Some people assumed that Daniel's disability would cause him to have problems in other areas of his life. By showing people that he could achieve remarkable things, even though he was "technically disabled," Daniel wanted to show that their assumptions were wrong. His disability wasn't going to hold him back.

1 Read the quotes from Daniel and Kim. Complete the sentences with assumptions that people have made about them.

   1. Daniel: "It was also the first time I was introduced as 'Daniel' rather than 'the guy who can do weird stuff in his head.'" (*paragraph 18*)

      Others didn't think that Daniel was _____

   2. Kim: "You don't have to be handicapped to be different—everybody's different." (*paragraph 11*)

   _____ friends." (*paragraph 19*)

   _____ thing that I do. I really feel that there is an _____." (*paragraph 19*) relationship to numbers _____

   _____ and in my own style, so an office with targets and _____ (*h 8*)

   _____ out sentences, words, or phrases that helped

MyEnglishLab

NorthStar 4 Reading & Writing

Home | Help | Sign out

Focus on Reading

Attempt **1**

Reading Practice: Distinguishing Voice in Quotations

Read the news article below about savant Stephen Wiltshire. The quotations are missing. Put the numbers corresponding to the quotations where they belong to add validity, to provide details or examples, or to continue the story in another voice for interest.

1. "I'm going to live in New York [some day]. I've designed my penthouse on Park Avenue."

2. "He is possibly the best child artist in Britain."

3. "These drawings testify to an assured draughtsmanship and an ability to convey complex perspective with consummate ease. But more importantly, they reveal his mysterious creative ability to capture the sensibility of a building and that which determines its character and its voice. It is this genius which sets him apart and confers upon him the status of artist. For a child who was once locked within the prison house of his own private world, unable to speak, incapable of responding to others, this thrilling development of language, laughter, and art is a miracle."

4. "I noticed early on that Stephen wasn't speaking other than random sounds. At the playground he would sit in the dirt while the other toddlers ran around."

5. "Young Stephen was an exceptional drawer even at five years old. He was able to accurately sketch animals, cars, and architectural drawings of imaginary cityscapes."

Stephen Wiltshire was born in London, England in 1974. At age three, his parents noticed developmental dela...

He was then diagnosed with autism. His parents quickly enrolled him in the Queensmill School in London. It ... there that one of his teachers noticed his affinity and talent for art. [ ] At age ten, he used his expertise to ... *The London Alphabet*. It is a collection of drawings depicting famous London landmarks in alphabet order. A... result, he began to emerge as a renowned artist and savant. Hugh Casson, a former president of London's R... Academy of Arts, noted his talents. [ ] Wiltshire's first trip abroad was to New York. Wiltshire had always dr... of New York and its famed skyscrapers. [ ] While in New York, he sketched the famous skyline. At sixteen, ... the floating cities of Europe with writer Oliver Sacks who he met in New York. Wiltshire's drawings were so impressive that they were compiled into a book, *Floating Cities*. Oliver Sacks wrote the forward highlighting Wiltshire's great talent. [ ] Wiltshire has gone on to publish several other texts with his drawings. He has also ventured into the world of music, having a perfect pitch. Stephen Wiltshire is just one more example of how savants transform our world.

Back to course   Save   Submit

MyEnglishLab

Key reading skills are reinforced and practiced in new contexts. Autograded skills-based activities provide instant scores, allowing teachers and students to identify where improvement is needed.

3 FOCUS ON WRITING

Productive vocabulary targeted in the unit is reviewed, expanded upon, and used creatively.

Grammar presentations focus on skills that are used in the readings and applied in the final writing task. A concise grammar skills box serves as a reference point for students throughout the unit and beyond.

MyEnglishLab
Auto-graded vocabulary and grammar practice activities reinforce meaning, form, and function. Meaningful and instant feedback guides students to self-correct and provides students and teachers with essential information to monitor progress.

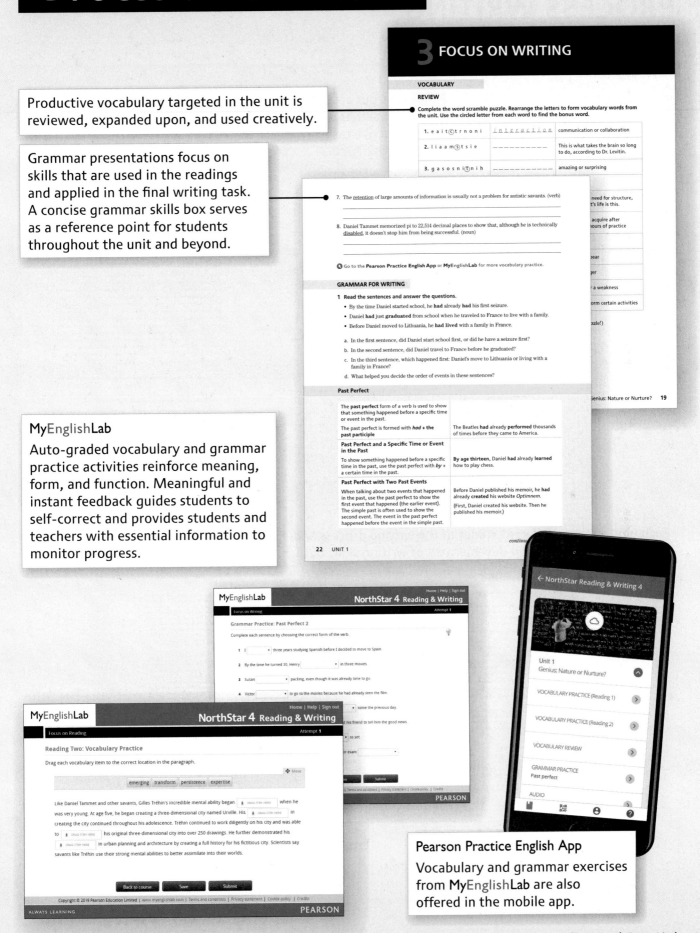

3 FOCUS ON WRITING

VOCABULARY

REVIEW

Complete the word scramble puzzle. Rearrange the letters to form vocabulary words from the unit. Use the circled letter from each word to find the bonus word.

1. e a i t ⓒ t r n o n i	i n t e r a c t i o n	communication or collaboration
2. l i a a m ⓢ t s i e	_ _ _ _ _ _ _ _ _ _	This is what takes the brain so long to do, according to Dr. Levitin.
3. g a s o s n i ⓣ n i h	_ _ _ _ _ _ _ _ _	amazing or surprising

7. The retention of large amounts of information is usually not a problem for autistic savants. (verb)

_____

8. Daniel Tammet memorized pi to 22,514 decimal places to show that, although he is technically disabled, it doesn't stop him from being successful. (noun)

_____

🔊 Go to the **Pearson Practice English App** or **MyEnglishLab** for more vocabulary practice.

GRAMMAR FOR WRITING

1 Read the sentences and answer the questions.
- By the time Daniel started school, he **had** already **had** his first seizure.
- Daniel **had** just **graduated** from school when he traveled to France to live with a family.
- Before Daniel moved to Lithuania, he **had lived** with a family in France.

a. In the first sentence, did Daniel start school first, or did he have a seizure first?
b. In the second sentence, did Daniel travel to France before he graduated?
c. In the third sentence, which happened first: Daniel's move to Lithuania or living with a family in France?
d. What helped you decide the order of events in these sentences?

Past Perfect

The **past perfect** form of a verb is used to show that something happened before a specific time or event in the past.	
The past perfect is formed with *had* + the **past participle**	The Beatles **had** already **performed** thousands of times before they came to America.
Past Perfect and a Specific Time or Event in the Past	
To show something happened before a specific time in the past, use the past perfect with *by* + a certain time in the past.	**By age thirteen,** Daniel **had** already **learned** how to play chess.
Past Perfect with Two Past Events	
When talking about two events that happened in the past, use the past perfect to show the first event that happened (the earlier event). The simple past is often used to show the second event. The event in the past perfect happened before the event in the simple past.	Before Daniel published his memoir, he **had** already **created** his website *Optimnem*. (First, Daniel created his website. Then he published his memoir.)

continu...

22   UNIT 1

Genius: Nature or Nurture?   19

MyEnglishLab — NorthStar 4 Reading & Writing

Home | Help | Sign out

Focus on Writing   Attempt 1

Grammar Practice: Past Perfect 2

Complete each sentence by choosing the correct form of the verb.

1   I [____] three years studying Spanish before I decided to move to Spain.
2   By the time he turned 30, Henry [____] in three movies.
3   Susan [____] packing, even though it was already time to go
4   Victor [____] to go to the movies because he had already seen the film

MyEnglishLab — NorthStar 4 Reading & Writing

Home | Help | Sign out

Focus on Reading   Attempt 1

Reading Two: Vocabulary Practice

Drag each vocabulary item to the correct location in the paragraph.

➕ Move

| emerging | transform | persistence | expertise |

Like Daniel Tammet and other savants, Gilles Tréhin's incredible mental ability began [DRAG ITEM HERE] when he was very young. At age five, he began creating a three-dimensional city named Urville. His [DRAG ITEM HERE] in creating the city continued throughout his adolescence. Tréhin continued to work diligently on his city and was able to [DRAG ITEM HERE] his original three-dimensional city into over 250 drawings. He further demonstrated his [DRAG ITEM HERE] in urban planning and architecture by creating a full history for his fictitious city. Scientists say savants like Tréhin use their strong mental abilities to better assimilate into their worlds.

Back to course   Save   Submit

Copyright © 2019 Pearson Education Limited | www.myenglishlab.com | Terms and conditions | Privacy statement | Cookie policy | Credits

ALWAYS LEARNING   PEARSON

← NorthStar Reading & Writing 4

Unit 1
Genius: Nature or Nurture?

VOCABULARY PRACTICE (Reading 1) >
VOCABULARY PRACTICE (Reading 2) >
VOCABULARY REVIEW >
GRAMMAR PRACTICE
Past perfect >
AUDIO

Pearson Practice English App
Vocabulary and grammar exercises from MyEnglishLab are also offered in the mobile app.

A TASK-BASED APPROACH TO PROCESS WRITING

APPLY calls out activities that get students to use new skills in a productive task.

A final writing task gives students an opportunity to integrate ideas, vocabulary, and grammar presented in the unit.

Each unit presents different stages of the writing process and encourages the structured development of writing skills both practical and academic.

FINAL WRITING TASK: A Summary Paragraph 🔍 APPLY

In this unit, you read about different geniuses and how they achieved their expertise.

You are going to *write a summary paragraph about a genius. This person can be alive now or from the past. Be sure to include why this person is considered a genius and how he or she achieved expertise.*

For an alternative writing topic, see page 31.

PREPARE TO WRITE: Group Brainstorming

Group brainstorming is a good way to get ideas for writing. In brainstorming, you think of as many ideas as you can. Don't think about whether the ideas are good or bad. Just write down all ideas.

1 Work in a small group. Brainstorm a list of geniuses. The person can be from any time period or culture. Don't stop to discuss the genius. Focus on thinking of as many examples as possible.

1. _____ 6. _____
2. _____ 7. _____
3. _____ 8. _____
4. _____ 9. _____
5. _____ 10. _____

2 Now work individually. Choose one genius that you find interesting and want to write about. Research this person to find information about his or her life and achievements. Be sure to include why this person is considered a genius and how he or she achieved expertise. Take notes about what you find out. Make sure the notes are in your own words and not copied word-for-word.

WRITE

Writing a Summary Paragraph

A **paragraph** is a group of sentences that are related and deal with a single topic. A **summary paragraph** identifies and extracts the main idea from a text, leaving out less important details. All summary paragraphs have a **topic sentence** with a **controlling idea**.

The **topic sentence** is an essential part of all well-written paragraphs. The topic sentence controls the content of the rest of the paragraph. This control helps the writer focus on supporting ideas in the paragraph that are directly related to the topic sentence. The first step in writing a topic sentence is to choose a topic and find a point of view or **main idea** about it.

Topics	Main Idea
Mozart	Mozart is considered a prodigy.
Autistic savants	Autistic savants have specific abilities or skills.
Malcolm Gladwell	Malcolm Gladwell has written a fascinating book.

continued on next page

26 UNIT 1

The next step is to narrow the main idea even more by finding a **controlling idea**. The controlling idea is the idea you want to explain, illustrate, or describe in the paragraph. It makes a specific statement about a topic. The controlling ideas in the topic sentences below are underlined.

Main Idea	Main Idea + Controlling Idea = Topic Sentence
Mozart is considered a prodigy.	Mozart is considered a prodigy because he achieved huge musical accomplishments at a very young age.
Autistic savants have specific abilities or skills.	Although autistic savants may have specific abilities or skills, they may have other limitations, especially problems with social interactions.
Malcolm Gladwell has written a fascinating book.	Malcolm Gladwell has written a fascinating book, which emphasizes the importance of hard work.

1 Read this paragraph about autistic savants. Then answer the questions.

> Autistic savants have specific abilities or skills, but they are not without certain limitations in other areas of life. An autistic savant is a person with an unusual ability, skill, or knowledge that is much more developed than that of an average person. In fact, many savants have highly developed mathematical skills. Others are able to retain large amounts of information in their memory. For example, some autistic savants can recite entire dictionaries or telephone books word-for-word. Still others are able to draw detailed maps of an area after flying over it once in a helicopter. Despite the fact that the autistic savant has these specific abilities or skills, he or she may have difficulties with other types of mental or physical tasks and social interactions. For instance, some savants may have trouble doing simple tasks, such as tying their shoes or driving a car. Additionally, an autistic savant may have problems talking to people or even making eye contact. So, despite their advanced skills and abilities in certain areas, savants may encounter difficulty with seemingly simple tasks.

1. What is the topic of this paragraph? _____

2. The first sentence is the topic sentence. What two ideas are presented in this sentence? _____

3. How does the content of the rest of the paragraph relate to the topic sentence? _____

Genius: Nature or Nurture? 27

---

2 Each paragraph is missing a topic sentence. Choose the topic sentence that best fits the paragraph.

1. Daniel suffered an epileptic seizure when he was very young, which may be the cause of his savant abilities. Soon after, when he was four, his mother gave him a counting book, and his love of mathematics was born. From an early age, he has been able to solve complicated mathematical problems in his head. Recently, he has been able to memorize pi to 22,514 digits.

   a. Daniel Tammet is very good at math and has a great memory.
   b. Daniel Tammet is an autistic savant with exceptional memory and mathematical abilities.
   c. Daniel Tammet is an autistic savant who loves solving mathematical problems.

2. What Levitin has found is that it appears that 10,000 hours of practice are required to reach world-class expertise in any field. In fact, he has found no world-class expert who has not put in at least that many hours of preparation. He believes that this is because it takes that much time for the brain to assimilate everything necessary to reach this level of expert.

   a. Daniel Levitin, a neurologist, has extensively studied what is needed to reach success.
   b. Reaching world-class expertise requires a lot of time and practice.
   c. Daniel Levitin believes that it takes the brain a long time to assimilate the information necessary to be an expert.

3. Parents create these hothouse kids because they are attempting to create a "genius." They may begin by playing classical music for the hothouse child when he or she is still in the crib. The parents start working with their children on math and language skills at an early age, using flashcards. They also enroll their children in music and dance lessons, often as early as age three or four. In addition, they try to get their kids into the most academically challenging preschools.

   a. Hothouse kids learn math and music at an early age.
   b. Parents take a variety of approaches to ensure that their kids become geniuses and can get into the best preschools.
   c. "Hothouse kids" is a term used to define children whose parents push them to learn more quickly and earlier than a "typical" child by providing a rich educational environment.

3 Read the paragraphs. The underlined topic sentences are incomplete because they do not have a controlling idea. Rewrite each topic sentence to include both a topic and a controlling idea.

1. Wolfgang Amadeus Mozart was a genius. For one thing, Mozart was a child prodigy who was playing the violin and piano by age four and composing by age six. Another reason that he is considered a genius is that he was able to create more than 600 compositions—including symphonies, chamber music, sonatas, and choral music—in his thirty-four-year lifetime. Additionally, he is said to have been able to compose entire symphonies in his head. He could imagine the sounds of all the different instruments without using a piano to help him compose. He was not only the best pianist of his day in Europe but also one of the top three or four violinists.

_____

28 UNIT 1

---

2. Scientists debate the importance of nature versus nurture. In other words, the debate of nature versus nurture asks the question: "What part does nature—the genetic information that you have inherited from your parents—play in your development? And, conversely, what part does environment—what you eat, where you went to school, how your parents raised you—play?" In an effort to understand the importance of each of these factors, there have been many studies using twins who were separated at birth. While these studies are not conclusive, there were instances where the separated twins had developed in a remarkably similar manner. Nevertheless, the reasons for this may also have to do with environment (nurture). Even though they were raised by different families, the environments could have been quite similar.

_____

3. Malcolm Gladwell is a talented author. His book *Outliers* was published in 2008 and was number one on the *New York Times* bestseller list for eleven straight weeks. It followed *The Tipping Point*, which was published in 2000. *The Tipping Point* addresses the individual's ability to change society. This non-fiction bestseller was followed by *Blink* in 2005. *Blink* is about thinking. Why are some people able to make brilliant decisions in the blink of an eye while others seem to always make the wrong decision? *Blink* also was a non-fiction bestseller.

_____

4 Use your outline and your notes from Prepare to Write on page 26 and Organize on page 18 to write the first draft of your summary paragraph. Make an organizer to help you plan your ideas.

- Make sure to include a clear topic sentence and content that supports it.
- Write a topic sentence that introduces the genius that you are going to write about and includes a controlling idea.
- Use the past perfect and time words to show the correct order of events.

REVISE: Identifying and Correcting Sentence Fragments

1 Choose the correct sentence.

   a. When Mozart, who was a child prodigy, wrote his first composition for piano.
   b. Before he went to Lithuania, Daniel Tammet had started to study the language.
   c. Malcolm Gladwell who wrote the book *Outliers*.

Genius: Nature or Nurture? 29

Students continue through the writing process to learn revision techniques that help them move toward coherence and unity in their writing. Finally, students edit their work with the aid of a checklist that focuses on essential outcomes.

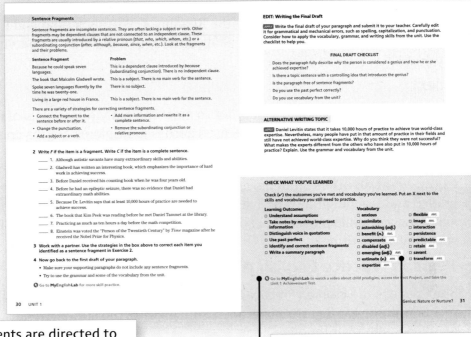

At the end of the unit, students are directed to MyEnglishLab to watch a video connected to the theme, access the Unit Project, and take the Unit Achievement Test.

Academic Word List words are highlighted with **AWL** at the end of the unit.

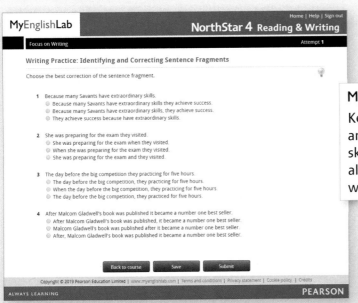

MyEnglishLab
Key writing skills and strategies are reinforced and practiced in new contexts. Autograded skills-based activities provide instant scores, allowing teachers and students to identify where improvement is needed.

COMPONENTS

Students can access the following resources on the Pearson English Portal.

- **Classroom Audio and Videos**

  Classroom audio (the readings for the Reading & Writing strand and the listenings and exercises with audio for the Listening & Speaking strand) and the end-of-unit videos are available on the portal.

- **Etext**

  Offering maximum flexibility in order to meet the individual needs of each student, the digital version of the student book can be used across multiple platforms and devices.

- **MyEnglishLab**

  MyEnglishLab offers students access to additional practice online in the form of both auto-graded and teacher-graded activities. Auto-graded activities support and build on the academic and language skills presented and practiced in the student book. Teacher-graded activities include speaking and writing.

- **Pearson Practice English App**

  Students use the **Pearson Practice English App** to access additional grammar and vocabulary practice, audio for the listenings and readings from the student books, and the end-of-unit videos on the go with their mobile phone.

INNOVATIVE TEACHING TOOLS

With instant access to a wide range of online content and diagnostic tools, teachers can customize learning environments to meet the needs of every student. Digital resources, all available on the Pearson English Portal, include **MyEnglishLab** and ExamView.

Using **MyEnglishLab**, *NorthStar* teachers can

Deliver rich online content to engage and motivate students, including

- student audio to support listening and speaking skills, in addition to audio versions of all readings.
- engaging, authentic video clips tied to the unit themes.
- opportunities for written and recorded reactions to be submitted by students.

Use diagnostic reports to

- view student scores by unit, skill, and activity.
- monitor student progress on any activity or test as often as needed.
- analyze class data to determine steps for remediation and support.

Access Teacher Resources, including

- unit teaching notes and answer keys.
- downloadable diagnostic, achievement and placement tests, as well as unit checkpoints.
- printable resources including lesson planners, videoscripts, and video activities.
- classroom audio.

Using **ExamView**, teachers can customize Achievement Tests by

- reordering test questions.
- editing questions.
- selecting questions from a bank.
- writing their own questions.

SCOPE AND SEQUENCE

	1 Genius: Nature or Nurture? Pages: 2–31 Reading 1: A Genius Explains Reading 2: 10,000 Hours to Mastery	**2 Facing Life's Obstacles** Pages: 32–59 Reading 1: A Life of Twists and Turns: The Story of Frank McCourt Reading 2: Marla Runyan Has Never Lost Sight of Her Goals
Inference	Understanding assumptions	Inferring the meaning of idioms and expressions
Note-Taking	Taking notes by marking important information	Taking notes on main ideas with questions
Reading	Distinguishing voice in quotations	Recognizing positive redundancy
Grammar	Past perfect	Gerunds and infinitives
Revise	Identifying and correcting sentence fragments	Choosing appropriate supporting sentences
Final Writing Task	A summary paragraph	A biographical paragraph
Video	Child prodigies	A girl with autism

Assessments	Pre-Unit Diagnostic:
	   Check What You Know
	Checkpoint 1
	Checkpoint 2
	Unit Achievement Test
		Pre-Unit Diagnostic:
		   Check What You Know
		Checkpoint 1
		Checkpoint 2
		Unit Achievement Test

Unit Project	Write a report on a genius	Write a biographical essay on a famous person who has overcome an obstacle

3 Making Medical Decisions	4 Instinct or Intellect?
Pages: 60–85 Reading 1: Genetic Testing and Disease: Would You Want to Know? Reading 2: Norman Cousins's Laughter Therapy	Pages: 86–115 Reading 1: Extreme Perception and Animal Intelligence Reading 2: How Smart are Animals?
Inferring degree of support	Inferring the use of hedging
Taking notes on cause and effect with a graphic organizer	Taking notes with outlining
Organizing the sequence of events in a time line	Recognizing the role of quoted speech
Past unreal conditionals	Adjective clauses
Writing introductions and hooks	Paraphrasing
An opinion essay	A summary in journalistic style
Sleep deprivation and health issues	Talking to animals

Pre-Unit Diagnostic:
  Check What You Know
Checkpoint 1
Checkpoint 2
Unit Achievement Test
	Pre-Unit Diagnostic:
	  Check What You Know
	Checkpoint 1
	Checkpoint 2
	Unit Achievement Test

Prepare a written presentation on genetic testing	Write a research summary on a famous animal

SCOPE AND SEQUENCE

	5 Too Much of a Good Thing? Pages: 116–143 Reading 1: Death Do Us Part Reading 2: Toward Immortality: The Social Burden of Longer Lives	**6 Making a Difference** Pages: 144–175 Reading 1: Justin Lebo Reading 2: Some Take the Time Gladly Problems with Mandatory Volunteering
Inference	Inferring attitudes and feelings	Inferring people's reactions
Note-Taking	Taking notes with signposts	Taking compare and contrast notes with a t-chart
Reading	Using titles and headings to identify main ideas	Recognizing persuasive language
Grammar	Simple past, present perfect, and present perfect progressive	Concessions
Revise	Using figurative language	Writing introductions and thesis statements
Final Writing Task	A descriptive essay	A persuasive essay
Video	The long lives of the residents of Acciaroli	Philanthropy

Assessments	Pre-Unit Diagnostic:
	  Check What You Know
	Checkpoint 1
	Checkpoint 2
	Unit Achievement Test
		Pre-Unit Diagnostic:
		  Check What You Know
		Checkpoint 1
		Checkpoint 2
		Unit Achievement Test

Unit Project	Write a report about a part of the world where people live long lives using questions as guides	Create a powerpoint presentation or poster about philanthropy in your community

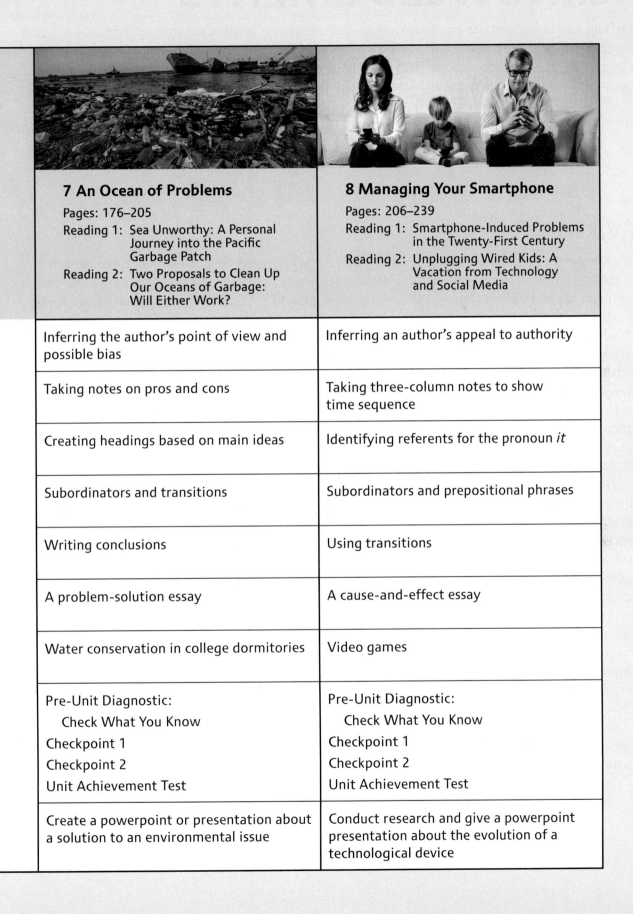

ACKNOWLEDGMENTS

We would like to express our gratitude to the entire *NorthStar* team of authors, editors, and assistants. Special thanks go to Carol Numrich for her vision and especially her ideas and guidance. We are, as always, honored to work with her. Thanks also to Andrea Bryant for her unending support and attention to detail. In addition, thanks to Kelly Sanabria for her timely help researching articles. Lastly, kudos to Peter West for all his hard work, ideas, and support bringing this fifth edition to fruition; we wouldn't have been able to do it without your help.

—Andrew K. English and Laura Monahon English

REVIEWERS

Chris Antonellis, Boston University – CELOP; Gail August, Hostos; Aegina Barnes, York College; Kim Bayer, Hunter College; Mine Bellikli, Atilim University; Allison Blechman, Embassy CES; Paul Blomquist, Kaplan; Helena Botros, FLS; James Branchick, FLS; Chris Bruffee, Embassy CES; Joyce Cain University of California at Fullerton; Nese Cakli, Duzce University; Molly Cheny, University of Washington; María Cordani Tourinho Dantas, Colégio Rainha De Paz; Jason Davis, ASC English; Lindsay Donigan, Fullerton College; Mila Dragushanskaya, ASA College; Bina Dugan, BCCC; Sibel Ece Izmir, Atilim University; Érica Ferrer, Universidad del Norte; María Irma Gallegos Peláez, Universidad del Valle de México; Vera Figueira, UC Irvine; Rachel Fernandez, UC Irvine; Jeff Gano, ASA College; Emily Ellis, UC Irvine; María Genovev a Chávez Bazán, Universidad del Valle de México; Juan Garcia, FLS; Heidi Gramlich, The New England School of English; Phillip Grayson, Kaplan; Rebecca Gross, The New England School of English; Rick Guadiana, FLS; Sebnem Guzel, Tobb University; Esra Hatipoglu, Ufuk University; Brian Henry, FLS; Josephine Horna, BCCC; Judy Hu, UC Irvine; Arthur Hui, Fullerton College; Zoe Isaacson, Hunter College; Kathy Johnson, Fullerton College; Marcelo Juica, Urban College of Boston; Tom Justice, North Shore Community College; Lisa Karakas, Berkeley College; Eva Kopernacki, Embassy CES; Drew Larimore, Kaplan; Heidi Lieb, BCCC; Patricia Martins, Ibeu; Cecilia Mora Espejo, Universidad del Valle de México; Oscar Navarro University of California at Fullerton; Eva Nemtson, ASA College; Kate Nyhan, The New England School of English; Julie Oni, FLS; Willard Osman, The New England School of English; Olga Pagieva, ASA College; Manish Patel, FLS; Paige Poole, Universidad del Norte; Claudia Rebello, Ibeu; Amy Renehan, University of Washington; Lourdes Rey, Universidad del Norte; Michelle Reynolds, FLS International Boston Commons; Mary Ritter, NYU; Ellen Rosen University of California at Fullerton; Dana Saito-Stehiberger, UC Irvine; Dariusz Saczuk, ASA College; Miryam Salimov, ASA College; Minerva Santos, Hostos; Sezer Sarioz, Saint Benoit PLS; Gail Schwartz, UC Irvine; Ebru Sinar, Tobb University; Beth Soll, NYU (Columbia); Christopher Stobart, Universidad del Norte; Guliz Uludag, Ufuk University; Debra Un, NYU; Hilal Unlusu, Saint Benoit PLS; María del Carmen Viruega Trejo, Universidad del Valle de México; Reda Vural, Atilim University; Douglas Waters, Universidad del Norte; Emily Wong, UC Irvine; Leyla Yucklik, Duzce University; Jorge Zepeda Porras, Universidad del Valle de México

LEARNING OUTCOMES

> Understand assumptions
> Take notes by marking important information
> Distinguish voice in quotations

> Use past perfect
> Identify and correct sentence fragments
> Write a summary paragraph

Go to **MyEnglishLab** to check what you know.

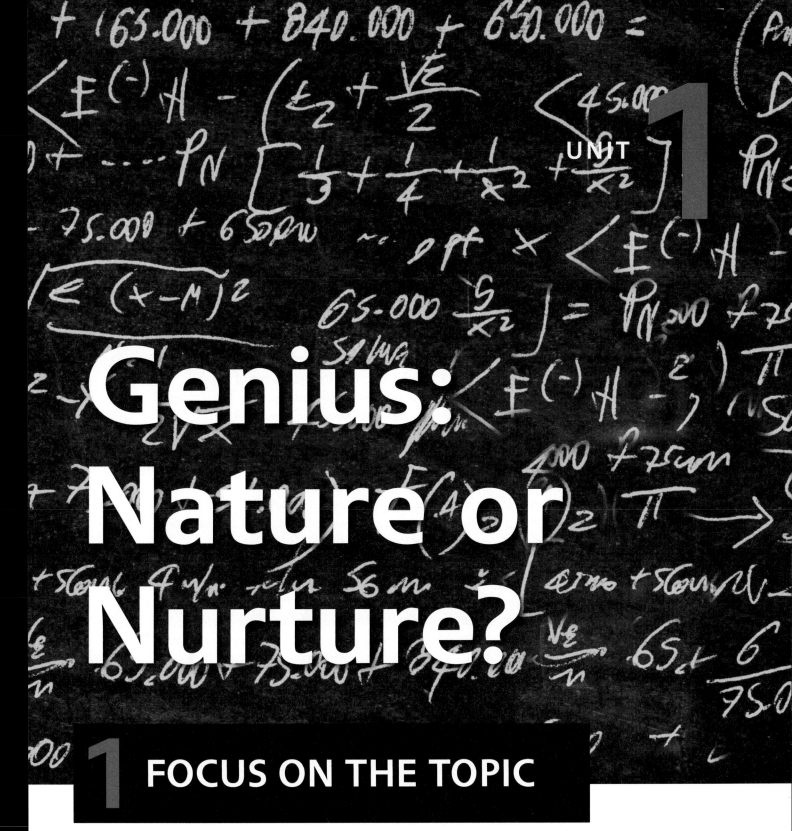

UNIT 1

Genius: Nature or Nurture?

1 FOCUS ON THE TOPIC

1. Why are some people geniuses and others are not? Does the environment a person is raised in create a genius (nurture), or was the person simply born that way (nature)?

2. What would it be like to be a genius? Describe the advantages and disadvantages.

2 FOCUS ON READING

READING ONE | A Genius Explains

VOCABULARY

1 Read this piece about Daniel Tammet, who is considered by many to be a genius. Being a genius does not mean that all aspects of your life are easy or even that you are good at everything. Daniel is very successful with some things but challenged by others. Pay attention to the boldfaced words.

Autism and autistic spectrum disorder (ASD) are names given to groups of complex developmental disorders involving the brain. Some of the symptoms of these disorders are problems with verbal and non-verbal social **interaction**, the display of repetitive behavior, and an inability to be **flexible**. Many people with ASD **compensate** for these challenges and are able to be high-functioning and lead "typical" lives. Others are more **disabled** by the disorder.

ASD is an umbrella term that includes many subcategories. One subcategory is autistic **savant**. Psychologists **estimate** that 10 percent of people with ASD have some savant abilities. An autistic savant is a person with an unusual ability, skill, or knowledge that is much more developed than that of an average person. Many savants are able to **retain** large amounts of information in their memory. For example, some autistic savants can recite entire dictionaries or telephone books word-for-word. Others are able to draw detailed maps of an area after flying over it once in a helicopter. Although autistic people with savant abilities have these specific skills, they may have difficulty with other types of mental or physical tasks.

Daniel Tammet is an autistic savant. For Daniel, as for many people with ASD, leading a **predictable** life has many **benefits**. In other words, life is easier for him if it has structure and routine. If it does not, he may become **anxious**. One of Daniel's special abilities is in mathematics. He is able to solve complex math problems almost immediately. When he does this, he sees each number he is calculating as an **image**. These images transform into a third image, which is the sum.

Why autistic savants have these **astonishing** abilities is a question that still has no definitive answer.

2 **Complete the sentences with the words from the boxes.**

compensate	estimate	retain

1. No one is sure of the exact number of autistic savants with extraordinary abilities there are in the world, but experts _____ that there are fewer than 100.

2. Studies indicate that one hemisphere of a savant's brain may _____ for damage to the other hemisphere.

3. With the number of passwords needed for everyday life, it is sometimes difficult to _____ all of them in your memory.

anxious	disabled	flexible	predictable

4. Children may feel _____ about their first day in a new school because they don't know what to expect.

5. For me, it is very hard to change my plans because I am not very _____ .

6. Although savants have amazing abilities and knowledge, in other areas of their lives they may be _____ .

7. Because I know him so well, Sam's reaction to my suggestion was very _____ .

astonishing	benefit	image	interaction	savant

8. It is sometimes hard for people who are shy to engage in social _____ , especially with people they don't know well.

9. Daniel Tammet's ability to instantaneously solve complex mathematical problems is _____ .

10. A(n) _____ can exhibit amazing mental powers and is able to memorize huge amounts of information.

11. One _____ of my new job is health insurance, and another is two weeks of paid vacation.

12. Even though Daniel had not been to Paris in many years, he still had a clear _____ in his mind of what his hotel looked like.

Go to the **Pearson Practice English App** or **MyEnglishLab** for more vocabulary practice.

PREVIEW

You are going to read an article about Daniel Tammet, an autistic savant. Before you read, look at the statements. Check (✓) three things about Daniel that you think you will read in the article.

_____ 1. He can't drive a car.

_____ 2. He has trouble remembering things.

_____ 3. He loves going to the beach.

_____ 4. He has lots of friends.

_____ 5. He has invented his own language.

_____ 6. He lives with his parents.

READ

Read the article about Daniel Tammet on the next page. Create a chart like the one below to take notes.

TAKE NOTES

Main Ideas	Details
Tammet is good at math and counting	started after epileptic fit at age 3
	obsessed with counting – even counts stitches
	figures out cube roots quickly
	sees numbers as shapes, colors + textures
Tammet is an autistic savant	extraordinary mental abilities
	most struggle with language - not Daniel
	created own language
	speaks 8 languages
	incredible memory

Go to **MyEnglishLab** to view example notes.

The Guardian
A GENIUS EXPLAINS

By Richard Johnson

Daniel Tammet

1   **D**aniel Tammet is talking. As he talks, he studies my shirt and counts the stitches. Ever since the age of three, when he suffered an epileptic fit[1], Tammet has been obsessed with counting. Now he is twenty-six and a mathematical genius who can figure out cube roots quicker than a calculator and recall pi to 22,514 decimal places. He also happens to be autistic, which is why he can't drive a car, wire a plug, or tell right from left. He lives with extraordinary ability and disability.

2   Tammet is calculating 377 multiplied by 795. Actually, he isn't "calculating": there is nothing conscious about what he is doing. He arrives at the answer instantly. Since his epileptic fit, he has been able to see numbers as shapes, colors, and textures. The number two, for instance, is a motion, and five is a clap of thunder. "When I multiply numbers together, I see two shapes. The **image** starts to change and evolve, and a third shape emerges. That's the answer. It's mental imagery. It's like maths without having to think."

3   Tammet is a "**savant**," an individual with an **astonishing**, extraordinary mental ability. An **estimated** 10 percent of the autistic population— and an estimated 1 percent of the non-autistic population— have savant abilities, but no one knows exactly why.

4   Scans of the brains of autistic savants suggest that the right hemisphere might be **compensating** for damage in the left hemisphere. While many savants struggle with language and comprehension (skills associated primarily with the left hemisphere), they often have amazing skills in mathematics and memory (primarily right hemisphere skills). Typically, savants have a limited vocabulary, but there is nothing limited about Tammet's vocabulary.

5   Tammet is creating his own language, strongly influenced by the vowel and image-rich languages of northern Europe. (He already speaks French, German, Spanish, Lithuanian, Icelandic, and Esperanto.) The vocabulary of his language— "Mänti," meaning a type of tree—reflects the relationships between different things. The word "ema," for instance, translates as "mother," and "ela" is what a mother creates: "life." "Päike" is "sun," and "päive" is what the sun creates: "day." Tammet hopes to launch Mänti in academic circles later this year, his own personal exploration of the power of words and their inter-relationship.

---

[1] **epileptic fit:** (also referred to as an epileptic seizure) a brief symptom of epilepsy which may include loss of consciousness, convulsions, or losing muscle tone and slumping to the ground

continued on next page

6 Last year, Tammet broke the European record for recalling pi, the mathematical constant[2], to the furthest decimal point. He found it easy, he says, because he didn't even have to "think." To him, pi isn't an abstract set of digits; it's a visual story, a film projected in front of his eyes. He learnt the number forwards and backwards and, last year, spent five hours recalling it in front of an adjudicator[3]. He wanted to prove a point. "I memorised pi to 22,514 decimal places, and I am technically **disabled**. I just wanted to show people that disability needn't get in the way."

7 Tammet is softly spoken and shy about making eye contact, which makes him seem younger than he is. He lives on the Kent coast, but never goes near the beach—there are too many pebbles to count. The thought of a mathematical problem with no solution makes him feel uncomfortable. Trips to the supermarket are always a chore. "There's too much mental stimulus. I have to look at every shape and texture. Every price and every arrangement of fruit and vegetables. So instead of thinking, 'What cheese do I want this week?,' I'm just really uncomfortable."

8 Tammet has never been able to work 9 to 5. It would be too difficult to fit around his daily routine. For instance, he has to drink his cups of tea at exactly the same time every day. Things have to happen in the same order: He always brushes his teeth before he has his shower. "I have tried to be more **flexible**, but I always end up feeling more uncomfortable. **Retaining** a sense of control is really important. I like to do things in my own time and in my own style, so an office with targets and bureaucracy just wouldn't work."

9 Instead, he has set up a business on his own, at home, writing email courses in language learning, numeracy, and literacy for private clients. It has had the fringe **benefit** of keeping human **interaction** to a minimum. It also gives him time to work on the verb structures of Mänti.

10 Few people on the streets have recognised Tammet since his pi record attempt. But, when a documentary about his life is broadcast on Channel 5 later this year, all that will change. "The highlight of filming was to meet Kim Peek, the real-life character who inspired the film *Rain Man*. Before I watched *Rain Man*, I was frightened. As a nine-year-old schoolboy, you don't want people to point at the screen and say, 'That's you.' But I watched it and felt a real connection. Getting to meet the real-life Rain Man was inspirational."

11 Peek was shy and introspective, but he sat and held Tammet's hand for hours. "We shared so much—our love of key dates from history, for instance. And our love of books. As a child, I regularly took over a room in the house and started my own lending library. I would separate out fiction and non-fiction, and then alphabetise them all. I even introduced a ticketing system. I love books so much. I've read more books than anyone else I know, so I was delighted when Kim wanted to meet in a library." Peek can read two pages simultaneously, one with each eye. He can also recall, in exact detail, the 7,600 books he has read. When he is at home in Utah, he spends afternoons at the Salt Lake City public library, memorising phone books and address directories. "He is such a lovely man," says Tammet. "Kim says, 'You don't have to be handicapped to be different—everybody's different.' And he's right."

12 As a baby, he (Tammet) banged his head against the wall and cried constantly. Nobody knew what was wrong. His mother was **anxious**, and would swing him to sleep in a blanket. She breastfed him for two years. The only thing the doctors could say was that perhaps he was understimulated. Then, one afternoon when he was playing with his brother in the living room, he had an epileptic fit.

13 "I was given medication—round blue tablets—to control my seizures and told not to go out in direct sunlight. I had to visit the hospital every month for

---

[2] **mathematical constant:** a special number that is usually a real number and is considered "significantly interesting is some way"

[3] **adjudicator:** a judge or arbitrator, especially in a dispute or competition

continued on next page

regular blood tests. I hated those tests, but I knew they were necessary. To make up for it, my father would always buy me a cup of squash[4] to drink while we sat in the waiting room. It was a worrying time because my dad's father had epilepsy and actually died of it, in the end. They were thinking, 'This is the end of Daniel's life.' "

14 He remembers being given a Ladybird book called *Counting* when he was four. "When I looked at the numbers, I 'saw' images. It felt like a place I could go where I really belonged. That was great. I went to this other country whenever I could. I would sit on the floor in my bedroom and just count. I didn't notice that time was passing. It was only when my mum shouted up for dinner or someone knocked at my door, that I would snap out of it."

15 One day his brother asked him a sum[5]. "He asked me to multiply something in my head—like 'What is 82 x 82 x 82 x 82?' I just looked at the floor and closed my eyes. My back went very straight, and I made my hands into fists. But after five or ten seconds, the answer just flowed out of my mouth. He asked me several others, and I got every one right. My parents didn't seem surprised. And they never put pressure on me to perform for the neighbours. They knew I was different but wanted me to have a normal life as far as possible."

16 Tammet could see the car park of his infant school from his bedroom window, which made him feel safe. "I loved assembly because we got to sing hymns. The notes formed a pattern in my head, just like the numbers did." The other children didn't know what to make of him and would tease him. The minute the bell went for playtime, he would rush off. "I went to the playground, but not to play. The place was surrounded by trees. While the other children were playing football, I would just stand and count the leaves."

17 Tammet may have been teased at school, but his teachers were always protective. "I think my parents must have had a word with them, so I was pretty much left alone." He found it hard to socialise with anyone outside the family, and, with the advent of adolescence, his shyness got worse.

18 After leaving school with three A-levels (History, French and German, all grade Bs), he decided he wanted to teach—only not the **predictable**, learn-by-rote type of teaching. For a start, he went to teach in Lithuania, and he worked as a volunteer. "It was also the first time I was introduced as 'Daniel' rather than 'the guy who can do weird stuff in his head.' It was such a pleasant relief." Later, he returned home to live with his parents and found work as a maths tutor.

19 When he isn't working, Tammet likes to hang out with his friends on the church quiz team. His knowledge of popular culture lets him down, but he's a shoo-in when it comes to the maths questions. "I do love numbers," he says. "It isn't only an intellectual or aloof thing that I do. I really feel that there is an emotional attachment, a caring for numbers. I think this is a human thing—in the same way that a poet humanises a river or a tree through metaphor, my world gives me a sense of numbers as personal. It sounds silly, but numbers are my friends."

Note: This article originally appeared in *The Guardian*, a British news publication. Several words in the article are written using British spelling and terms, which is sometimes different from American usage.

---

[4] **squash:** fruit syrup mixed with sugar and water or carbonated water
[5] **sum:** (in British English) a calculation

Articles and textbooks often contain paragraph headings. A paragraph heading is like a title for the paragraph. It tells readers what they can expect to read about. Choose the best paragraph heading for each section in the article.

1. Paragraphs 1 and 2

    a. Daniel Tammet—mathematical genius

    b. Daniel Tammet's abilities and disabilities

    c. Math—how he does it

2. Paragraphs 4 and 5

    a. The autistic brain

    b. Mänti—Daniel's language

    c. Not the typical savant

3. Paragraphs 7 and 8

    a. Everyday life can be challenging

    b. Overstimulation can be a problem

    c. Daniel's daily routine

4. Paragraphs 10 and 11

    a. Kim Peek and Daniel's similarities

    b. Kim Peek and Daniel's love of books

    c. Daniel and Kim Peek connect

5. Paragraphs 14 and 15

    a. Daniel starts counting

    b. Daniel's math skills emerge

    c. Numbers as images

6. Paragraphs 16 and 17

    a. Daniel's love of singing

    b. Daniel's shyness

    c. Problems in school

DETAILS

1 Reading One gives information about Daniel's abilities and disabilities. Read the categories on the left in the chart. Then write the details and examples from the box next to the correct categories. Finally, identify each detail or example as either an ability or a disability. Use your notes to help you. Share your completed chart with a partner.

He feels uncomfortable in the supermarket.

He can recall pi to 22,514 decimal points.

He is able to read a lot of books.

He doesn't go to the beach because there are too many pebbles to count.

He can easily remember key dates in history.

~~He has invented his own language.~~

He must drink his tea at exactly the same time every day.

He has trouble making eye contact.

He always has to brush his teeth before he showers.

He speaks eight languages.

~~He can calculate cube roots faster than a calculator.~~

It is hard for him to socialize with anyone outside his family.

He can multiply 377 × 795 in his head.

The thought of a mathematical problem with no solution makes him uncomfortable.

CATEGORY	DETAILS OR EXAMPLES	ABILITY	DISABILITY
Math	1. He can calculate cube roots faster than a calculator.	X	
	2.		
	3.		
	4.		
Language	1. He has invented his own language.	X	
	2.		
	3.		
Memory	1.		
	2.		
Social Interaction	1.		
	2.		
	3.		
Need for Order	1.		
	2.		

2 Look at your notes and at your answers in Preview. How did they help you understand the article?

Understanding Assumptions

An **inference** is an **educated guess** about something that is **not directly stated** in a text. *A Genius Explains* includes quotes from Daniel Tammet and Kim Peek that show what others might assume about the two men's disabilities. What assumptions can you infer from these quotations?

Look at the example and read the assumption and the explanation.

> "I just wanted to show people that disability needn't get in the way." (*paragraph 6*)

Assumption: People think that someone with a disability cannot do as much as someone without a disability.

Some people assumed that Daniel's disability would cause him to have problems in other areas of his life. By showing people that he could achieve remarkable things, even though he was "technically disabled," Daniel wanted to show that their assumptions were wrong. His disability wasn't going to hold him back.

1 Read the quotes from Daniel and Kim. Complete the sentences with assumptions that people have made about them.

1. Daniel: "It was also the first time I was introduced as 'Daniel' rather than 'the guy who can do weird stuff in his head.'" (*paragraph 18*)

    Others didn't think that Daniel was _____

    _____

2. Kim: "You don't have to be handicapped to be different—everybody's different." (*paragraph 11*)

    Others think that _____

    _____

3. Daniel: "It sounds silly, but numbers are my friends." (*paragraph 19*)

    Other people probably think that numbers _____

    _____

4. Daniel: "It isn't only an intellectual or aloof thing that I do. I really feel that there is an emotional attachment, a caring for numbers." (*paragraph 19*)

    Other people probably assume that Daniel's relationship to numbers _____

    _____

5. Daniel: "I like to do things in my own time and in my own style, so an office with targets and bureaucracy just wouldn't work." (*paragraph 8*)

    Other people might expect Daniel to _____

    _____

2 Discuss your answers with a partner. Point out sentences, words, or phrases that helped you find the answers.

Use your notes to support your answers with information from the reading.

Work in a small group. Choose one of the questions. Discuss your ideas. Then choose one person in your group to report the ideas to the class.

1. Which of Daniel's abilities would be advantageous? Which would be less advantageous? Why? Have you ever met anyone with this combination of advantage and disadvantage?

2. William James, the American psychologist and philosopher (1842–1910) said, "Genius means nothing more than the faculty of perceiving in an unhabitual way." How does this quotation apply to Daniel Tammet?

➤ Go to **MyEnglishLab** to give your opinion about another question.

READING TWO | 10,000 Hours to Mastery

PREVIEW

1 **Look at the title of the reading and the picture. Write two questions that you think will be answered in this reading.**

_____

_____

2 **Look at the boldfaced words in the reading. Which words do you know the meanings of?**

1 Read the article about Malcolm Gladwell's book, *Outliers: The Story of Success.* As you read, guess the meanings of the words that are new to you. Remember to take notes on main ideas and details.

10,000 HOURS TO MASTERY by Harvey Mackay

1 For years, I have preached the importance of hard work, determination, **persistence**, and practice—make that perfect practice—as key ingredients of success. A nifty new book seems to support my theory.

2 Malcolm Gladwell has written a fascinating study, *Outliers: The Story of Success* (Little, Brown & Co.), which should make a lot of people feel much better about not achieving instant success. In fact, he says it takes about ten years, or 10,000 hours, of practice to attain true **expertise**.

3 "The people at the very top don't just work harder or even much harder than everyone else," Gladwell writes. "They work much, much harder." Achievement, he says, is talent plus preparation. Preparation seems to play a bigger role.

4 For example, he describes the Beatles: They had been together seven years before their famous arrival in America. They spent a lot of time playing in strip clubs in Hamburg, Germany, sometimes for as long as eight hours a night. Overnight sensation? Not exactly. Estimates are the band performed 1,200 times before their big success in 1964. By comparison, most bands don't perform 1,200 times in their careers.

5 Neurologist Daniel Levitin has studied the formula for success extensively and shares this finding: "The **emerging** picture from such studies is that 10,000 hours of practice is required to achieve the level of mastery associated with being a world-class expert in anything. In study after study of composers, basketball players, fiction writers, ice skaters, concert pianists, chess players, master criminals, and what have you, the number comes up again and again. Of course, this doesn't address why some people get more out of their practice sessions than others do. But no one has yet found a case in which true world-class expertise was accomplished in less time. It seems it takes the brain this long to **assimilate** all that it needs to know to achieve true mastery."

6 Two computer giants, Bill Joy, who co-founded Sun Microsystems, and Bill Gates, co-founder of

The Beatles

Microsoft, also were proof of the 10,000-hour theory.

7 As Gladwell puts it, "Practice isn't the thing you do once you're good. It's the thing you do that makes you good."

8 Consider these thoughts from successful folks in all walks of life:

9 • "No one can arrive from being talented alone. God gives talent; work **transforms** talent into genius."—Anna Pavlova, ballerina.

10 • "I know the price of success: dedication, hard work, and an unremitting devotion to the things you want to see happen."—Frank Lloyd Wright, architect.

11 • "The way to learn to do things is to do things. The way to learn a trade is to work at it. Success teaches how to succeed. Begin with the determination to succeed, and the work is half done already."—Mark Twain, writer and humorist.

12 Do you detect a theme here?

13 The abilities these people possessed were far-ranging, yet the formula for success was the same: hard work and lots of it. I don't know anyone who has succeeded any other way. Some people just make it look easy. Of course, you probably didn't see the first 9,999 hours of hard work. And you don't just have to work hard; you have to work smart, too.

14 **Mackay's Moral:** Some people dream about success, and others wake up and do something about it.

2 Compare your notes on main ideas and details with a partner's. How can you improve your notes next time?

🎧 Go to the **Pearson Practice English App** or **MyEnglishLab** for more vocabulary practice.

NOTE-TAKING SKILL

Taking Notes by Marking Important Information

When you mark a text, you identify important information. This helps you read more carefully. You can also look back at the information you marked to help you study for tests and complete assignments.

You can underline or highlight information. Only mark the important words. For example, these marks focus on the author's use of experts' words (or appealing to authority) to support his thesis that success is based on hard work, determination, and persistence.

> Malcolm Gladwell has written a fascinating study, *Outliers: The Story of Success* (Little, Brown, & Co.), which should make a lot of people feel much better about not achieving instant success. In fact, he says it takes about ten years, or 10,000 hours of practice to attain true expertise.

1 **Mark the expert's words in this paragraph that support the author's thesis that success is based on hard work, determination, and persistence. Share your answers with a partner.**

"The people at the very top don't just work harder or even much harder than everyone else," Gladwell writes. "They work much, much harder." Achievement, he says, is talent plus preparation. Preparation seems to play a bigger role.

2 **Look at Reading Two again. Mark the information that you think is most important.**

 Go to **MyEnglishLab** for more note-taking practice.

COMPREHENSION

1 **Complete each statement according to information in the article. Use your notes from Reading Two to help you. Discuss your answers with a partner.**

1. According to Gladwell, achievement is _____

_____

2. The Beatles were different from most other bands because _____

_____

3. Regarding success, Daniel Levitin says that _____

_____

4. Levitin believes success takes so long to achieve because _____

_____

2 **Review the boldfaced words from the reading with a partner. Use a dictionary or ask your teacher for any meanings you still do not know.**

READING SKILL

1 Go back to Reading Two. Underline the quotations. Why do you think Mackay includes these quotations?

Distinguishing Voice in Quotations

Distinguishing voice is an important reading skill, as it is not always clear whether we are reading the author's words or someone else's words. One indication of a change in voice is the use of quotation marks. Another indication is a change in pronouns, for example, from third person (*he, she*, or *they*) to first person (*I* or *we*). In order to fully comprehend a text, you need to notice when a shift in voice takes place to make sure you know who is speaking.

Authors often shift the voice in their writing by using quoted speech.

- Quotations add first-hand validity to a point the author has made.

- Quotations often provide details or examples of what the author has been talking about.

- Quotations can continue the story in another voice for added interest.

In paragraph 3 of Reading Two, Mackay includes two quotations from Malcolm Gladwell's book. This adds validity to what Mackay says, as the words are Gladwell's. In paragraph 5, the author includes an extended quotation from Daniel Levitin. This quotation gives several details and examples of how much time it takes for true mastery to occur.

2 Read the excerpts from Reading One. All quotation marks have been removed. Underline the sections where the voice changes from the author's to someone else's. Add quotation marks where necessary. Then discuss these questions with a partner:

- How do you know where the change in voice occurs?

- Who is speaking where you added quotation marks?

- Why might the author have chosen to use quotations in the examples?

1. To [Tammet], pi isn't an abstract set of digits; it's a visual story, a film projected in front of his eyes. He learnt the number forwards and backwards and, last year, spent five hours recalling it in front of an adjudicator. He wanted to prove a point. I memorised pi to 22,514 decimal places, and I am technically disabled. I just wanted to show people that disability needn't get in the way. (*paragraph 6*)

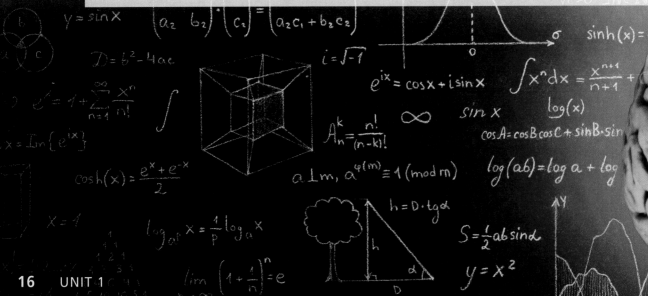

2. [Tammet] lives on the Kent coast, but never goes near the beach—there are too many pebbles to count. The thought of a mathematical problem with no solution makes him feel uncomfortable. Trips to the supermarket are always a chore. There's too much mental stimulus. I have to look at every shape and texture. Every price and every arrangement of fruit and vegetables. So instead of thinking, 'What cheese do I want this week?,' I'm just really uncomfortable. (*paragraph 7*)

3. Peek was shy and introspective, but he sat and held Tammet's hand for hours. We shared so much—our love of key dates from history, for instance. And our love of books. . . . I've read more books than anyone else I know, so I was delighted when Kim wanted to meet in a library. Peek can read two pages simultaneously, one with each eye. He can also recall, in exact detail, the 7,600 books he has read. . . . He is such a lovely man, says Tammet. Kim says, 'You don't have to be handicapped to be different—everybody's different.' And he's right. (*paragraph 11*)

4. He remembers being given a Ladybird book called *Counting* when he was four. When I looked at the numbers, I 'saw' images. It felt like a place I could go where I really belonged. (*paragraph 14*)

Go to **MyEnglishLab** for more skill practice.

ORGANIZE

Reading One (R1) and Reading Two (R2) both talk about genius. A Venn diagram can be used to show where the ideas about genius are found. Read the statements in the box. Write the statement in the correct part of the diagram. Include the paragraph number where the information is found.

1. "Genius" may be the result of brain chemistry.

2. A person can be a genius and also be disabled.

3. People at the top (experts) work harder than other people.

4. Genius = talent + hard work.

5. "Genius" is being studied by scientists.

6. Expertise requires a lot of practice.

7. Special talents can also cause problems.

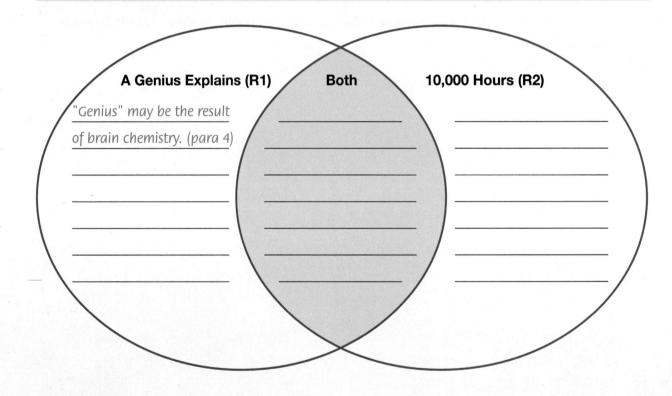

A Genius Explains (R1)

"Genius" may be the result of brain chemistry. (para 4)

Both

10,000 Hours (R2)

SYNTHESIZE

Look back at the readings about Daniel Tammet and Malcolm Gladwell's theory and at the work you did in Organize. Based on this information, write two paragraphs. One paragraph will be about Daniel Tammet. The other paragraph will be about Malcolm Gladwell's idea of what makes a person an expert, including examples of some of the people he mentions. You may also write a third paragraph discussing any similarities between the two readings.

▶ Go to **MyEnglishLab** to check what you learned.

REVIEW

Complete the word scramble puzzle. Rearrange the letters to form vocabulary words from the unit. Use the circled letter from each word to find the bonus word.

1. e a i t ©t r n o n i	_interaction_	communication or collaboration
2. l i a a m ⓢt s i e	_ _ _ _ _ _ _ _ _ _	This is what takes the brain so long to do, according to Dr. Levitin.
3. g a s o s n i ⓣn i h	_ _ _ _ _ _ _ _ _ _	amazing or surprising
4. f r o a m t r ⓝs	_ _ _ _ _ _ _ _ _	to change
5. e ⓟi r d b t e a l c	_ _ _ _ _ _ _ _ _ _ _	Because of his need for structure, Daniel Tammet's life is this.
6. p e i e e x ⓢt r	_ _ _ _ _ _ _ _	what you may acquire after thousands of hours of practice
7. f n i t b e ⓔ	_ _ _ _ _ _ _	an advantage
8. n m ⓡi e g g e	_ _ _ _ _ _ _ _	starting to appear
9. u n x a o ⓘs	_ _ _ _ _ _ _	nervous or eager
10. m p n o ⓔs a t e c	_ _ _ _ _ _ _ _ _ _	to make up for a weakness
11. b l d s i ⓔd a	_ _ _ _ _ _ _ _	unable to perform certain activities

Bonus Word (This is the quality you might need to have to complete this puzzle!)

_ _ _ _ _ _ _ _ _ _ _

EXPAND

1 Complete the chart with the correct word forms. Some categories can have more than one form. Use a dictionary if necessary. An X indicates that you do not need to put a form in that category.

NOUN	VERB	ADJECTIVE	ADVERB
		predictable	
		estimated	X
		1. astonishing 2.	X
	X	anxious	
		flexible	
interaction			
	transform	1. 2. 3.	X
	retain		X
benefit			X
		disabled	X
1. expertise 2.	X		
	assimilate		X
		emerging	X
		persistent	
	compensate	X	X

2 Complete the sentences with the words in the boxes. You may need to change the word form.

expertise	flexible	persistence	predictable	transform

1. According to Anna Pavlova, work has the _____ effect of turning talent into genius.

2. A lack of _____ is one of the symptoms of ASD.

3. Daniel Tammet's life is very _____ ; he always drinks his tea at the same time.

4. Gladwell believes that to achieve mastery you must _____ in your practice and never give up.

5. Gladwell says it takes about ten years to attain true world-class _____ .

anxious	compensate	emerging	estimated	interaction

6. Mathematical problems with no solution cause a feeling of _____ for Daniel Tammet.

7. Scientists _____ that there are fewer than 100 autistic savants alive today.

8. Daniel Tammet's choosing to work at home instead of in an office is a type of

   _____ for the fact that he needs structure.

9. Tammet also chooses to work at home because he has trouble with social

   _____ .

10. The symptoms of ASD usually begin to _____ when a child is two or three years old.

CREATE

APPLY **Rewrite the sentences by replacing the underlined word with the form of the word noted in parentheses. Make any necessary grammatical changes.**

1. Because I know Daniel Tammet well, I can <u>predict</u> how he will react in certain situations. (adjective)

   Because I know Daniel Tammet well, how he will react in certain situations is very predictable.

2. Many people who suffer from ASD have problems with <u>flexibility</u>. (adjective)

   _____

   _____

3. According to Gladwell, the <u>transformation</u> of talent into expertise requires at least 10,000 hours. (verb)

   _____

   _____

4. A lack of structure can cause <u>anxiety</u> for Daniel Tammet. (adjective)

   _____

   _____

5. For many people with ASD, being able to <u>interact</u> socially is difficult. (noun)

   _____

   _____

6. Brain scans of autistic savants suggest that there might be <u>compensation</u> being done by the right hemisphere for damage to the left. (verb)

   _____

   _____

7. The <u>retention</u> of large amounts of information is usually not a problem for autistic savants. (verb)

_____

_____

8. Daniel Tammet memorized pi to 22,514 decimal places to show that, although he is technically <u>disabled</u>, it doesn't stop him from being successful. (noun)

_____

_____

> ↻ Go to the **Pearson Practice English App** or **MyEnglishLab** for more vocabulary practice.

GRAMMAR FOR WRITING

1 Read the sentences and answer the questions.

- By the time Daniel started school, he **had** already **had** his first seizure.
- Daniel **had** just **graduated** from school when he traveled to France to live with a family.
- Before Daniel moved to Lithuania, he **had lived** with a family in France.

a. In the first sentence, did Daniel start school first, or did he have a seizure first?

b. In the second sentence, did Daniel travel to France before he graduated?

c. In the third sentence, which happened first: Daniel's move to Lithuania or living with a family in France?

d. What helped you decide the order of events in these sentences?

Past Perfect

The **past perfect** form of a verb is used to show that something happened before a specific time or event in the past.	
The past perfect is formed with **had** + the **past participle**	The Beatles **had** already **performed** thousands of times before they came to America.
Past Perfect and a Specific Time or Event in the Past	
To show something happened before a specific time in the past, use the past perfect with **by** + a certain time in the past.	**By age thirteen,** Daniel **had** already **learned** how to play chess.
Past Perfect with Two Past Events	
When talking about two events that happened in the past, use the past perfect to show the first event that happened (the earlier event). The simple past is often used to show the second event. The event in the past perfect happened before the event in the simple past.	Before Daniel published his memoir, he **had** already **created** his website *Optimnem*. (First, Daniel created his website. Then he published his memoir.)

continued on next page

Time words	
After and *as soon as* are used to introduce the first event (past perfect).	**As soon as** Daniel **had learned** Lithuanian, he was able to communicate more easily. (First, he learned Lithuanian. Then he communicated more easily.)
Before and *by the time* are used to introduce the second event (simple past).	The Beatles **had performed** more than 1,200 times **by the time** they came to America. (First, they performed over 1,200 times. Then they came to America.)
When can be used to introduce either the first or second event. Notice the difference.	Daniel **had cooked dinner when** Kim Peek arrived. (First, he cooked dinner. Then Kim Peek arrived.)
	Daniel cooked dinner **when Kim Peek had arrived.** (First, Kim Peek arrived. Then Daniel cooked dinner.)
Adverbs often used with Past Perfect – *Already, Just, Never, Yet,* and *Ever*	
In addition to using time words, *already, just,* and *never* are often used in affirmative sentences with the past perfect to emphasize the event that happened first.	Daniel **had *just* graduated** when he decided to travel to France. (He graduated and immediately decided to travel to France.)
	Daniel **had *already* learned** to play chess before he graduated from secondary school. (First, he learned to play chess. Then, he graduated.)
Yet and *ever* are usually used in negative sentences or in questions. *Yet* is used for something that hasn't happened until this point, but likely will happen in the future.	It was 2002. Daniel Tammet **hadn't *yet* broken** the record for memorizing pi. (Not in 2002, but he would in the future.)
	The Beatles **hadn't *ever* been** in America before 1964. (Never / not ever before 1964. Maybe they went after that, but the sentence doesn't address that.)
Punctuation with the Past Perfect	
As in all sentences with two clauses, when the sentence begins with the dependent clause (the clause beginning with the time word, such as *after, before,* etc.), use a comma to separate it from the main clause.	**Before Daniel published his memoir,** he had already created his website *Optimnem.*
When the sentence begins with an independent clause, do not use a comma.	Daniel had already created his website *Optimnem* **before he published his memoir.**

2 Each of these sentences talks about two events that happened in the past. Which event happened first? Write *1* for the first event and *2* for the second event.

1. By the time Malcolm Gladwell wrote *Outliers*, he had already published two other books.

   _____ Malcolm Gladwell wrote *Outliers*.

   _____ Malcolm published two other books.

2. Before the Beatles became famous, they had worked in Hamburg, Germany.

   _____ The Beatles became famous.

   _____ The Beatles worked in Hamburg, Germany.

3. Daniel Tammet went to the playground as soon as the school bell had rung.

   _____ Daniel went to the playground.

   _____ The school bell rang.

4. Frank Lloyd Wright had already married his first wife when he opened his architecture firm.

   _____ Frank Lloyd Wright married his first wife.

   _____ Frank Lloyd Wright opened his architecture firm.

5. Anna Pavlova had decided to live in London by the time she performed *Sleeping Beauty* in New York City.

   _____ Anna Pavlova decided to live in London.

   _____ Anna Pavlova performed *Sleeping Beauty* in New York City.

6. Before Mark Twain published *The Adventures of Huckleberry Finn*, he had already worked as a riverboat pilot on the Mississippi River.

   _____ Mark Twain published *The Adventures of Huckleberry Finn*.

   _____ Mark Twain worked as a riverboat pilot on the Mississippi River.

7. After Malcolm Gladwell had worked for the *Washington Post*, he started working for *The New Yorker* magazine.

   _____ Malcolm Gladwell worked for the *Washington Post*.

   _____ Malcolm Gladwell started working for *The New Yorker* magazine.

8. When Daniel Tammet met Kim Peek, Peek had already read over 7,000 books.

   _____ Daniel Tammet met Kim Peek.

   _____ Kim Peek read over 7,000 books.

9. Anna Pavlova moved to London as soon as she had started her own ballet company.

   _____ Anna Pavlova moved to London.

   _____ Anna Pavlova started her own ballet company.

10. By the time Mark Twain started working as a riverboat pilot, he had worked as a printer in New York and Philadelphia.

    _____ Mark Twain started working as a riverboat pilot.

    _____ Mark Twain worked as a printer in New York and Philadelphia.

3 **APPLY** Study the timeline of Daniel Tammet's life. Use the information in the timeline to complete the sentences using the past perfect or simple past.

DANIEL TAMMET'S LIFE	
1979 – born in East London, England	1999 – returns to England
1983 – has first seizure	2002 – creates website, *Optimnem*
1984 (September 7) – starts school	2004 (May) – breaks record for memorizing pi
1984 (September 20) – sister, Claire, born	2004 (September) – learns Icelandic language in one week
1988 – starts learning foreign languages	2005 – appears on American TV shows
1990 – starts secondary school	2006 – publishes memoir, *Born on a Blue Day*
1992 – learns to play chess	2008 – moves to France
1995 (June 10) – graduates from secondary school	2009 – second book, *Embracing the Wide Sky*, becomes a bestseller in France
1995 (July 22) – travels to France to live with family	2012 – third book is published
1998 – moves to Lithuania to teach English	2016 – writes first book in French, *Mishenka*

1. After Daniel had had his first seizure, *he started school* .

2. Before Daniel learned to play chess, _____ .

3. As soon as _____ , his sister, Claire, was born.

4. _____ by the time he moved to France.

5. By 2005, _____ .

6. When _____ .

7. Daniel had already _____ .

8. _____ before _____ .

9. _____ as soon as _____ .

Go to the **Pearson Practice English App** or **MyEnglishLab** for more grammar practice.
Check what you learned in **MyEnglishLab**.

In this unit, you read about different geniuses and how they achieved their expertise.

You are going to *write a summary paragraph about a genius. This person can be alive now or from the past. Be sure to include why this person is considered a genius and how he or she achieved expertise.*

For an alternative writing topic, see page 31.

PREPARE TO WRITE: Group Brainstorming

Group brainstorming is a good way to get ideas for writing. In brainstorming, you think of as many ideas as you can. Don't think about whether the ideas are good or bad. Just write down all ideas.

1 Work in a small group. Brainstorm a list of geniuses. The person can be from any time period or culture. Don't stop to discuss the genius. Focus on thinking of as many examples as possible.

1. _____   6. _____
2. _____   7. _____
3. _____   8. _____
4. _____   9. _____
5. _____   10. _____

2 Now work individually. Choose one genius that you find interesting and want to write about. Research this person to find information about his or her life and achievements. Be sure to include why this person is considered a genius and how he or she achieved expertise. Take notes about what you find out. Make sure the notes are in your own words and not copied word-for-word.

WRITE

Writing a Summary Paragraph

A **paragraph** is a group of sentences that are related and deal with a single topic. A **summary paragraph** identifies and extracts the main idea from a text, leaving out less important details. All summary paragraphs have a **topic sentence** with a **controlling idea**.

The **topic sentence** is an essential part of all well-written paragraphs. The topic sentence controls the content of the rest of the paragraph. This control helps the writer focus on supporting ideas in the paragraph that are directly related to the topic sentence. The first step in writing a topic sentence is to choose a topic and find a point of view or **main idea** about it.

Topics	Main Idea
Mozart	Mozart is considered a prodigy.
Autistic savants	Autistic savants have specific abilities or skills.
Malcolm Gladwell	Malcolm Gladwell has written a fascinating book.

continued on next page

The next step is to narrow the main idea even more by finding a **controlling idea**. The controlling idea is the idea you want to explain, illustrate, or describe in the paragraph. It makes a specific statement about a topic. The controlling ideas in the topic sentences below are underlined.

Main Idea	Main Idea + Controlling Idea = Topic Sentence
Mozart is considered a prodigy.	Mozart is considered a prodigy <u>because he achieved huge musical accomplishments at a very young age.</u>
Autistic savants have specific abilities or skills.	Although autistic savants have specific abilities or skills, <u>they may have other limitations, especially problems with social interactions.</u>
Malcolm Gladwell has written a fascinating book.	Malcolm Gladwell has written a fascinating book, <u>which emphasizes the importance of hard work.</u>

1 Read this paragraph about autistic savants. Then answer the questions.

> Autistic savants have specific abilities or skills, but they are not without certain limitations in other areas of life. An autistic savant is a person with an unusual ability, skill, or knowledge that is much more developed than that of an average person. In fact, many savants have highly developed mathematical skills. Others are able to retain large amounts of information in their memory. For example, some autistic savants can recite entire dictionaries or telephone books word-for-word. Still others are able to draw detailed maps of an area after flying over it once in a helicopter. Despite the fact that the autistic savant has these specific abilities or skills, he or she may have difficulties with other types of mental or physical tasks and social interactions. For instance, some savants may have trouble doing simple tasks, such as tying their shoes or driving a car. Additionally, an autistic savant may have problems talking to people or even making eye contact. So, despite their advanced skills and abilities in certain areas, savants may encounter difficulty with seemingly simple tasks.

1. What is the topic of this paragraph? _____
   _____

2. The first sentence is the topic sentence. What two ideas are presented in this sentence?
   _____
   _____

3. How does the content of the rest of the paragraph relate to the topic sentence?
   _____
   _____

2 Each paragraph is missing a topic sentence. Choose the topic sentence that best fits the paragraph.

1. Daniel suffered an epileptic seizure when he was very young, which may be the cause of his savant abilities. Soon after, when he was four, his mother gave him a counting book, and his love of mathematics was born. From an early age, he has been able to solve complicated mathematical problems in his head. Recently, he has been able to memorize pi to 22,514 digits.

   a. Daniel Tammet is very good at math and has a great memory.

   b. Daniel Tammet is an autistic savant with exceptional memory and mathematical abilities.

   c. Daniel Tammet is an autistic savant who loves solving mathematical problems.

2. What Levitin has found is that it appears that 10,000 hours of practice are required to reach world-class expertise in any field. In fact, he has found no world-class expert who has not put in at least that many hours of preparation. He believes that this is because it takes that much time for the brain to assimilate everything necessary to reach this level of expertise.

   a. Daniel Levitin, a neurologist, has extensively studied what is needed to reach success.

   b. Reaching world-class expertise requires a lot of time and practice.

   c. Daniel Levitin believes that it takes the brain a long time to assimilate the information necessary to be an expert.

3. Parents create these hothouse kids because they are attempting to create a "genius." They may begin by playing classical music for the hothouse child when he or she is still in the crib. The parents start working with their children on math and language skills at an early age, using flashcards. They also enroll their children in music and dance lessons, often as early as age three or four. In addition, they try to get their kids into the most academically challenging preschools.

   a. Hothouse kids learn math and music at an early age.

   b. Parents take a variety of approaches to ensure that their kids become geniuses and can get into the best preschools.

   c. "Hothouse kids" is a term used to define children whose parents push them to learn more quickly and earlier than a "typical" child by providing a rich educational environment.

3 Read the paragraphs. The underlined topic sentences are incomplete because they do not have a controlling idea. Rewrite each topic sentence to include both a topic and a controlling idea.

1. <u>Wolfgang Amadeus Mozart was a genius.</u> For one thing, Mozart was a child prodigy who was playing the violin and piano by age four and composing by age six. Another reason that he is considered a genius is that he was able to create more than 600 compositions—including symphonies, chamber music, sonatas, and choral music—in his thirty-four-year lifetime. Additionally, he is said to have been able to compose entire symphonies in his head. He could imagine the sounds of all the different instruments without using a piano to help him compose. He was not only the best pianist of his day in Europe but also one of the top three or four violinists.

_____

_____

2. <u>Scientists debate the importance of nature versus nurture.</u> In other words, the debate of nature versus nurture asks the question: "What part does nature—the genetic information that you have inherited from your parents—play in your development? And, conversely, what part does environment—what you eat, where you went to school, how your parents raised you—play?" In an effort to understand the importance of each of these factors, there have been many studies using twins who were separated at birth. While these studies are not conclusive, there were instances where the separated twins had developed in a remarkably similar manner. Nevertheless, the reasons for this may also have to do with environment (nurture). Even though they were raised by different families, the environments could have been quite similar.

_____

_____

3. <u>Malcolm Gladwell is a talented author.</u> His book *Outliers* was published in 2008 and was number one on the *New York Times* bestseller list for eleven straight weeks. It followed *The Tipping Point*, which was published in 2000. *The Tipping Point* addresses the individual's ability to change society. This non-fiction bestseller was followed by *Blink* in 2005. *Blink* is about thinking. Why are some people able to make brilliant decisions in the blink of an eye while others seem to always make the wrong decision? *Blink* also was a non-fiction bestseller.

_____

_____

4 **Use your outline and your notes from Prepare to Write on page 26 and Organize on page 18 to write the first draft of your summary paragraph. Make an organizer to help you plan your ideas.**

- Make sure to include a clear topic sentence and content that supports it.

- Write a topic sentence that introduces the genius that you are going to write about and includes a controlling idea.

- Use the past perfect and time words to show the correct order of events.

REVISE: Identifying and Correcting Sentence Fragments

1 Choose the correct sentence.

   a. When Mozart, who was a child prodigy, wrote his first composition for piano.

   b. Before he went to Lithuania, Daniel Tammet had started to study the language.

   c. Malcolm Gladwell who wrote the book *Outliers*.

Sentence Fragments

Sentence fragments are incomplete sentences. They are often lacking a subject or verb. Other fragments may be dependent clauses that are not connected to an independent clause. These fragments are usually introduced by a relative pronoun (*that, who, which, whom,* etc.) or a subordinating conjunction (*after, although, because, since, when,* etc.). Look at the fragments and their problems.

Sentence Fragment	Problem
Because he could speak seven languages.	This is a dependent clause introduced by *because* (subordinating conjunction). There is no independent clause.
The book that Malcolm Gladwell wrote.	This is a subject. There is no main verb for the sentence.
Spoke seven languages fluently by the time he was twenty-one.	There is no subject.
Living in a large red house in France.	This is a subject. There is no main verb for the sentence.

There are a variety of strategies for correcting sentence fragments.

- Connect the fragment to the sentence before or after it.
- Change the punctuation.
- Add a subject or a verb.

- Add more information and rewrite it as a complete sentence.
- Remove the subordinating conjunction or relative pronoun.

2 Write *F* if the item is a fragment. Write *C* if the item is a complete sentence.

_____ 1. Although autistic savants have many extraordinary skills and abilities.

_____ 2. Gladwell has written an interesting book, which emphasizes the importance of hard work in achieving success.

_____ 3. Before Daniel received his counting book when he was four years old.

_____ 4. Before he had an epileptic seizure, there was no evidence that Daniel had extraordinary math abilities.

_____ 5. Because Dr. Levitin says that at least 10,000 hours of practice are needed to achieve success.

_____ 6. The book that Kim Peek was reading before he met Daniel Tammet at the library.

_____ 7. Practicing as much as ten hours a day before the math competition.

_____ 8. Einstein was voted the "Person of the Twentieth Century" by *Time* magazine after he received the Nobel Prize for Physics.

3 Work with a partner. Use the strategies in the box above to correct each item you identified as a sentence fragment in Exercise 2.

4 Now go back to the first draft of your paragraph.

- Make sure your supporting paragraphs do not include any sentence fragments.
- Try to use the grammar and some of the vocabulary from the unit.

 Go to **MyEnglishLab** for more skill practice.

EDIT: Writing the Final Draft

APPLY Write the final draft of your paragraph and submit it to your teacher. Carefully edit it for grammatical and mechanical errors, such as spelling, capitalization, and punctuation. Consider how to apply the vocabulary, grammar, and writing skills from the unit. Use the checklist to help you.

FINAL DRAFT CHECKLIST

☐ Does the paragraph fully describe why the person is considered a genius and how he or she achieved expertise?

☐ Is there a topic sentence with a controlling idea that introduces the genius?

☐ Is the paragraph free of sentence fragments?

☐ Do you use the past perfect correctly?

☐ Do you use vocabulary from the unit?

ALTERNATIVE WRITING TOPIC

APPLY Daniel Levitin states that it takes 10,000 hours of practice to achieve true world-class expertise. Nevertheless, many people have put in that amount of practice in their fields and still have not achieved world-class expertise. Why do you think they were not successful? What makes the experts different from the others who have also put in 10,000 hours of practice? Explain. Use the grammar and vocabulary from the unit.

CHECK WHAT YOU'VE LEARNED

Check (✔) the outcomes you've met and vocabulary you've learned. Put an X next to the skills and vocabulary you still need to practice.

Learning Outcomes

☐ **Understand assumptions**

☐ **Take notes by marking important information**

☐ **Distinguish voice in quotations**

☐ **Use past perfect**

☐ **Identify and correct sentence fragments**

☐ **Write a summary paragraph**

Vocabulary

☐ **anxious**

☐ **assimilate**

☐ **astonishing** (*adj.*)

☐ **benefit** (*n.*) AWL

☐ **compensate** AWL

☐ **disabled** (*adj.*)

☐ **emerging** (*adj.*) AWL

☐ **estimate** (*v.*) AWL

☐ **expertise** AWL

☐ **flexible** AWL

☐ **image** AWL

☐ **interaction**

☐ **persistence**

☐ **predictable** AWL

☐ **retain** AWL

☐ **savant**

☐ **transform** AWL

➤ Go to **MyEnglishLab** to watch a video about child prodigies, access the Unit Project, and take the Unit 1 Achievement Test.

LEARNING OUTCOMES

> Infer the meaning of idioms and expressions
> Take notes on main ideas with questions
> Recognize positive redundancy

> Use gerunds and infinitives
> Choose appropriate supporting sentences
> Write a biographical paragraph

🖱 Go to **MyEnglishLab** to check what you know.

Facing Life's Obstacles

FOCUS ON THE TOPIC

1. There are many different kinds of obstacles that people face in their lives: Physical and economic are two examples. What are some other examples of the kinds of obstacles that people face?

2. What are some ways that people overcome their obstacles?

READING ONE | A Life of Twists and Turns: The Story of Frank McCourt

VOCABULARY

1 Read the passage about author Frank McCourt. Try to understand the boldfaced words from the context.

Frank McCourt was born in Brooklyn, New York, in 1930. His parents, Angela and Malachy, had moved to New York from Ireland in search of a better life. Unfortunately, life was not easy in New York. His father could not earn enough money to support his family. The McCourts returned to Ireland hoping their life would improve. Again, it didn't. Life in Ireland was equally hard, if not harder than in New York. Three of Frank's siblings died as babies. Eventually, his father **abandoned** the family, which forced his four sons and Angela to live a very **meager** existence.

Frank's childhood was filled with **misery**. There was never enough food. Their house was small, dirty, and very cold in the winter. When it rained, the floor would flood with water. Frank and his brothers **yearned for** a better life.

Frank was a **curious** boy and found reading as one way to escape from his **tormented** childhood. Because his house was falling apart and had no electricity, he would read under the street lamp outside his home. He also had an excellent sense of humor. Humor was the McCourts' defense against their life of relentless **poverty** and **hopelessness**. Even though they often felt **humiliated**, the McCourts could usually find something to laugh about.

In 1949, Frank returned to the United States. He was nineteen years old and only had an eighth-grade education. He was full of **shame** about his past and often invented stories about his unhappy childhood instead of telling the truth. However, Frank was never **defeated** by his obstacles. In fact, Frank eventually used his humor and his storytelling talents to overcome the challenges life had set before him. He enjoyed much success until his death in 2009 at the age of seventy-eight.

2 Write each boldfaced word from the reading passage next to its synonym.

1. _____ sadness

2. _____ poor, sparse

3. _____ embarrassment (*n.*)

4. _____ beaten, overcome by

5. _____ strongly desired, wanted

6. _____ painful

7. _____ embarrassed, mortified (*adj.*)

8. _____ having little money or few material things

9. _____ left someone behind

10. _____ being without hope

11. _____ inquisitive

➤ Go to the **Pearson Practice English App** or **MyEnglishLab** for more vocabulary practice.

PREVIEW

Read the first two paragraphs of *A Life of Twists and Turns: The Story of Frank McCourt* on the next page. Answer the questions.

1. The reading on the previous page said that Frank McCourt returned to New York in 1949, and the reading on the next page describes what he was doing in 1958. What do you think happened to him between 1949 and 1958?

2. Do you think McCourt was nervous? Explain.

3. What do you think he did "to show the class who was boss"?

READ

Read the article about Frank McCourt on the next page. Create a chart like the one below to take notes.

TAKE NOTES

Main Ideas	Details
Frank McCourt – 1st day teaching	1958 – McKee Voc.Tech. HS
	recent NYU grad – English
	nervous – knows he must control class

➤ Go to **MyEnglishLab** to view example notes.

A Life of Twists and Turns: The Story of Frank McCourt

By Greg Russos

1 On the first day of his first-ever teaching job, Frank McCourt went to his classroom early. Waiting for his students at the McKee Vocational and Technical High School in New York's Staten Island, he gazed at the rows of empty seats that lay before him and pondered[1] his role. The year was 1958, and McCourt had graduated from New York University not long before. He had earned a bachelor's degree in English, and now it was time to share his enthusiasm for the subject with bright young minds.

2 McCourt watched his students file in and tried to project confidence. "Make one mistake your first day and it takes months to recover," he'd been told. Suddenly, McCourt had a problem. One boy, Petey, had thrown his sandwich at another student. McCourt reflected, "Professors of education at New York University never lectured on how to handle flying-sandwich situations." Although he had no idea what to do, he did know that he had to show the class who was boss.

3 Just then, McCourt had an idea. He strode across the classroom and picked the sandwich up off the floor. In his first act of classroom management, McCourt unwrapped the sandwich. He noticed that the bread was homemade and saw that it contained rich layers of baloney, tomato, and onions. So, he took a bite, followed by another. Moments later, the sandwich was gone. "Yo, teacher, that's my sandwich you et [sic]," came Petey's accusation. "Shaddup [sic]," the rest of the class rejoined. "Can't you see the teacher is eating?"

4 Students quickly came to see McCourt as an unconventional[2] teacher, and a humorous one, too.

After this unusual beginning, he went on to spend the next thirty years working in high schools all over New York. At many moments he questioned his teaching abilities. Yet by the time he retired in 1987, he had earned the admiration of thousands of students.

5 In his book *Teacher Man*, published in 2005, McCourt recounted the anecdote about the sandwich with characteristic playfulness. After he captured the attention of the class, he claimed, "I felt like a champion." However, there is more to this incident than meets the eye. At least part of the motivation for McCourt's response came from the deprivation he experienced when he was young. His childhood had taught him that food was not to be wasted. McCourt was born in New York in 1930, at the beginning of the Great Depression, and his earliest years were defined by **poverty** and hardship.

6 At the start of the twentieth century, millions of Irish people made their way to the United States. McCourt's parents, Malachy and Angela, were part of this wave of immigrants. They **yearned for** a better life and imagined New York to be a sort of paradise. At certain moments, their vision was realized. For example, in his 1996 memoir *Angela's Ashes*, McCourt described the meals that his mother would prepare when his father managed to find work. He cast his mind back to "a breakfast of eggs, fried tomatoes and fried bread, tea with lashings of sugar and milk and, later in the day, a big dinner of mashed potatoes, peas and ham, [even] a trifle[3]."

7 But this memory aside, the McCourts often struggled to make ends meet. Malachy had a

---

[1] **pondered:** considered, contemplated, wondered about
[2] **unconventional:** unusual, not typical
[3] **trifle:** a dessert made with fruit and cake covered with jam and cream

continued on next page

tendency to squander his **meager** wages, leaving the family hungry. At that time, the McCourts had four other children besides Frank. To feed them, Angela resorted to buying on credit and begged for milk from local bars. The McCourts were seeing that their new home was not the exalted[4] land they had imagined. In 1934, the McCourts' youngest child, Margaret, died after coming down with a dangerous fever. This tragedy, together with the family's financial difficulties, left the McCourts **defeated**. Later that same year, they made the tough decision to return to Ireland.

8 Back home, the family's troubles continued. At first, they hoped they might be taken in by Malachy's relatives in the north of the country. However, Malachy's parents and siblings had problems of their own and wasted no time turning them away. Next, the McCourts journeyed south, where Angela's family was based. A similarly cold reception by Angela's mother left them feeling **humiliated** and alone. Eventually, they ended up in a city called Limerick, in a one-room apartment infested with fleas.

9 At that stage of his life, McCourt was **tormented** by rain. To summarize his childhood he wrote that, "Above all—we were wet." The intensity of Ireland's storms was such that, for months, "the walls of Limerick glistened with damp." Diseases such as bronchitis, pneumonia, and tuberculosis were a constant worry. Home remedies did little to relieve these **miseries**. In Limerick, McCourt's younger brother, Oliver, died of scarlet fever. Oliver's twin, Eugene, passed away soon after. Angela fell into a deep depression. On her darkest days she could barely get out of bed.

10 Over the following years, the McCourts continued to struggle. Food was scarce, and a typical dinner consisted of just bread and tea. Sometimes, the family had to wander the streets looking for coal, which they needed for heat. When Angela could afford food, she had to be careful not to be cheated by shop owners. Charitable groups helped the family get by, but they also made them feel **shame** at their situation. In other words, adversaries were everywhere. Meanwhile, Malachy was excluded from many jobs because his accent marked him as an outsider. There was also the troubling issue of his character: He did little to help the family, and he later **abandoned** them completely.

11 In spite of the **hopelessness** that surrounded him, McCourt was determined to make something of himself. He was an inquisitive child, **curious** about everything. A classmate, Mikey Molloy, made a big impression on him. Mikey's father brought Mikey books from the library, and McCourt saw him as someone who "knows everything." McCourt dreamed of being able to read books like Mikey did. He got his chance when, at the age of ten, he was admitted to hospital with typhoid fever. In the three and a half months that he spent on bed rest, he read night and day. He had befriended a hospital worker who, though illiterate, had picked up on his love of learning and found him a box filled with classic texts.

12 McCourt's interest in reading grew into a love of writing, and soon he realized that words could be a way for him to earn money. First, he began reading novels out loud for an elderly neighbor, Mr. Timoney. Later, he got a job with a moneylender, Mrs. Finucane, who needed help composing letters to people in her debt. McCourt was so keen to impress her that he began to throw in words that he didn't even really understand. One way to think about this detail is as another example of McCourt's humor. On the other hand, it also shows how his circumstances were forcing him to come up with creative solutions to the problems he faced. Mrs. Finucane was thrilled with McCourt's efforts, and the money she paid him eventually enabled him to purchase a ticket back to New York. Throughout these years, McCourt's parents encouraged his education. Even his father, for all his shortcomings[5], wanted his son to get ahead.

---

[4] **exalted:** glorious, dignified

[5] **shortcomings:** fault or failure to meet a certain standard, typically in a person's character, a plan, or a system

continued on next page

Facing Life's Obstacles **37**

13 McCourt reached New York in 1949, but he would experience other challenges before finally landing his job at McKee. First, he began working as a janitor at a luxury hotel in downtown Manhattan. He was miserable there but couldn't seek better employment because he didn't have a high school diploma. Then, in 1951, he was drafted into the army to serve in the Korean War. As part of his military service he trained as a clerk, giving him his first exposure to professional life. At this point, he got it into his head that he wanted to become a teacher. However, in spite of his newfound skills, he frequently questioned this ambition. In Ireland, he'd always been told that he shouldn't attempt to "get above himself." In addition to the material obstacles McCourt faced, another issue was his low self-esteem.

14 Following his time in the army, McCourt set about getting the qualifications he needed for a career in education. Still, he was plagued by doubts, and he very nearly gave up on his dream. After he graduated from New York University he backpedaled, and took a job working in shipyards. In his words, "I didn't think I was cut out for the life of a teacher." He was spending his days loading and unloading merchandise on the Manhattan, Hoboken, and Brooklyn piers when a chance conversation with a fellow worker changed his perspective. Confused by McCourt's choices, his colleague demanded to know: "What's the use of a college education [if] you just gonna stand on the platform checking off sacks of peppers?" That was when McCourt decided he might as well give teaching a shot.

15 In the classroom, McCourt discovered that his personal experiences were of great interest to his students. He began telling them stories about his upbringing and life in Ireland. This approach encouraged his students to study and motivated them to open up about their own lives. This, in turn, helped them to become better writers, which was one of McCourt's most important aims. On occasion, McCourt's colleagues criticized his methods. Teachers had a right to privacy, they claimed. But in McCourt's view, any strategy that enabled him to teach effectively was acceptable.

16 After his time at McKee, McCourt went on to teach at five other schools around New York. In 1972, he landed at the elite Stuyvesant High School, where he remained until the end of his career. As the years went by, he became one of the most popular teachers at Stuyvesant, and any student who wanted to be a writer was invariably told that they had to enroll in his classes. Remarkably, McCourt had earned this reputation in spite of the fact that he had, until that point, done little writing of his own.

17 McCourt was known for telling people, "Dance your dance. Tell your tale." After he finally retired, he began to think that he should follow his own advice. He set his sights on crafting a memoir although he didn't see himself as a writer. The result of his efforts was *Angela's Ashes*, which told the story of his childhood—a story McCourt had been hesitant to write while his mother was alive as he did not want to embarrass her. In the book, McCourt wanted to portray a young person's perception of the adult world. He chose to narrate his experiences in the present tense, a decision which lent the book an air of innocence and made it easy for readers to relate to his story. The book was a runaway success, selling millions of copies and winning McCourt both a Pulitzer Prize and the National Book Critics Circle Award. Afterwards, two other memoirs were published (*'Tis* and *Teacher Man*). A film deal also followed. McCourt's rapid rise to fame caught him off guard, and he often reflected on the ways his life had changed. According to people who knew him, although he took great pride in his many successes, he still remained humble.

18 McCourt passed away in 2009 after a battle with melanoma[6]. His death prompted moving tributes from friends and family, as well as from former students and fans around the world. Many people asked themselves how they should remember him. Was he more of a teacher or more of a writer? Or perhaps he should be thought of just as someone who loved stories. It is in these reflections that McCourt's greatest lesson can be found. Each of us has the opportunity to wear more than one hat, and it is up to us to make the most of the years we have. In each of the many chapters of his long life, McCourt made an indelible[7] mark. There is no reason why we can't do the same.

19 In keeping with his wishes, McCourt's ashes were scattered in Limerick, amidst the ruins of a thirteenth century castle. In 2010, a New York City high school was named after him.

---

[6] **melanoma:** a type of skin cancer
[7] **indelible:** unforgettable

MAIN IDEAS

Complete the timeline with information from Vocabulary on page 34 and Reading One.
Use your notes to help you.

1930	*Frank McCourt born in Brooklyn, New York*
1934	
1949	
1951	
1958	
1972	
1996	
2009	

DETAILS

1 Complete the left side of the chart using information from Main Ideas. Then complete
the right side of the chart with details about why the event took place and what
happened as a result. Look at Vocabulary on page 34 and Reading One for the
information. Use your notes to help you.

1934 Event *Sister Margaret dies and Frank McCourt's family returns to Ireland.*	*The McCourts wanted a better life, so they returned to Ireland. Irish family didn't welcome them. Their life was still very hard. Two other children died. The family remained very poor and very hungry. Father abandoned the family.*
1949 Event	
1951 Event	
1958 Event	
1972 Event	
1996 Event	
2009 Event	

2 Look at your notes and at your answers in Preview. How did they help you understand
the article?

Inferring the Meaning of Idioms and Expressions

An **inference** is an **educated guess** about meaning that is **not directly stated** in a text. Readers can often infer the meaning of idioms and expressions from the context of a story. Closely reading the information in the sentence where the idiom or expression is used, as well as reading the sentences before and after that sentence, will help readers to determine the meaning of an idiom or expression.

Look at the example and read the explanation.

What does the boldfaced idiom mean?

> The McCourts often struggled **to make ends meet**. Malachy had a tendency to squander his meager wages, leaving the family hungry. At that time, the McCourts had four other children besides Frank. To feed them, Angela resorted to buying on credit and begged for milk from local bars. (*paragraph 7*)

In the excerpt, we read that Malachy didn't earn much money and what he did earn he wasted. This left the family of seven hungry, so Angela had to beg for milk and buy on credit. It is clear that the McCourts didn't have enough money to survive. We can guess that the meaning of the idiom is "to have enough money to buy what you need to live."

1 Find the idioms and expressions in the paragraphs noted in parentheses. Read the idioms and expressions in context and use context clues to determine their meaning. Write a synonym or definition for each.

1. more to something than meets the eye (*paragraph 5*)

_____

2. cast his mind back to (*paragraph 6*)

_____

3. turning them away (*paragraph 8*)

_____

4. (to) get by (*paragraph 10*)

_____

5. to make something of himself (*paragraph 11*)

_____

6. got it into his head (*paragraph 13*)

_____

7. get above himself (*paragraph 13*)

_____

8. was cut out for (*paragraph 14*)

_____

9. open up about (*paragraph 15*)

_____

10. caught off guard (*paragraph 17*)

_____

11. to wear more than one hat (*paragraph 18*)

_____

2 **Compare your answers with a partner. Discuss the context clues, sentences, words, or phrases in the paragraphs that helped you figure out the meanings.**

DISCUSS 🔍

USE YOUR NOTES

Use your notes to support your answers with information from the reading.

Work in a small group. Choose one of the questions. Discuss your ideas. Then choose one person in your group to report the ideas to the class.

1. Frank McCourt had many obstacles in his life. What do you think was Frank McCourt's greatest obstacle? How did he overcome it?

2. How did Frank McCourt's students give him the courage he had been lacking to overcome his obstacles?

🔾 Go to **MyEnglishLab** to give your opinion about another question.

READING TWO │ Marla Runyan Has Never Lost Sight of Her Goals

PREVIEW

Marla Runyan is an accomplished athlete who is legally blind. Despite her blindness, she has excelled in many fields in addition to athletics. How has she been able to do so much? She explains it by saying, "A poor attitude can be far more disabling than blindness."

1 **Read the title and the first paragraph of the reading. Write two questions that you think will be answered in this reading.**

_____

_____

2 **Look at the boldfaced words in the reading. Which words do you know the meanings of?**

1 Read the article about Marla Runyan. As you read, guess the meaning of the words that are new to you. Remember to take notes on main ideas and details.

Marla Runyan Has Never Lost Sight of Her Goals

1 Marla Runyan is a woman used to questions. There are the interviews about how she made history chasing an Olympic dream, runners who want to know how she trains, people looking for advice on how to overcome the obstacles in their lives. They come to her looking for answers sometimes mundane and sometimes profound. But since she was a child, there has been one question that has followed her above all others: What do you see?

2 At the age of nine, Runyan was diagnosed with Stargardt's disease. It's a genetic condition that causes progressive vision loss, and most who suffer from it have their sight degenerate[1] to the point of legal blindness.

3 Now forty-four, Runyan's vision is reduced to shadows and indistinct shapes, though she retains some peripheral sight.

4 "Here's what I do see: a permanent blot in front of my eyes that almost has physical properties," she described in her autobiography, *No Finish Line: My Life As I See It*. "Imagine that some-one took a flash picture, and the flash got in your eyes. For a few moments, you'd see a purplish or grey splotch. In a few minutes it would fade away, and the world around you would appear normal again. For me, it stays."

5 However, she has refused to be defined by her condition. Today she holds the Paralympic World Records in the B3 division for the 100-meter, 200-meter, 400-meter, 800-meter, 1500-meter, High Jump, Long Jump, and Pentathlon.

6 Her success has extended far beyond athletics. She has been a teacher, a public speaker, a coach, the race director for the Camarillo Half Marathon, a philanthropist[2] for Camp Ability, and, with the publication of her autobiography *No Finish Line: My Life As I See It*, a bestselling author.

7 This was not the life most thought Runyan would have. As a child, the specialists told her to lower her expectations. They told her she shouldn't expect to get the same grades as her fellow students because she wouldn't be able to learn the way they did. They told her that meant she likely wouldn't get into a good college.

8 While Runyan may not have been graced with perfect eyes, she was given a loving mother who instilled in her a sense of hard work, **self-reliance**, and pride.

---

[1] **degenerate:** to become worse
[2] **philanthropist:** a person who donates his or her time or money to help others

Continued on next page

9 "A poor attitude can be far more disabling than blindness," Runyan would later say.

10 All of the specialists were wrong. Runyan refused to give up because of her disability. In 1987, she graduated from Adolfo Camarillo High School, then went on to attend the University of San Diego to complete her master's degree in 1994. She studied education for deaf and blind students.

11 Still, none of it came easily.

12 As an adult, Runyan admitted to struggling in the classroom because schoolwork was so **laborious** for her. However, one place she felt free was on the field. She'd always been an athletic girl, and, in college, she found herself drawn to the track.

13 When she was running, the divisions between herself and the students with perfect vision fell away. She felt as if she could do as well as everyone else.

14 It was a feeling she would chase the rest of her life, and following it would lead her into history.

15 In 2000, when she journeyed to Sydney, she became the first legally blind person ever to compete in the Olympic Games.

16 Then, in 2002, she finished the New York City Marathon in fourth place with a time of 2 hours, 27 minutes, and ten seconds, becoming the fastest American in that year's competition and the second fastest American woman ever to cross the finish line.

17 In preparation for those games, Runyan told reporters that her biggest challenge was to keep track of the people just ahead of her as she navigated the field.

18 To compensate for her handicap, Runyan prepared for a style of racing she described as "fast and tactical—a combination of both."

19 The one thing she didn't plan for, or want, was sympathy.

20 "I don't expect any mercy, no mercy whatsoever," she said. "They're not going to say, 'Go ahead Marla.' That's not going to happen."

21 Runyan's unique story put her in the international spotlight and brought her fans across the globe.

22 Runyan explained to reporters that, though she loves knowing that she inspires people, seeing how strongly some people react to her story can be shocking.

23 In that interview, Runyan went on to recount how she received an email from a woman whose son wanted to be a skateboarder but had also been diagnosed with Stargardt's. At first, the mother refused to allow him, but once she read Runyan's story, she told him, "Go get the ramp."

24 As much as these stories inspire Runyan to continue her example, she admits that even reading them can be a **struggle**. Reading is extremely difficult, and she can only do so with a voice output system on her computer. The words have to be enlarged so much that sometimes only three letters at a time can fit on the screen.

25 There are moments when she simply **gives up** for the day. Even the simple act of reading an email is too much.

26 Those moments never last long.

27 "I've never known anyone to be successful if all they do is blame, if they choose to be a victim," she told reporters. "If you choose to be a victim of this or that, or of what others have done to you, or what you believe to be someone else's fault, [you're] just constantly making excuses. I think the secret to achieving something is holding yourself **accountable** for your choices, good and bad, and learning from your mistakes, and then re-grouping and moving on. It's an ongoing process."

2 Compare your notes on main ideas and details with a partner's. How can you improve your notes next time?

⬤ Go to the **Pearson Practice English App** or **MyEnglishLab** for more vocabulary practice.

Taking Notes on Main Ideas with Questions

When you generate key questions from a text, you are identifying main ideas. Thinking about what question a section of a text answers will help you comprehend the text. These questions can also serve as a study aid for a test or help you complete an assignment.

You can write these questions directly in the margins of the text if you own the book. If the book is not yours, use post-it notes or write on a separate piece of paper or your computer or tablet.

Look at paragraph 2. What question is answered in this paragraph?

The question could be:

What is Marla's condition?

According to paragraph 2, Marla has Stargardt's disease, which causes vision loss.

Go back to Reading Two and write questions for paragraphs 4, 7, 8 and 9, 12, and 24. Share your questions with a partner and see if they can answer them.

1. Paragraph 4: _____ ?

2. Paragraph 7: _____ ?

3. Paragraphs 8 and 9: _____ ?

4. Paragraph 12: _____ ?

5. Paragraph 24: _____ ?

🔾 Go to **MyEnglishLab** for more note-taking practice.

COMPREHENSION

1 Two of the three answers for each question are correct. Circle the two correct answers and cross out the incorrect answer. Use your notes from Reading Two to help you. Discuss your answers with a partner.

1. What does Marla "see"?

    a. She sees a permanent blot.

    b. She sees shadows and indistinct shapes.

    c. She sees blindness.

2. How has her life defied the experts' predictions?

    a. She graduated from college.

    b. She struggled in the classroom.

    c. She became a bestselling author.

3. How did she feel on the field?

    a. She felt equal to everyone else.

    b. She felt free.

    c. She felt she needed sympathy.

4. What strategies have helped her to be successful?

    a. She lowered her expectations.

    b. She had a good attitude.

    c. She worked hard.

5. How does she feel about her effect on other people?

    a. She is shocked.

    b. She is inspired.

    c. She is self-reliant.

2 **Review the boldfaced words from the reading with a partner. Use a dictionary or ask your teacher for any meanings you still do not know.**

READING SKILL

1 Look at Reading Two again. How many synonyms and antonyms can you find?

Recognizing Positive Redundancy

Authors often use synonyms and antonyms in their writing for **positive redundancy.** This use of synonyms and antonyms exposes readers to ideas more than once but with different vocabulary. In this way, meaning is reinforced, but language is new. The writer's ideas stay with the reader as related vocabulary is threaded through a text.

Reread paragraph 4 of Reading Two:

> "Here's what I do see: a permanent ***blot*** in front of my eyes that almost has physical properties," she described in her autobiography, *No Finish Line: My Life As I See It*. "Imagine that someone took a flash picture, and the flash got in your eyes. For a few moments, you'd see a purplish or grey splotch. In a few minutes it would fade away, and the world around you would appear normal again. For me, it stays."

In the first sentence, Marla uses the word *blot*. What synonym for the word *blot* does she use later in the paragraph?

The synonym *splotch* adds interest to her description. Instead of repeating the word *blot*, the author uses a synonym to repeat an idea, but with new language.

Noticing synonyms and antonyms will help you see where the author emphasizes important information and ideas.

2 Work with a partner. Identify synonyms and antonyms for the words given. Discuss the effect of using different language rather than repeating the same words or expressions.

1. In paragraph 3, the author mentions *shadows*. What similar expression is also used in this paragraph?

   _____

2. In paragraph 8, the author uses the word *graced*. What synonym is also used in this paragraph?

   _____

3. In paragraph 10, the author uses the phrase *give up*. What antonym is also used in this paragraph?

   _____

4. In paragraph 12, the author talks about *struggling*. What two-word expression with an opposite meaning is also used in this paragraph?

   _____

5. In paragraph 19, the author uses the word *sympathy*. What synonym is used in paragraph 20?

   _____

6. In paragraph 24, the author says reading can be a *struggle*. What similar phrase is also used in this paragraph?

   _____

7. In paragraph 27, the author talks about *blame*. What similar expression is also used in this paragraph?

   _____

🔊 Go to **MyEnglishLab** for more skill practice.

ORGANIZE

Both Frank McCourt in Reading One (R1) and Marla Runyan in Reading Two (R2) faced many obstacles and challenges in their lives. These same challenges also helped them to discover and develop their talent and become successful. Complete the chart comparing Frank McCourt and Marla Runyan.

USE YOUR NOTES

Review your notes from Reading One and Two. Use the information in your notes to complete the chart.

	FRANK MCCOURT (R1)	MARLA RUNYAN (R2)
1. Obstacles they faced		
2. Person or people who influenced and inspired them		
3. Personal values, traits, or characteristics that helped them face their obstacles		
4. Talent or gift that resulted from the challenges they faced		

SYNTHESIZE

Write a short paragraph comparing the lives of Frank McCourt and Marla Runyan. Use the information from Organize. Describe their obstacles and triumphs.

🕩 Go to **MyEnglishLab** to check what you learned.

3 FOCUS ON WRITING

VOCABULARY

REVIEW

Look at the chain diagram showing the three stages of overcoming obstacles: facing an obstacle, dealing with an obstacle, and overcoming an obstacle. Write the words from the box in the correct circles. Some words may go in more than one circle.

abandoned	exalted	humiliated	misery	shame
accountable	free	inquisitive	poverty	struggle
curious	give up	laborious	pride	tormented
defeated	hopelessness	meager	self-reliance	yearning for

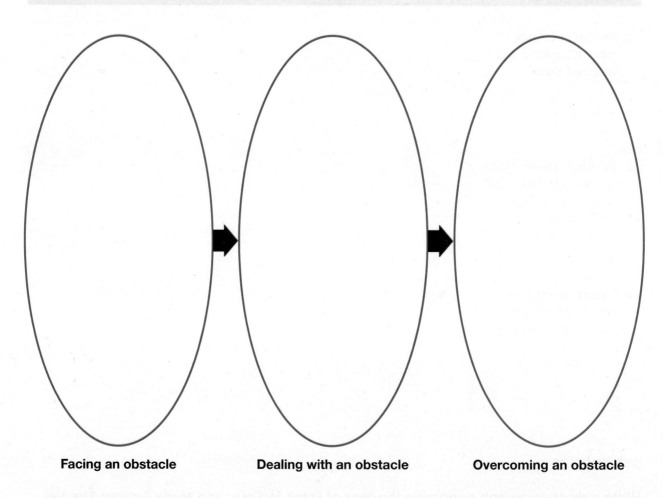

Facing an obstacle   Dealing with an obstacle   Overcoming an obstacle

EXPAND

An **analogy** is a comparison between two words that seem similar or are related in some way. In this exercise, the word pairs are either synonyms or antonyms. For example, in question 1, *struggle* is a synonym of *fight*; in the same way, *embarrassment* is a synonym of *shame*.

Work with a partner. Discuss the relationship between the words. Circle the word that best completes each analogy. Then circle *synonym* or *antonym* for each set of words. Use a dictionary if you need help.

1. struggle : fight = embarrassment : _____
   a. expectation   b. sadness   (c. shame)   (synonym)   antonym

2. confusion : understanding = hopeful : _____
   a. defeated   b. enlivened   c. liberated   synonym   antonym

3. exalted : noble = free : _____
   a. embarrassed   b. confused   c. liberated   synonym   antonym

4. poverty : wealth = misery : _____
   a. hopelessness   b. happiness   c. yearning   synonym   antonym

5. yearning : longing = self-reliance : _____
   a. inquisitiveness   b. independence   c. pride   synonym   antonym

6. laborious : difficult = inquisitive : _____
   a. curious   b. prestigious   c. humiliated   synonym   antonym

7. inquisitiveness : indifference = give up : _____
   a. struggle   b. continue   c. compensate   synonym   antonym

8. meager : plentiful = accountable : _____
   a. irresponsible   b. humiliated   c. inquisitive   synonym   antonym

9. darkest : unhappiest = mortified : _____
   a. tormented   b. liberated   c. humiliated   synonym   antonym

CREATE

APPLY Choose one of the situations. Write a letter using words and phrases from Review and Expand.

1. Imagine you are the mother of the skateboarder with Stargardt's disease. Write a letter to Marla Runyan. Explain how she helped and inspired you and your son.

2. Imagine you are one of Frank McCourt's former students. You have just graduated from college. Write a letter to Frank McCourt. Explain how he helped and inspired you to overcome an obstacle.

Go to the **Pearson Practice English App** or **MyEnglishLab** for more vocabulary practice.

GRAMMAR FOR WRITING

1 Read the sentences. Think about the meanings of the boldfaced words and answer the questions.

a. **Teaching** was the most exalted profession I could imagine.

b. McCourt enjoyed **writing** about his childhood.

c. McCourt had done a lot of **reading**.

d. Marla Runyan refused **to give up** because of her disability.

e. McCourt persuaded New York University **to enroll** him.

f. After McCourt's mother died, he felt free **to write** his memoirs.

g. Marla Runyan has the ability **to inspire** others with her actions.

1. In sentence *a*, what is the subject?

2. In sentence *b*, what is the object of the verb *enjoyed*?

3. In sentence *c*, what word follows the preposition *of*?

4. Look at the boldfaced words in *a*, *b*, and *c*. They are gerunds. How are gerunds formed?

5. In sentence *d*, the main verb is *refused*. What is the verb that follows it?

6. In sentence *e*, the main verb is *persuaded*. What is the object of the main verb? What is the verb that follows it?

7. In sentence *f*, what is the verb that follows the adjective *free*?

8. In sentence *g*, what is the verb that follows the noun *ability*?

9. Look at the boldfaced words in *d*, *e*, *f*, and *g*. They are infinitives. How are infinitives formed?

Gerunds and Infinitives

Gerunds	
To form a gerund, **use the base form of the verb + -ing.**	read + ing = reading write + ing = writing* [*Note that for verbs ending in a consonant and final e, drop the e before adding -ing.]
1. Use the gerund as the **subject** of a sentence.	**Writing** is very important to Frank McCourt.
2. Use the gerund as the **object** of a sentence after certain verbs (such as *enjoy, acknowledge, recall*).	Frank McCourt *enjoys* **writing**. McCourt *recalled* **not wanting** to offend his mother, and that held him back.
3. Use the gerund **after a preposition** (such as *of, in, for, about*).	Frank McCourt is interested *in* **writing**.
Infinitives	
To form an infinitive, **use *to* + the base form of the verb.**	to read to write
4. Use the infinitive **after certain verbs.**	
a. some verbs are followed directly by an infinitive (such as *learn, decide, agree, refuse*)	McCourt's students *learned* **to write** about their personal experiences.
b. some verbs are followed by an object + an infinitive (such as *urge, persuade*)	McCourt *urged* **his students to write** about their personal experiences.
c. some verbs are followed by an infinitive or an object + an infinitive (such as *want, ask, need*)	McCourt *wanted* **to write** about his personal experiences. McCourt *wanted* **them to write** their personal experiences.
5. Use the infinitive **after certain adjectives** (such as *free, able, hard*).	McCourt's students were *free* **to write** about whatever they wanted.
6. Use the infinitive **after certain nouns** (such as *ability, freedom*).	McCourt's students had the *freedom* **to write** about whatever they wanted.

2 Underline the gerund or infinitive in each sentence. Write the number of the rule from the grammar chart that applies to each sentence.

___1___ a. <u>Doing</u> schoolwork was very laborious for Marla Runyan.

_____ b. Marla Runyan has the ability to run as fast as sighted competitors.

_____ c. McCourt acknowledged not going to high school.

_____ d. Marla Runyan was able to compete in the 2000 Olympics.

_____ e. A professor asked McCourt to describe an object from his childhood.

_____ f. Marla Runyan has refused to be defined by her condition.

_____ g. Many people don't feel free to write about their lives.

_____ h. Recounting his experiences inspired McCourt's students.

_____ i. McCourt couldn't think about writing his memoirs while his mother was alive.

_____ j. McCourt's students urged him to write a book.

3 [APPLY] Read the information about Frank McCourt and Marla Runyan. Rewrite each situation using a form of the first verb given and the gerund or infinitive form of the second verb. There may be more than one way to rewrite each sentence.

1. McCourt was worried that his memoirs would embarrass his mother. After she died, he didn't have to worry about this. (feel free / write) *After his mother died, McCourt felt free* *to write his memoirs.*

2. Before Marla runs a marathon, she spends many months preparing. It takes a long time to get ready for a 26-mile race. (need / train) _____

   _____

3. McCourt's classmate, Mikey Molloy, had lots of books that interested McCourt. McCourt asked and asked if could borrow one of them. Molloy finally said he could. (persuade / lend)

   _____

4. Marla's unique story has brought her fans from around the globe. She is happy that her story is helping others. (enjoy / inspire) _____

   _____

5. The McCourts didn't have a lot of money when Frank was growing up. His mother was afraid that the children would be hungry. (worry about / feed) _____

   _____

6. At first, the boy's mother did not want him to skateboard, but after she read about Marla's story, she changed her mind. (decide / let) _____

   _____

7. After McCourt had graduated from New York University, he still was working menial jobs at the shipyard. His co-worker told him to look for a job as a teacher. (urge / become) _____

   _____

8. Because Marla is legally blind, it is a struggle for her to read the words on a computer screen. (be hard / see) _____

   _____

9. McCourt remembered the breakfast of eggs and fried tomatoes his mother sometimes made. He could see and imagine what it tasted like. (recall / eat) _____

_____

10. Specialists told Marla she couldn't expect to get good grades. Despite their predictions, Marla attended college and completed her master's degree. (be able / graduate) _____

_____

Go to the **Pearson Practice English App** or **MyEnglishLab** for more grammar practice. Check what you learned in **MyEnglishLab**.

FINAL WRITING TASK: A Biography Paragraph 🔍 APPLY

In this unit, you read personal accounts of how people overcame major obstacles.

You are going to *write a biographical paragraph about how you or someone you know overcame an obstacle*.

For an alternative writing topic, see page 59.

PREPARE TO WRITE: Listing

Listing is a prewriting activity in which you list information about a topic or category before you begin to write a paragraph or essay. Your list doesn't have to be written in complete sentences. Write quickly. You can always organize your ideas later.

Look back at Connect the Readings on page 47 to complete the left column of the chart. In the right column, write three or more obstacles that you or someone you know has faced.

OBSTACLES FACED BY FRANK MCCOURT AND MARLA RUNYAN	OBSTACLES FACED BY ME OR SOMEONE I KNOW

WRITE

Writing a Biographical Paragraph

A **paragraph** is a group of sentences that are related and that support a controlling idea. A **biographical paragraph** describes a person's life and sometimes focuses on one particular aspect. All paragraphs have three parts: the **topic sentence**, the **supporting sentences**, and the **concluding sentence**.

Topic Sentence

The **topic sentence** introduces the main idea and the controlling idea, which is your idea or opinion about the main idea. The topic sentence controls what you write in the rest of the paragraph. All the sentences in the paragraph must relate to, describe, or illustrate the controlling idea in the topic sentence.

Supporting Sentences

The second part of the paragraph includes **supporting sentences** that give details or examples that develop your ideas about the topic. This is usually the longest part of the paragraph since it discusses and explains the controlling idea.

Concluding Sentence

The **concluding sentence** is the last part of the paragraph. It can do one or more of the following: summarize the paragraph, offer a solution to the problem, restate the topic sentence, or offer an opinion.

Note: For more information on topic sentences and controlling ideas, see Unit 1, Write, page 26.

1 Read the paragraph. Then answer the questions.

Michael Jordan said, "Obstacles don't have to stop you. If you run into a wall, don't turn around and give up. Figure out how to climb it, go through it, or work around it." This attitude can be seen all around us. Many people have faced great obstacles in their lives but have found ways to overcome and actually benefit from these obstacles. For example, Greg Barton, the 1984, 1988, and 1992 U.S. Olympic medalist in kayaking, was born with a serious disability. He had clubfoot: his toes pointed inward, and as a result, he could not walk easily. Even after a series of operations, he still had limited mobility. Even so, Greg was never defeated. First, he taught himself to walk, and even to run. Then he competed on his high school running team. He knew, though, he would never become an Olympic runner, so he looked for other sports that he could play. Happily, he discovered kayaking, a perfect sport for him because it required minimal leg and foot muscles. Using his upper body strength, he was able to master the sport. Finally, after many years of training and perseverance, Greg made the 1984 Olympic team. He says of his accomplishments, "Each step of the road has been made easier by looking just as far as necessary—yet not beyond that." In short, even though that road was paved with obstacles, he was able to overcome them and achieve the impossible.

1. What is the topic of the paragraph? How do you know?

_____

_____

2. What is the controlling idea?

_____

_____

3. Underline the sentences that support the topic and controlling ideas. How do they relate to the controlling idea?

_____

_____

4. What is the concluding sentence? What does it do?

_____

_____

2 Use the information from Prepare to Write on page 53 and complete the chart to plan your paragraph.

- Make sure you have a topic sentence, supporting sentences, and a concluding sentence.
- Check your use of gerunds and infinitives.

Topic Sentence:

1. _____

   _____

Supporting Sentences:

2. _____

   _____

3. _____

   _____

4. _____

   _____

5. _____

   _____

6. _____

   _____

Concluding Sentence:

7. _____

   _____

REVISE: Choosing Appropriate Supporting Sentences

1 Choose two sentences that help the reader understand the sentence, "Back home, the family's troubles continued." Why do these sentences help? Look at the other two sentences. Why are they not helpful?

- Malachy's parents and siblings had problems of their own, and wasted no time turning them away.

- They were a big family and were very poor; they hoped their parents and siblings could help them.

- Many of their friends were poor, too. Their neighbor had fourteen children, and the father did not have a job.

- Eventually, they ended up in a city called Limerick, in a one-room apartment infested with fleas.

Supporting Sentences

The **supporting sentences** in a paragraph help the reader to better understand the controlling idea. Supporting sentences provide examples, details, and facts and must relate directly to the topic sentence.

Look at this paragraph from Reading Two. Note how the supporting sentences offer examples of how Marla's successes go beyond her athletics.

> Marla's success has extended far beyond athletics. She has been a teacher, a public speaker, a coach, the race director for the Camarillo Half Marathon, a philanthropist for Camp Ability, and, with the publication of her autobiography *No Finish Line: My Life As I See It*, a bestselling author.

2 Read each topic sentence. Two ideas support the topic sentence and one does not. Circle the two correct answers and cross out the incorrect answer.

1. Ever since Greg Barton was in high school, he longed to be an Olympic champion.

   a. Greg's sports records

   b. How Greg trained for the Olympics

   c. Greg's academic achievements

2. The achievements of people like Greg Barton and Marla Runyan have inspired many others.

   a. Explanation of how they have inspired others

   b. How many people have read about Greg Barton and Marla Runyan

   c. Greg Barton's and Marla Runyan's obstacles

3. The poverty-stricken lives of Frank McCourt's students deeply affected him.

   a. How Frank saw himself in his students

   b. How Frank taught his students to write

   c. How the students inspired Frank to write

4. Training to run a marathon is a very difficult and time-consuming process.

   a. The patience needed to run a marathon

   b. Reasons why people should run a marathon

   c. The amount of practice and time needed to run a marathon

3 **Read the paragraphs. Each paragraph has one supporting sentence that does not directly relate to the topic sentence. Cross out the sentence and explain why it is unrelated.**

1. Helen Keller lost her sight at a very early age and, so, was very frustrated as a child. First of all, because she could neither hear nor speak, she couldn't understand what was happening around her. She felt her mother's lips moving as she spoke, but this made no sense to her. She couldn't understand what her mother was doing. ~~Her mother could hear and speak.~~ Secondly, once she learned what words were, she felt she could never communicate with them as quickly as sighted people could. As a result of all her frustration, she would often cry and scream until she was exhausted.

   Explanation: _The sentence focuses on her mother's abilities, not Helen's frustrations._

2. Succeeding in sports liberated Marla Runyan and Greg Barton. They both faced overwhelming obstacles, but sports freed them from their hardest struggles. For example, when Marla was on the field, she finally felt she could do as well as everyone else. Similarly, when Greg found the best sport for his physical limitations, he excelled. In addition, Marla has become a bestselling author. They are both great athletes who were freed from their struggles by sports.

   Explanation: _____

   _____

3. Some of the world's most talented and famous people have overcome some of the hardest obstacles. For example, Ludwig van Beethoven became deaf at age forty-six. Franklin D. Roosevelt was paralyzed by polio and was often in a wheelchair, but he was elected president of the United States four times. Finally, Stephen Hawking was a world-famous scientist who was completely paralyzed and couldn't speak. Furthermore, he lived in England. These people show us that we should never give up or let obstacles defeat us.

   Explanation: _____

   _____

4 **Now go back to the first draft of your paragraph.**

- Make sure your supporting sentences directly relate to your topic sentence.

- Try to use the grammar and some of the vocabulary from the unit.

🔊 Go to **MyEnglishLab** for more skill practice.

EDIT: Writing the Final Draft

APPLY Write the final draft of your paragraph and submit it to your teacher. Carefully edit it for grammatical and mechanical errors, such as spelling, capitalization, and punctuation. Consider how to apply the vocabulary, grammar, and writing skills from the unit. Use the checklist to help you.

FINAL DRAFT CHECKLIST

- ☐ Does the paragraph describe a person who was faced with challenges and overcame them?
- ☐ Is there a topic sentence stating the obstacle that the person overcame?
- ☐ Do all the supporting sentences relate directly to the topic sentence?
- ☐ Is there a concluding sentence that restates the main idea of the paragraph, offers an opinion, or suggests a solution?
- ☐ Do you use gerunds and infinitives correctly?
- ☐ Do you use vocabulary from the unit?

ALTERNATIVE WRITING TOPIC

APPLY "I've missed more than 9,000 shots in my career. I've lost almost 300 games. Twenty-six times, I've been trusted to take the game-winning shot and missed. I've failed over and over and over again in my life. And that is why I succeed."

—Michael Jordan

How does this quotation apply to a person you have read about in the unit, to another famous person, or to yourself? Write a paragraph responding to the question. Use the grammar and vocabulary from the unit.

CHECK WHAT YOU'VE LEARNED

Check (✔) the outcomes you've met and vocabulary you've learned. Put an X next to the skills and vocabulary you still need to practice.

Learning Outcomes
- ☐ Infer the meaning of idioms and expressions
- ☐ Take notes on main ideas with questions
- ☐ Recognize positive redundancy
- ☐ Use gerunds and infinitives
- ☐ Choose appropriate supporting sentences
- ☐ Write a biographical paragraph

Vocabulary
- ☐ abandon (v.) AWL
- ☐ accountable
- ☐ curious
- ☐ defeated (adj.)
- ☐ hopelessness
- ☐ humiliated (adj.)
- ☐ laborious
- ☐ meager
- ☐ misery
- ☐ poverty
- ☐ self-reliance
- ☐ shame (n.)
- ☐ struggle (n.)
- ☐ tormented (adj.)

Multi-word Units
- ☐ give up
- ☐ yearn for

⬥ Go to **MyEnglishLab** to watch a video about a girl with autism, access the Unit Project, and take the Unit 2 Achievement Test.

LEARNING OUTCOMES

> Infer degree of support
> Take notes on cause and effect with a graphic organizer
> Organize the sequence of events in a timeline

> Use past unreal conditionals
> Write introductions and hooks
> Write an opinion essay

🔊 Go to **MyEnglishLab** to check what you know.

Making Medical Decisions

1 FOCUS ON THE TOPIC

1. Who is the person in the photo? What is he doing?

2. What role can genes play in medicine? Do you think medical treatment could be more effective if doctors had genetic information about their patients?

3. Genetic testing is now widely available and far less expensive than it has been in the past. What would be the advantage of someone's knowing he or she had a gene for a specific disease? What would be the disadvantage?

READING ONE | Genetic Testing and Disease: Would You Want to Know?

VOCABULARY

1 Read the timeline about the history of medicine and medical decision-making. Try to understand the boldfaced words from the context.

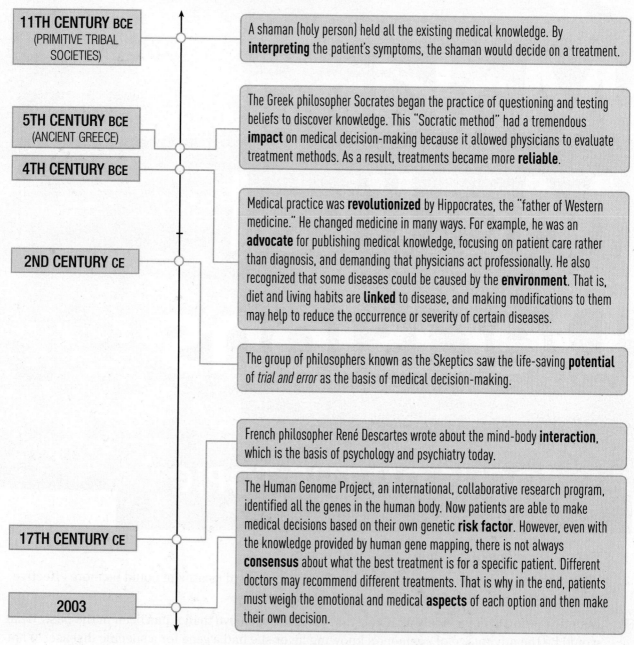

11TH CENTURY BCE
(PRIMITIVE TRIBAL SOCIETIES)

A shaman (holy person) held all the existing medical knowledge. By **interpreting** the patient's symptoms, the shaman would decide on a treatment.

5TH CENTURY BCE
(ANCIENT GREECE)

4TH CENTURY BCE

The Greek philosopher Socrates began the practice of questioning and testing beliefs to discover knowledge. This "Socratic method" had a tremendous **impact** on medical decision-making because it allowed physicians to evaluate treatment methods. As a result, treatments became more **reliable**.

2ND CENTURY CE

Medical practice was **revolutionized** by Hippocrates, the "father of Western medicine." He changed medicine in many ways. For example, he was an **advocate** for publishing medical knowledge, focusing on patient care rather than diagnosis, and demanding that physicians act professionally. He also recognized that some diseases could be caused by the **environment**. That is, diet and living habits are **linked** to disease, and making modifications to them may help to reduce the occurrence or severity of certain diseases.

The group of philosophers known as the Skeptics saw the life-saving **potential** of *trial and error* as the basis of medical decision-making.

French philosopher René Descartes wrote about the mind-body **interaction**, which is the basis of psychology and psychiatry today.

17TH CENTURY CE

The Human Genome Project, an international, collaborative research program, identified all the genes in the human body. Now patients are able to make medical decisions based on their own genetic **risk factor**. However, even with the knowledge provided by human gene mapping, there is not always **consensus** about what the best treatment is for a specific patient. Different doctors may recommend different treatments. That is why in the end, patients must weigh the emotional and medical **aspects** of each option and then make their own decision.

2003

2 Write each boldfaced word from the timeline next to its definition.

1. _____ something that is likely to hurt you or be dangerous

2. _____ the effect that an event or situation has on someone or something

3. _____ the possibility that something will develop or happen in a particular way

4. _____ the situations, things, people, etc. that surround people and affect the way in which they live and work

5. _____ a process in which two or more things have an effect on each other

6. _____ the parts of a situation, plan, or subject

7. _____ an opinion that everyone in a group agrees with or accepts

8. _____ someone who publicly supports someone or something

9. _____ explaining or deciding on the meaning of an event, statement, etc.

10. _____ able to be trusted; dependable

11. _____ related or connected, often because one strongly affects or causes the other

12. _____ to have completely changed the way people think or do things

⬆ Go to the **Pearson Practice English App** or **MyEnglishLab** for more vocabulary practice.

PREVIEW

Read the first two paragraphs of *Genetic Testing and Disease: Would You Want to Know?* Answer the questions.

1. Why do you think Kristen wants to know if she has the gene for Huntington's disease?

2. How can knowing if she has the gene for Huntington's disease help her live her life better?

3. What do you think Kristen's brother thinks about her being tested?

1 Read the article about genetic testing and disease. Create a chart like the one below to take notes.

TAKE NOTES

Main Ideas	Details
genetic testing for neurodegenerative diseases – like Huntington's	Kristen and Nate's mom had Huntington's Kristen – wants test, Nate – unsure
Researchers identified genes that play roles in diseases.	Genetic testing could revolutionize medicine.

▶ Go to **MyEnglishLab** to view example notes.

Genetic Testing and Disease: Would You Want to Know?

By Janice Lloyd, USA TODAY

1 Kristen Powers finishes packing her lunch and opens the kitchen door to leave for high school with her brother, Nate, in tow[1]. "I drive but always let him pick the music," she says, smiling. He gives her a gentle nudge[2] and they set off to the car.

2 Nothing like having a kid brother behind you, especially when you are embarking[3] on a courageous journey. Kristen, 18, is having blood work done May 18 to find out whether she inherited the defective gene for Huntington's disease, a fatal, neurodegenerative disorder that can debilitate victims as early as their mid-thirties. The siblings have a fifty-fifty chance of developing the rare disease, which claimed their mother's life last year at age forty-five.

3 Nate, 16, doesn't know whether he'll follow his sister's lead. Only people eighteen or older can be tested, unless they're exhibiting symptoms, because a positive result can be shattering news. There's also no cure. Huntington's is devastating on so many levels: People lose coordination, developing wild jerky movements; they suffer behavioral changes, often becoming depressed and psychotic; and in the end, they develop dementia and require total care. One of their last images of their mother was in a wheelchair in a nursing home.

4 Nate "has been amazingly supportive of my wanting to get tested," Kristen says. "He is interested in the whole process, but he's been hesitant over the years to commit to testing, while I've known since I was fifteen that I wanted to do this."

5 "Know thyself" has taken on a scientific meaning for a growing number of people who, like Kristen, want a crystal ball to look into their DNA. Ever since the Human Genome Project identified the 20,000 to 25,000 genes in 2003, researchers have continued to identify the ones that play roles in diseases, from Alzheimer's to type-2 diabetes to certain types of cancer. Though lifestyle and environment are big pieces of the puzzle, consider this: Genetic tests could become part of standard care for everyone and **revolutionize** the way medicine is practiced, proponents say.

6 Gone would be the days of waiting to develop a disease. People would know about diseases they are at risk for and could change their living habits or consider treatments. Opponents warn about the **potential** for invasion of privacy—threatening employment and insurance—and the possibility that people equipped with the knowledge of their genetic makeup might make risky and unhealthy decisions.

[1] **in tow:** following closely behind someone or something
[2] **nudge:** push
[3] **embarking:** starting something new, difficult, or exciting

continued on next page

7 Kristen has had counseling at the University of North Carolina to prepare her for dealing with her testing news, and she copes with stress by walking with her rescue dog, Jake. "Walking is critical for me," she says. She will return to the campus at the end of May with her father, Ed Powers, to get the results.

8 "She's always wanted to take matters into her own hands," her father says. "She's constantly asking what we can do to make things better. I am her biggest backer and want to be there for her every step of the way during this."

Leaning on social media

9 Kristen leans on her kitchen table and explains in a quiet, clear voice that she is ready to handle the news and has no plans to keep it secret. "I started out trying to find answers on the internet about Huntington's disease," she says, "but I quickly became very disappointed. There's not a good video or an **advocate** for it, like Michael J. Fox is for Parkinson's disease."

10 She has raised $17,580 on the website Indiegogo.com and hired a video crew to make a documentary about the emotional and medical **aspects** of testing on her and her family. "Social media can be a real unifier. There's not much out there yet for young people on Huntington's. I want to change that."

11 Her mother, Nicola Powers, was diagnosed in 2003 after struggling with symptoms for several years. "I remember watching her stumble and walk like a drunk person at times," Kristen says. "That was before we knew what was wrong with her. She was really struggling. It was very scary."

12 Nicola Powers didn't know the disease ran in her family. She grew apart from her biological father after her parents divorced. Once she looked into his medical history because of her symptoms, she discovered he had Huntington's.

13 Kristen doesn't want the gene to be passed on again. She says she won't have children if she tests positive: "I can be candid with potential partners and be responsible," she says.

14 Genetic counselors warn about the emotional **impact** of testing on the person and family. "Some people like to plan everything out," says Brenda Finucane, president of the National Society of Genetic Counselors. "They think the information is empowering, while some people want to see how life plays out."

15 Robert Green has found that most people will not seek out risk information about late-onset Alzheimer's disease if they're not psychologically prepared to handle it. But "it turns out many people handle this kind of information quite well," says Green, associate director for research in genetics at Brigham and Women's Hospital in Boston. "Some changed their wills[4], and some made lifestyle changes. Taking these tests is all about actionability[5]."

16 Timing can be tricky, though. Kristen's father and stepmother, Betsy Banks Saul, suggested she hold off until she has a support system at college. "She's a very intelligent, strong young woman, and we trust her, but we wish we could be nearby to support her," Betsy says.

17 After high school graduation in June, she will attend Stanford, in California—far from her farm, family, and friends. Kristen listened to her parents' concerns and considered putting off testing, "but I am a type A person who has always craved getting information. I want to know."

Not all tests are equal

18 Her test will look for the single gene that causes Huntington's, but most diseases have a more complicated genetic profile. A growing number of tests look at multiple genes that might increase or decrease a person's risk for developing thousands of diseases. Companies market the tests for as little as $100 on the internet and don't require a physician's signature. But those kinds of results are not always **reliable**, says Ardis Dee Hoven, former chair of the American Medical Association.

19 "In the absence of a medical professional, a patient might have difficulty **interpreting** the test and make decisions that are not healthy decisions," Hoven says. For instance, someone who tests negative for BRCA1 and BRCA2—genes that put people at a higher risk for developing certain breast and ovarian cancers—might not know there are other **risk factors**. Unless the patient has a physician guiding her, Hoven says, she might think she's home-free[6] and skip routine screening tests.

20 David Agus, author of the new book *The End of Illness*, says that's why the company he co-founded, Navigenics, requires customers to get a signature from their doctors before being tested. Navigenics also offers genetic counseling as part of the $300–$400 fee. "Genetics are a small piece of the puzzle, but they're a very important piece," says Agus, head of the Center for Applied Molecular Medicine at the University of Southern California.

21 A cancer specialist, Agus discovered he has an above-average risk for cardiovascular disease and a slightly lower-than-average risk for colon cancer. His doctor put him on a statin to help prevent heart disease, and, he says, "My kids took it upon themselves to keep me away from french fries." He also had a colonoscopy at age forty-three, earlier than medical standards call for, and had a polyp removed. "Could my polyp have turned into cancer? Who knows? But why should I wait for that to happen? Unless our country can focus on prevention, which testing is all about, our health care costs will be completely out of control."

22 A study of 1,200 patients that was presented in March at an American College of Cardiology meeting found that those who

---

[4] **wills:** legal documents that show whom you want to have your money and property after you die
[5] **actionability:** being able to act upon
[6] **home-free:** safe and without problems

continued on next page

were told they had a gene **linked** to heart disease improved their adherence to statin therapy by 13 percent compared with those who had not been tested for the gene.

23 "I could see how testing could become embedded[7] in how we treat our patients," Hoven says. "It's always better to prevent disease than to treat it, and quality of life is so much better for people."

How accessibility could change

24 Since the human genome was unraveled[8] a dozen years ago, genetic testing has been cost-prohibitive for the average person. The promise was that this breakthrough would lead to a better understanding of myriad[9] diseases and, ultimately, individualized treatments. Whole genome testing studies the **interaction** of our 20,000 to 25,000 genes with one another and with a person's **environment**. The $10,000 price tag, though, is expected to drop to $1,000 within the decade. When the tests become mainstream, doctors could face a dilemma[10].

25 A study in March reports that ten of sixteen specialists (62%) favored telling a patient he carried the gene for Huntington's if the finding was incidental to why the test was ordered. The study noted that the specialists unanimously agreed on disclosing twenty-one of ninety-nine commonly ordered genetic conditions for adults, and "multiple expert panels" might be needed to agree on what to tell patients.

26 "This is one of the toughest issues facing the rollout of clinical sequencing (whole genome sequencing)," Green says. He adds that after the study, he co-chaired a forum March 28 of the American College of Medical Genetics to discuss how to form a **consensus**.

27 That's a non-issue for Kristen. She knows she will get an answer. One of her hardest decisions has been picking who will be in the room when she gets her results. She knows she wants the videographers taping. At first, she didn't want her father to be there, but she relented when he asked her to reconsider.

28 "I know I can take the news," she says, "Knowledge is power. But I didn't think I could get a positive result and then watch my father cry. I've never seen him cry before."*

*Kristin tested negative for Huntington's disease.

---

[7] **embedded:** believed in very strongly
[8] **was unraveled:** something very complicated was understood or explained

[9] **myriad:** a very large number of something
[10] **dilemma:** situation in which you have to make a difficult choice between two or more actions

MAIN IDEAS

Reading One presents the pros and cons of genetic testing. Complete the chart with the information in the box.

Can choose appropriate treatment plan	There are other risk factors in addition to genes.	Can change lifestyle	Positive result can lead to risky, unhealthy decisions.
Can prevent diseases rather than just treat them	Positive result can be shattering for patient and family.	Patient may interpret test results incorrectly.	May threaten employment and insurance

POSITIVE	NEGATIVE
I. Can revolutionize medicine a. b. Quality of life is better.	I. Emotional and physical impact a. b.
II. Information is empowering for patient. a. b.	II. Invasion of privacy a.
	III. Results are not always reliable.
	IV. Professional interpretation is not required. a. b.

DETAILS

1 Reading One mentions many people, places, and names of diseases connected with genetic testing. Match the people, places, and diseases on the left with the information on the right.

1. _____ Ardis Dee Hoven

2. _____ Robert Green

3. _____ Human Genome Project

4. _____ Alzheimer's disease

5. _____ David Agus

6. _____ BRCA1 & BRCA2

7. _____ Huntington's disease

8. _____ University of North Carolina

9. _____ Indiegogo.com

10. _____ Brenda Finucane

11. _____ Michael J. Fox

a. A progressive, degenerative disorder that attacks the brain's nerve cells, or neurons, resulting in loss of memory, thinking and language skills, and behavioral changes. It can be identified through genetic testing.

b. Head of the Center for Applied Molecular Medicine at the University of Southern California, author of *The End of Illness*, and co-founder of Navigenics, a genetic testing company

c. Location of the counseling center that Kristen Powers has attended

d. An incurable fatal, neurodegenerative disorder that can debilitate victims as early as their mid-30s. It can be identified through genetic testing.

e. A 2003 study which identified the 20,000–25,000 genes in the human body

f. A well-known advocate for Parkinson's disease

g. Website where Kristen Powers raised money to hire a video crew

h. Former chair of the American Medical Association who warned that genetic test results are not always reliable

i. President of the National Society of Genetic Counselors who talks about the emotional impact of testing

j. Genes that indicate a high-risk factor for developing certain breast and ovarian cancers

k. Associate director for research in genetics at Brigham and Women's Hospital. He talks about using the test results to take (positive) action.

2 Look at your notes and at your answers in Preview. How did they help you understand the article?

Inferring Degree of Support

Some texts deal with controversial topics, meaning that people probably have strong feelings about the topic. For these controversial texts, it is important to be able to infer the degree of support that different people express about the topic. Some may be more supportive than others. Some may not be supportive at all. How do we "read between the lines" to get a sense of how supportive a person is? What language is used? How often does a statement of support occur? What doubts or uncertainties are expressed?

Look at the example and read the explanation.

Reading One deals with genetic testing. This is clearly a controversial topic as shown by the difference in viewpoints of the people mentioned in the story.

How strong is Kristen's support of genetic testing? Look at the scale.

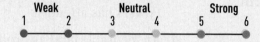

In paragraph 4, she notes, "I've known since I was 15 that I wanted to do this." She adds in paragraph 17, "I am a type A person who has always craved getting information. I want to know." Finally, in paragraph 28, she states, "I know I can take the news. Knowledge is power."

From these statements, we can infer that Kristen's support of genetic testing is very strong, so on the scale about a 5 or 6.

Understanding the position of people mentioned in a text concerning controversial topics enables the reader to understand the text more thoroughly.

1 **Think about the people mentioned in Reading One. Rate their support of genetic testing, based on what they say and do, by putting an X on the scales. Reread the indicated paragraph(s) to support your choice. Compare your answers with a partner's.**

1. Nate, Kristen's brother
   (paragraph 3)

2. Kristen's father
   (paragraphs 7, 8)

3. Brenda Finucane
   (paragraph 14)

4. Robert Green
   (paragraphs 15, 26)

5. Betsy Bank Saul
   (paragraph 18)

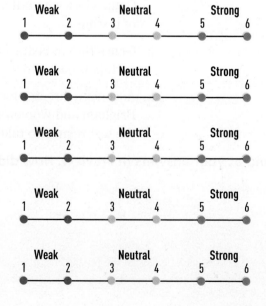

6. Ardis Dee Hoven
   (*paragraphs 18, 19*)

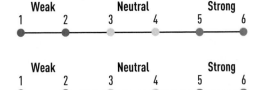

Weak		Neutral		Strong	
1	2	3	4	5	6

7. David Agus
   (*paragraphs 20, 21*)

Weak		Neutral		Strong	
1	2	3	4	5	6

2 Discuss your answers with a partner. Point out sentences, words, or phrases in the paragraphs that helped you find the answers.

DISCUSS 🔍

USE YOUR NOTES

Use your notes to support your answers with information from the reading.

Work in a small group. Choose one of the questions. Discuss your ideas. Then choose one person in your group to report the ideas to the class.

1. What reasons did Kristen give for her decision to be tested? Do you agree with these reasons? Why or why not?

2. Do you think genetic testing has more potential benefits than possible problems? Explain using evidence from the text.

🔾 Go to **MyEnglishLab** to give your opinion about another question.

READING TWO | Norman Cousins's Laughter Therapy

PREVIEW

Reading Two talks about Norman Cousins, a well-known American writer and editor. When diagnosed with a serious illness, he was not content to let the doctor make all his medical decisions. He decided to use his own type of alternative therapy, which focused on the importance of a positive attitude in healing. After writing about his successful recovery, he received mail from all over the world. Many letters came from doctors who supported his ideas.

1 Look at the title and read the first paragraph of the reading on the next page. Write two questions that you think will be answered in the reading.

_____

_____

2 Look at the boldfaced words in the reading. Which words do you know the meanings of?

1 Read the article about Norman Cousins. As you read, guess the meanings of the words that are new to you. Remember to take notes on main ideas and details.

2 Compare your notes on main ideas and details with a partner's. How can you improve your notes next time?

Norman Cousins's Laughter Therapy

1 In the summer of 1964, well-known writer and editor Norman Cousins became very ill. His body ached, and he felt constantly tired. It was difficult for him to even move around. He **consulted** his physician, who did many tests. Eventually, he was diagnosed as having ankylosing spondylitis, a very serious and destructive form of arthritis[1]. His doctor told him that he would become immobilized[2] and eventually die from the disease. He was told he had only a one in 500 chance of survival.

2 Despite the diagnosis[3], Cousins was determined to overcome the disease and survive. He had always been interested in medicine and had read the work of organic chemist Hans Selye, *The Stress of Life* (1956). This book discussed the idea of how body chemistry and health can be damaged by emotional stress and negative attitudes. Selye's book made Cousins think about the possible benefits of positive attitudes and emotions. He thought, "If negative emotions produce (negative) changes in the body, wouldn't positive emotions produce positive chemical changes? Is it possible that love, hope, faith, laughter, confidence, and the will to live have positive therapeutic value?"

3 He decided to concentrate on positive emotions as a remedy to heal some of the symptoms of his ailment. In addition to his **conventional** medical treatment, he tried to put himself in situations that would **elicit** positive emotions. "Laughter Therapy" became part of his treatment. He scheduled time each day for watching comedy films, reading humorous books, and doing other activities that would bring about laughter and positive emotions. Within eight days of starting his "Laughter Therapy" program, his pain began to decrease, and he was able to sleep more easily. His body chemistry even improved. Doctors were able to see an improvement in his condition! Within a few months' time, he was able to walk wearing a metal brace. Soon after that, he was able to return to work. He actually reached complete recovery in a few years. He lived for twenty-six years after he became ill. He died in 1990 at the age of seventy-five.

4 **Skeptical** readers may question the doctor's preliminary diagnosis, but Cousins believed his recovery was the result of a mysterious mind-body interaction. His "Laughter Therapy" is a good example of one of the many **alternative**, or nonconventional, medical treatments people look to today.

---

[1] **arthritis:** a disease that causes pain and swelling in the joints of the body

[2] **immobilized:** not able to move

[3] **diagnosis:** identification, usually by a doctor, of what illness a person has

 Go to the **Pearson Practice English App** or **MyEnglishLab** for more vocabulary practice.

Taking Notes on Cause and Effect with a Graphic Organizer

When you create a graphic organizer, you are making a visual representation of the text structure. A graphic organizer can be used in note-taking to help you understand the different relationships among people, events, and ideas in a text. Using a graphic organizer is an excellent way to show the text structure of a cause / effect relationship.

Look at paragraph 1 of Reading Two. What is the first cause / effect relationship you can find in this paragraph?

Cousins becomes ill → his body ached

This relationship could be depicted as

However, there are many more cause / effect relationships in paragraph 1.

Sometimes one cause can have multiple effects

- Cousins becomes ill → his body ached
- Cousins becomes ill → he felt tired
- Cousins becomes ill → it was difficult to move

Sometimes the effect of one cause can become the cause of another effect, and so on.

- Cousins becomes ill → his body ached, felt tired, and it was difficult to move
- Cousins's body ached, felt tired, and it was difficult to move → he consulted a physician
- He consulted a physician → he was diagnosed with ankylosing spondylitis
- He was diagnosed with ankylosing spondylitis → he learned his chances for survival were only 1 in 500

Using a graphic organizer can make it clearer how all of these different events are related.

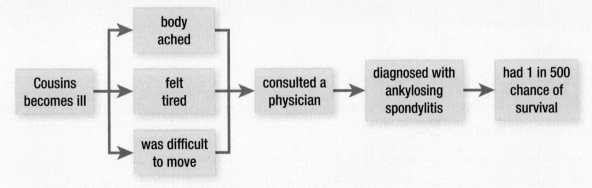

Go back to Reading Two and create a graphic organizer for paragraph 3. Compare your organizer with a partner's.

Go to **MyEnglishLab** for more note-taking practice.

COMPREHENSION

1 Answer the questions. Use your notes from Reading Two to help you. Discuss your answers with a partner.

1. What was Norman Cousins's original diagnosis, and how did he respond?

2. What is the connection between mind and body in Laughter Therapy?

3. What are some examples of what Cousins did for Laughter Therapy?

4. How did Cousins benefit from his Laughter Therapy?

2 Review the boldfaced words from the reading with a partner. Use a dictionary or ask your teacher for any meanings you still do not know.

⬦ Go to the **Pearson Practice English App** or **MyEnglishLab** for more vocabulary practice.

READING SKILL

1 In Reading Two, the author describes a number of events that take place around the year 1964: Cousins's diagnosis with arthritis, his reading of books by Hans Selye, and his invention of Laughter Therapy. What is the order in which these events take place? How do you know?

Organizing the Sequence of Events in a Timeline

Making a timeline of events in a narrative is a useful way to organize and remember information and understand a text. In the article about Norman Cousins, a number of events happen before, during, and after the summer of 1964.

Look at paragraph 3. The author states, "Within eight days of starting his 'Laughter Therapy' program, his pain began to decrease, and he was able to sleep more easily. His body chemistry even improved."

How would you complete the timeline?

Later in the summer of 1964	
8 days later	

What happened later in the summer of 1964?

Cousins was diagnosed with a severe form of arthritis and started his Laughter Therapy program.

What happened eight days later?

Cousins's pain decreased, he was able to sleep better, and his body chemistry improved.

Understanding how events are related chronologically will help you to better understand and remember the information you read. A timeline is a good visual representation of the chronology of events.

2 Go back to Reading Two. Complete the timeline using information from the article.

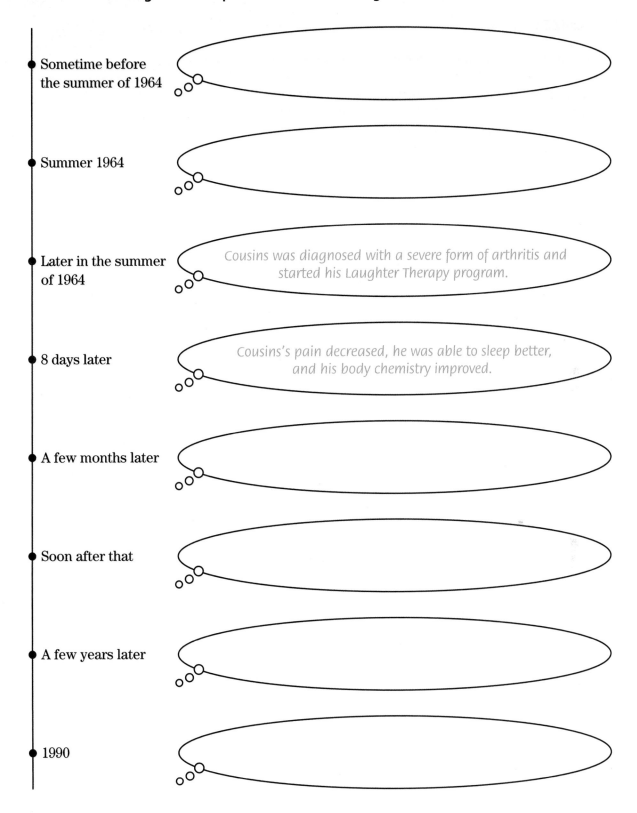

Sometime before the summer of 1964

Summer 1964

Later in the summer of 1964 — *Cousins was diagnosed with a severe form of arthritis and started his Laughter Therapy program.*

8 days later — *Cousins's pain decreased, he was able to sleep better, and his body chemistry improved.*

A few months later

Soon after that

A few years later

1990

⟩ Go to **MyEnglishLab** for more skill practice.

ORGANIZE

You have read about genetic testing in Reading One (R1) and Norman Cousins' Laughter Therapy in Reading Two (R2). What are the similarities and differences between them? Complete the Venn diagram with information from both readings. In the left circle, write notes that are true only about genetic testing. In the right circle, write notes that are true only about Norman Cousins. In the middle, write notes that are true for both.

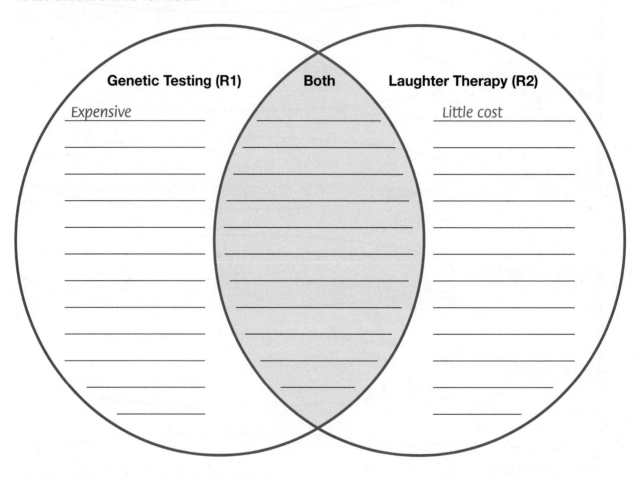

Genetic Testing (R1) — Expensive

Both

Laughter Therapy (R2) — Little cost

SYNTHESIZE

Write a short paragraph comparing the genetic testing story and Norman Cousins's story. Concentrate on the similarities between the two methods. Use the information from Organize.

▶ Go to **MyEnglishLab** to check what you learned.

VOCABULARY

REVIEW

Complete the paragraph using the words in the boxes.

advocates	impact	potential	revolutionize	risk factors

Many people believe that genetic testing will continue to _____ the practice
1.

of medicine. These _____ , who support genetic testing, believe it has the
2.

_____ to save many lives. They point out that after genetic testing, patients will know
3.

their _____ and will be able to better choose their treatment plans. These supporters
4.

acknowledge that the _____ of getting a positive test result could be devastating but
5.

point out that, with proper counseling, people will have the tools to make the best decisions for

their individual situations.

consult	environment	linked	reliable	skeptical

However, others are _____ of the value of genetic testing. For one thing, some
6.

people don't believe it is _____ . In addition, they note that without professional help
7.

to interpret the results, patients may experience more harm than good from the tests. Of course,

there wouldn't be a problem if patients were required to _____ with their doctors
8.

about the results. Another issue is that some diseases are not caused by genetics, but rather are

_____ to lifestyle, _____ , or a combination of the two.
9.   10.

alternative	consensus	conventional	interaction

A further area of concern is that doctors still do not fully understand the _____

11.

between specific genes and how this affects the possibility for disease. Although there may never

be complete _____ on the value of genetic testing, the way the public and the medical

12.

establishment view specific treatments and therapies may change over time. Don't forget that when

Norman Cousins first used Laughter Therapy in the summer of 1964, it was definitely viewed as

a(n) _____ therapy. Nowadays, it is used in many hospitals around the world and has

13.

entered the realm of _____ medicine.

14.

EXPAND

1 Write *S* if the word pairs have a similar meaning. Write *D* if they have a different meaning.

1. reliable / dependable _____

2. impact / interaction _____

3. conventional / alternative _____

4. interpret / elicit _____

5. revolutionize / change _____

6. environment / surroundings _____

7. treatment / diagnosis _____

8. linked / connected _____

9. elicit / produce _____

10. consensus / disagreement _____

11. consulted / asked advice of _____

12. potential / ability _____

13. aspect / factor _____

14. skeptical / doubtful _____

15. advocate / supporter _____

2 Circle the word that best completes each sentence.

1. Whole genome testing looks at the **impact / interaction** of our 20,000 genes with one another and our environment.

2. A medical professional can help a patient **elicit / interpret** genetic test results.

3. After the doctor told Norman Cousins he was suffering from ankylosing spondylitis, Cousins had to decide on his **treatment / diagnosis**.

4. The idea of genetic testing is still a controversial topic. There is ongoing **disagreement / consensus** on when it should be used.

5. When Norman Cousins first used Laughter Therapy, it was considered a(n) **alternative / conventional** treatment.

6. Norman Cousins watched comedy films as a way to **revolutionize / elicit** positive emotions.

7. Some people are skeptical of Cousins's original **diagnosis / treatment**. They don't think he was ever suffering from a severe form of arthritis.

CREATE

APPLY Imagine that you are going to interview Kristen Powers or Norman Cousins. Write four interview questions that you would like to ask. Use at least one word from the box in each question. Then work with a partner. Answer each other's questions as if you were Kristen Powers or Norman Cousins.

advocate	consensus	elicit	impact	link	revolutionize
alternative	consult	environment	interaction	potential	skeptical
aspect	conventional	factor	interpret	reliable	

Go to the **Pearson Practice English App** or **MyEnglishLab** for more vocabulary practice.

GRAMMAR FOR WRITING

1 Read the sentences. Write *Y* (yes) or *N* (no) to answer the questions that follow.

   a. If Kristen Power's mother **hadn't died** of Huntington's disease, Kristen **might not have wanted** to be tested.

   b. If Kristen's mother **had been** closer to her biological father, Kristen **could have known** earlier that Huntington's disease ran in her family.

   c. If Norman Cousins **hadn't read** Hans Selye's book, Cousins **wouldn't have invented** Laughter Therapy.

   1. _____ In sentence *a*: Did Kristen's mother die?

        _____ Did Kristen want to be tested?

   2. _____ In sentence *b*: Was Kristen's mother close to her father?

        _____ Did Kristen always know Huntington's disease ran in her family?

   3. _____ In sentence *c*: Did Norman Cousins read Hans Selye's book?

        _____ Did Norman Cousins invent Laughter Therapy?

Past Unreal Conditionals

1. A **past unreal conditional** sentence has two clauses: the **if clause,** which gives the condition, and the **result clause,** which gives the result. The *if* clause can be seen as a possible cause, and the result clause an effect. The sentence can begin with the *if* clause or the result clause, and the meaning is the same.

2. There are two important things to notice in past unreal conditional sentences:

   - the use of a comma when the *if* clause begins the sentence
   - the verb form used in each clause

If Clause	Result Clause

If + subject + past perfect,	subject + *would (not) have* + past participle
	                            could (not) have
	                            might (not) have

If Kristen's father **hadn't supported** her,	she **might not have wanted** a genetic test.

Result Clause	*If* Clause

Subject + *would (not) have* + past participle
                    could (not) have
                    might (not) have
	if + subject + past perfect

Norman Cousins **might not have survived**	if he **hadn't used** Laughter Therapy.

3. The past unreal conditional talks about past unreal, untrue, or imagined conditions and their results. Both parts of the conditional sentence describe events that are the opposite of what happened.

   Conditional statement: Kristen **could not have been tested if** the Human Genome Project **hadn't identified** all the genes in the human body.

   What really happened: Kristen **was tested.** The Human Genome Project **did identify** all the genes in the human body.

4. The past unreal conditional is often used to express possibility or uncertainty about the result. Use **might have** or **could have** in the result clause as in the sentence about Kristen in number 3 above.

   The past unreal conditional is also used to express regret about what really happened. In this case, use *wouldn't have* in the result clause. For example:

   I **wouldn't have** asked for a genetic test if I had thought the result would be positive.

2 Read the conditional sentences. Write *Y* (yes) or *N* (no) to answer the questions.

1. If David Agus hadn't taken a genetic test, he wouldn't have discovered his risk for cardiovascular disease.

   _____ Did he take a genetic test?

   _____ Did he discover his risk for cardiovascular disease?

2. If Norman Cousins had been healthy, he wouldn't have had to try Laughter Therapy.

_____ Was Norman Cousins healthy?

_____ Did he have to try Laughter Therapy?

3. Kristen's parents might not have been so worried if she had decided to go to a nearby college.

_____ Did Kristen decide to go to a nearby college?

_____ Were her parents worried?

4. The family wouldn't have understood Kristen's mother's symptoms if she hadn't been diagnosed with Huntington's disease.

_____ Did the family understand her symptoms?

_____ Was Kristen's mother diagnosed with Huntington's disease?

5. If there had been a famous advocate for Huntington's disease, Kristen might not have decided to make a documentary about her genetic testing.

_____ Was there a famous advocate for Huntington's disease?

_____ Did Kristen decide to make a documentary?

6. If Kristen hadn't had counseling, she might not have been prepared to deal with the test results.

_____ Did Kristen have counseling?

_____ Was Kristen prepared to deal with the test results?

7. If Norman Cousins hadn't survived for twenty-six more years, Laughter Therapy might not have received so much publicity.

_____ Did Norman Cousins survive for twenty-six more years?

_____ Did Laughter Therapy receive a lot of publicity?

8. If Norman Cousins hadn't believed in a mind-body interaction, Laughter Therapy would not have been effective for him.

_____ Did Norman Cousins believe in a mind-body interaction?

_____ Did Laughter Therapy work for him?

3 **APPLY** **Write a sentence about each situation. Use the past unreal conditional.**

1. Her sister chose a treatment plan based on her genetic test results. She soon felt better.

   If she hadn't chosen the correct treatment plan, she might not have felt better.

2. Kristen Powers always wanted all the information available. She chose to be genetically tested.

   _____

   _____

3. Norman Cousins read *The Stress of Life*. When he was diagnosed with ankylosing spondylitis, he already had ideas about the mind-body connection.

_____

_____

4. Norman Cousins tried to cure himself by using Laughter Therapy. He made a complete recovery.

_____

_____

5. David Agus found out that he was at risk for cardiovascular disease. His children made him change his diet.

_____

_____

6. Kristen's mom contacted her biological father. She learned that Huntington's disease ran in their family.

_____

_____

7. Cousins wasn't satisfied with his doctor's treatment plan. He developed his own Laughter Therapy treatment.

_____

_____

Go to the **Pearson Practice English App** or **MyEnglishLab** for more grammar practice. Check what you learned in **MyEnglishLab**.

FINAL WRITING TASK: An Opinion Essay 🔍 APPLY

In this unit, you have read about genetic testing. Genetic testing can be ordered and interpreted by medical professionals. Testing can also be done at home by sending saliva samples to private companies. In these cases, there is often no consultation or interpretation offered.

You are going to *write a four-paragraph opinion essay expressing your opinion on making medical decisions based on genetic testing*.

For an alternative writing topic, see page 85.

PREPARE TO WRITE: Tree Mapping

Tree mapping helps you to organize ideas about a topic. The topic is written on the top line. Your ideas are written in branches leading from the topic. You can include reasons and evidence on smaller branches.

Complete the tree map. Then discuss your tree map with a partner. Notice how the ideas become more detailed as the branches extend.

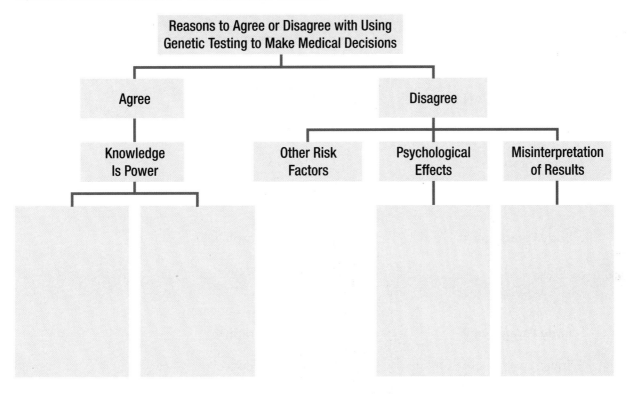

WRITE

Writing an Opinion Essay

An **essay** is a group of paragraphs about one topic. An **opinion essay** is written to persuade or convince the reader that your opinion is "the right way of thinking." An opinion essay has three parts: the **introduction**, the **body**, and the **conclusion**.

Introduction

The **introduction** is the first paragraph of an essay. It includes a thesis statement that introduces the topic and states the main idea. The introduction should capture the reader's attention and make them want to read on. Many introductions begin with general background information on the topic and end with the thesis statement as the last sentence of the paragraph. In an opinion essay, the thesis statement should state the writer's opinion about the topic. *Tip:* Some writers find it helpful to write their introductory paragraph after they have completed their essay.

Body

The **body** is one to three paragraphs. The body supports the thesis statement by giving examples, details, reasons, and facts to support the thesis statement. Each paragraph should start with a clearly stated topic sentence that relates to the thesis statement. In addition, because you are trying to convince your readers to accept your opinion, you need to give evidence to support your opinion. You also need to give reasons that explain why the evidence supports your opinion.

continued on next page

Conclusion

The **conclusion** should restate the thesis statement and include the writer's final thoughts on the topic. For example, the writer can give advice, suggest a solution to a problem, or predict what will happen in the future. The conclusion should not include new or unrelated topics.

Note: For more information on paragraph writing, see Unit 1, Write, page 26 and Unit 2, Write, page 54.

1 **Read the opinion essay. As you read, complete the essay organizer with information from each part of the essay.**

THREE PARTS OF AN ESSAY	NOTES
I. Introduction Thesis Statement:	**Background Information:**
II. Body Paragraph 1 Topic:	**Body Paragraph 1** Support/Evidence:
Body Paragraph 2 Topic:	**Body Paragraph 2** Support/Evidence:
III. Conclusion Restate the Thesis: Final Thought/Wrap Up:	

Home Genetic Testing

Disastrous. Depressing. These two words come to mind when reading about home genetic testing. Because of the many adverse effects it can cause, I cannot understand why this type of 'service' is available without stricter regulations. First, let me say that my great-grandfather and my grandmother both suffered from Huntington's disease. I am a well-educated college graduate with a master's degree in biology. I am thirty years old and, so far, show no signs of developing Huntington's. I don't think knowing whether I have the potential to develop an incurable disease will, in any way, enhance the quality of my life, nor would I be able to interpret the test results without the help of a medical professional. From this personal perspective, I believe that home genetic testing should be much more strictly regulated, if not prohibited altogether.

The first reason I disagree with the use of home genetic testing is that the results can be misinterpreted with devastating effects. I witnessed this first-hand when a fifty-five-year-old coworker of mine, whose family had a history of cancer, submitted a DNA sample to an online genetic testing company. He was told that he had an 83-percent chance of developing colon cancer. He was convinced that because of this test result, he was going to die. After the test, this was all he could think about. This fear of impending tragedy made it impossible for him to concentrate on his work. As a result, his work suffered, and eventually he was let go. Finally, he went to a doctor and was retested. The doctor was able to interpret the results and explain to him that by taking the correct medications and changing his lifestyle, he could expect to live for many more years and very possibly never develop colon cancer. This is exactly why genetic testing must have stricter regulations.

Another reason I disagree with the use of these tests is that genetic testing is currently in its infancy, and even doctors and researchers do not fully understand the interaction between different genes. It is rare that a single gene can prove that a person is definitely at risk of getting a specific disease, so, until the link between diseases and multiple genes has been further studied, there is the potential for false positives and false negatives. In addition, environmental factors play a large part in who develops a disease and who doesn't. DNA is rarely the only factor affecting disease. For example, some cancers and other diseases are caused by exposure to chemicals or even to the sun. They have nothing to do with genetics. Knowledge is power, but it is important that this knowledge be accurate.

If we, as a society, truly believe that genetic testing has more benefits than negative effects, it is our responsibility to regulate it so all testing includes counseling and interpretation by professionals. In this way, patients can choose the treatment that is appropriate and effective for their genetic profile and lifestyle. Do we, as a society, truly believe that home genetic testing can be an effective method of choosing treatment without professional counseling and interpretation?

Remember, the key is that to truly be able to make the best medical choices, medical professionals need to be involved in any decision.

2 Create an essay organizer like the one in Exercise 1 and fill it in with information for your opinion essay about making medical decisions based on genetic testing.

3 Use the information from Prepare to Write on page 81 and your essay organizer from Write to plan your essay.

- Make sure you have four paragraphs: an introductory paragraph, two body paragraphs, and one concluding paragraph.

- Use past unreal conditionals to describe causes and effects.

REVISE: Writing Introductions and Hooks

1 Is there a part of the first paragraph in the essay *Home Genetic Testing* on page 82 that grabs your attention and makes you want to keep reading? What is it? Is it effective? Why or why not? Share your answer with a partner.

Introductions and Hooks

The **introductory paragraph** is very important in all essays. The reader will decide whether or not your essay is worth the time and effort to read, depending on how interesting your introductory paragraph is. The introduction for an opinion essay should:

- give information on the topic and why your opinion is important
- provide background information about the topic
- provoke the reader's interest with a hook
- include a thesis statement

A **hook** is a sentence or two written with the goal of grabbing the reader's attention. There are many different ways to hook a reader, some include:

- a shocking or surprising sentence
- an anecdote (story)
- an interesting point
- a quote

2 Read the hooks from introductions of opinion essays. Check (✓) the hooks you think are effective. Discuss your answers with a partner.

1. _____ "Genetic testing definitely saved my life! If I hadn't been tested, I would never have known that I had an elevated risk of type-2 diabetes. Because of my test results, I was able to change my lifestyle before developing the disease," says Dr. Neville Clynes of Columbia Presbyterian Hospital.

2. _____ People are becoming more interested in genetic testing. Genetic testing can be very useful in making medical decisions.

3. _____ Stop! Don't go to the doctor! You can cure all problems with genetic testing. Or at least that's what people who believe in genetic testing would have you believe.

4. _____ People should stick with conventional medicine because it has been proven. There is no proof that genetic testing is an effective tool in making medical decisions.

5. _____ There are some studies that prove genetic testing can help with medical decision-making. This is why genetic testing should be a regular part of medical treatment.

6. _____ Dr. Robert Grasberger finally, after almost three months of consultation, understood what was wrong with his patient. What had he done? He had ordered a genetic test—the results explained everything.

7. _____ Imagine a world in which people are given jobs based entirely on their genes. Marriages are permitted only between couples whose genetic matchup ensures a "perfect" child. This is the future genetic testing will bring! Is this the future you want?

3 Now go back to the first draft of your essay.

- Look at your introductory paragraph. Make sure you have all the parts of an effective introduction. If you don't have a hook, add one.

- Try to use the grammar and some of the vocabulary from the unit.

🜂 Go to **MyEnglishLab** for more skill practice.

EDIT: Writing the Final Draft

APPLY Write the final draft of your essay and submit it to your teacher. Carefully edit it for grammatical and mechanical errors, such as spelling, capitalization, and punctuation. Consider how to apply the vocabulary, grammar, and writing skills from the unit. Use the checklist to help you.

FINAL DRAFT CHECKLIST

- ☐ Does the essay have an introduction, two body paragraphs, and a conclusion?
- ☐ Does the introduction include a thesis statement, background information about the topic, and a hook?
- ☐ Does each paragraph have a topic sentence?
- ☐ Do all the topic sentences support the thesis statement?
- ☐ Does the essay have a conclusion that restates the thesis and includes a final thought?
- ☐ Do you use the past unreal conditional correctly?
- ☐ Do you use vocabulary from the unit?

ALTERNATIVE WRITING TOPIC

APPLY Ethicists worry that genetic testing will be used not just to help make medical decisions but to discriminate against people. They foresee a world in which test results could prevent people from getting high-paying jobs, insurance and welfare benefits, and even being able to marry. Do you believe such uses of test results will happen and be a problem? If so, does this issue outweigh the potential medical benefits of genetic testing? Use the grammar and vocabulary from the unit.

CHECK WHAT YOU'VE LEARNED

Check (✔) the outcomes you've met and vocabulary you've learned. Put an X next to the skills and vocabulary you still need to practice.

Learning Outcomes
- ☐ **Infer degree of support**
- ☐ **Take notes on cause and effect with a graphic organizer**
- ☐ **Organize the sequence of events in a timeline**
- ☐ **Use past unreal conditionals**
- ☐ **Write introductions and hooks**
- ☐ **Write an opinion essay**

Vocabulary
- ☐ **advocate (n.)** AWL
- ☐ **alternative** AWL
- ☐ **aspect** AWL
- ☐ **consensus** AWL
- ☐ **consult (v.)** AWL
- ☐ **conventional** AWL
- ☐ **elicit**
- ☐ **environment** AWL
- ☐ **impact (n.)** AWL
- ☐ **interaction** AWL
- ☐ **interpret** AWL
- ☐ **link (v.)** AWL
- ☐ **potential (n.)** AWL
- ☐ **reliable** AWL
- ☐ **revolutionize** AWL
- ☐ **risk factor**
- ☐ **skeptical**

🔊 Go to **MyEnglishLab** to watch a video about sleep deprivation and health issues, access the Unit Project, and take the Unit 3 Achievement Test.

LEARNING OUTCOMES

> Infer the use of hedging
> Take notes with outlining
> Recognize the role of quoted speech

> Use adjective clauses
> Paraphrase
> Write a summary in journalistic style

Go to **MyEnglishLab** to check what you know.

UNIT 4

Instinct or Intellect?

1 FOCUS ON THE TOPIC

1. Is an animal's ability to imitate human behavior a sign of high intelligence? Explain.

2. Are domesticated animals (dogs, horses, monkeys, parrots) that can be trained more intelligent than animals living in the wild?

3. Which animals seem to exhibit higher levels of intelligence than others? What do they do that makes them seem intelligent?

READING ONE | Extreme Perception and Animal Intelligence

VOCABULARY

Reading One is an excerpt from the book *Animals in Translation* by Temple Grandin. In this excerpt, the author discusses animal intelligence. Many other scientists and researchers are also studying the growing field of animal intelligence.

Read an interview with a noted researcher in animal intelligence. Complete the interview with synonyms for the words in parentheses. Use the words in the box.

achieve	apparently	behavior	cognition	obvious	unconscious
acquired	approach	category	controversy	perception	unique

REPORTER: Can you tell us a little bit about your work studying animal intelligence?

RESEARCHER: Sure, but let me start by saying that there has always been

_____ about exactly what animal intelligence is. For many years,
   1. (serious disagreement)
those animals that could act most human were put into the _____
                                                              2. (group with shared characteristics)
of "intelligent."

REPORTER: But that is not really the case, is it? Maybe you could give us some historical

background.

RESEARCHER: Well, during the nineteenth and early twentieth centuries, people believed

animals possessed human emotions and mental abilities. Those animals that could be

trained to imitate human _____ were judged to be intelligent. In
                            3. (conduct)
fact, shows involving these trained animals were very popular. One such animal was the

famous horse, Clever Hans, who seemed to be able to solve mathematical problems. The

_____ conclusion was that he was intelligent. Actually, Clever Hans
          4. (clear)
was reacting to _____ movements made by people watching him.
                   5. (done without realizing it)
His answers had nothing to do with a knowledge of mathematics.

REPORTER: But doesn't the fact that an animal can be trained show that it is intelligent?

RESEARCHER: Not really. When trying to assess animal intelligence, it is easy to confuse trainability with _____. However, just because you can train an
6. (thinking)
animal to perform certain behaviors doesn't mean it really knows what it is doing. Dogs at airports around the world sniff suitcases and signal their handlers when they detect illegal drugs. These dogs are _____ behaving in an intelligent manner
7. (seeming to be true)
even though they have no concept of drugs being illegal.

REPORTER: So, what is actually happening?

RESEARCHER: These dogs possess extreme _____ with their sense
8. (use of senses)
of smell, but this doesn't necessarily make them intelligent. In fact, smell is not the only sense in which animals outdo humans. For example, eagles can clearly see a rabbit when flying almost a mile above it. They also see more colors than humans. In fact, eagles are not _____ in having extreme vision. Hammerhead sharks have a
9. (special)
visual field of 360 degrees. In other words, they can see fish both in front of and behind them, but, again, this alone does not make them intelligent.

REPORTER: So, how can we really know if an animal is intelligent?

RESEARCHER: As Albert Einstein said, "Everybody is a genius. But, if you judge a fish by its ability to climb a tree, it'll spend its whole life believing it is stupid." Therefore, in order to assess animal intelligence, it is important to test the animal in ways that are meaningful for their lives. This is the _____ most researchers are using in the
10. (method)
twenty-first century.

REPORTER: Using this method, how do researchers today define intelligence?

RESEARCHER: First of all, it is necessary to separate what animals are born with, instinct, from what they have _____ by learning. Learning how to respond
11. (developed / obtained)
to new situations in ways that allow them to _____ the goals that
12. (accomplish)
are important in their lives is the most effective way to measure their intelligence.

🅝 Go to the **Pearson Practice English App** or **MyEnglishLab** for more vocabulary practice.

You are going to read an article by Temple Grandin in which she talks about animals that are considered intelligent. She mentions two types of dogs that help people with medical problems: seizure[1] alert dogs and seizure response dogs. She also gives her own definition of animal intelligence. Answer the questions.

1. What do you think the difference is between a seizure response dog and a seizure alert dog?

   _____

   _____

   _____

2. Which of these dogs might the author think is showing more intelligence?

   _____

   _____

   _____

3. How do you think Temple Grandin might define intelligence in animals?

   _____

   _____

   _____

---

[1] **seizure:** a short time when someone is unconscious and cannot control the movements of his or her body

READ

Read the article about animal intelligence on the next page. Create a chart like the one below to take notes.

TAKE NOTES

Main Ideas	Details
Many animals have extreme perception.	forensic dogs: • 3X better than x-ray • 90% accuracy smelling drugs and explosives

⬤ Go to **MyEnglishLab** to view example notes.

EXTREME PERCEPTION AND ANIMAL INTELLIGENCE

By Temple Grandin and Catherine Johnson (from *Animals in Translation*)

1   Many animals have extreme **perception**. Forensic[1] dogs are three times as good as any x-ray machine at sniffing out contraband[2], drugs, or explosives, and their overall success rate is 90 percent.

2   The fact that a dog can smell things a person can't doesn't make him a genius—it just makes him a dog. Humans can see things dogs can't, but that doesn't make us smarter. But when you look at the jobs some dogs have invented for themselves using their advanced perceptual abilities, you're moving into the realm of true **cognition**, which is solving a problem under novel conditions. The seizure alert dogs are an example of an animal using advanced perceptual abilities to solve a problem no dog was born knowing how to solve. Seizure alert dogs are dogs who, their owners say, can *predict* a seizure before it starts. There's still **controversy** over whether you can train a dog to predict seizures, and so far people haven't had a lot of luck trying. But there are a number of dogs who have figured it out on their own. These dogs were trained as seizure response dogs, meaning they can help a person once a seizure has begun. The dog might be trained to lie on top of the person so he doesn't hurt himself or bring the person his medicine or the telephone. Those are all standard helpful **behaviors** any dog can be trained to perform.

3   But some of these dogs have gone from responding to seizures to perceiving signs of a seizure ahead of time. No one knows how they do this because the signs are invisible to people. No human being can look at someone who is about to have a seizure and see (or hear, smell, or feel) what's coming. Yet one study found that 10 percent of owners said their seizure response dogs had turned into seizure alert dogs.

4   The *New York Times* published a terrific article about a woman named Connie Standley, in Florida, who has two huge Bouvier de Flandres dogs who predict her seizures about thirty minutes ahead of time. When they sense Ms. Standley is heading into a seizure, they'll do things like pull on her clothes, bark at her, or drag on her hand to get her to someplace safe so she won't get hurt when the seizure begins. Ms. Standley says they predict about 80 percent of her seizures. Ms. Standley's dogs **apparently** were trained as seizure alert dogs before they came to her, but there aren't many dogs in that **category**. Most seizure alert dogs were trained to respond to seizures, not predict seizures.

5   The seizure alert dogs remind me of Clever Hans. Hans was the world-famous German horse in the early 1900s whose owner, Wilhelm von Osten, thought he could count. Herr von Osten could ask the horse questions like, "What's seven and five?" and Hans would tap out the number twelve with his hoof. Hans could even tap out answers to questions like, "If the eighth day of the

---

[1] **forensic:** relating to methods for finding out about a crime

[2] **contraband:** goods that are brought into or taken out of a country illegally

continued on next page

month comes on Tuesday, what is the date for the following Friday?" He could answer mathematical questions posed to him by complete strangers, too.

6 Eventually, a psychologist named Oskar Pfungst managed to show that Hans wasn't really counting. Instead, Hans was observing subtle, **unconscious** cues the humans had no idea they were giving off. He'd start tapping his foot when he could see it was time to start tapping. Then he'd stop tapping his foot when he could see it was time to stop tapping. His questioners were making tiny, unconscious movements only Hans could see. The movements were so tiny the humans making them couldn't even *feel* them.

7 Dr. Pfungst couldn't see the movements, either, and he was looking for them. He finally solved the case by putting Hans's questioners out of view and having them ask Hans questions they didn't know the answers to themselves. It turned out Hans could answer questions only when the person asking the question was in plain view and already knew the answer. If either condition was missing, his performance fell apart.

8 Psychologists often use the Clever Hans story to show that humans who believe animals are intelligent are deluding themselves. But that's not the **obvious** conclusion as far as I'm concerned. No one has ever been able to *train* a horse to do what Hans did. Hans trained himself. Is the ability to read a member of a different species as well as Hans was reading human beings really a sign that he was just a "dumb animal" who'd been classically conditioned to stamp his hoof? I think there is more to it than that.

9 What makes Hans similar to seizure alert dogs is that both Hans and the dogs **acquired** their skills without human help. As I mentioned, to my knowledge, so far no one has figured out how to take a "raw" dog and teach it how to predict seizures. About the best a trainer can do is reward the dogs for helping when a person is having a seizure and then leave it up to the dog to start identifying signs that predict the onset of a seizure on his own. That **approach** hasn't been hugely successful, but some dogs do it. I think those dogs are showing superior intelligence the same way a human who can do something few other people can do shows superior intelligence.

10 What makes the actions of the seizure alert dogs, and probably of Hans, too, a sign of high intelligence—or high talent—is the fact that they didn't have to do what they did. It's one thing for a dog to start recognizing the signs that a seizure is coming. You might chalk that up to **unique** aspects of canine hearing, smell, or vision, like the fact that a dog can hear a dog whistle while a human can't. But it's another thing for a dog to start to recognize the signs of an impending seizure and *then decide to do something about it*. That's what intelligence is in humans; intelligence is people using their built-in perceptual and cognitive skills to **achieve** useful and sometimes remarkable goals.

MAIN IDEAS

Read the statements. Check the three that represent the main ideas of Reading One. Then discuss the reasons for your choice.

☐ 1. Many animals have extreme perception.

☐ 2. True cognition, or intelligence, is defined as solving problems under novel conditions.

☐ 3. Ms. Standley's seizure alert dogs are able to predict about 80 percent of her seizures before they happen.

☐ 4. Some psychologists believe animals like Clever Hans are not really intelligent.

☐ 5. Some animals are able to read human behavior by observing subtle signs that even humans don't recognize.

☐ 6. The psychologist Oskar Pfungst was able to show that Hans wasn't really counting.

☐ 7. For Clever Hans to correctly answer a question, two conditions had to be met. He had to be able to see the person asking the question, and the person had to know the answer to the question.

☐ 8. Seizure alert dogs and Clever Hans are showing high intelligence because they are able to recognize a sign and then choose to do something about it.

DETAILS

1 Reading One mentions many people and animals connected with animal intelligence. Match the people and animals with their descriptions.

1. _____ forensic dogs

2. _____ seizure response dogs

3. _____ seizure alert dogs

4. _____ Ms. Connie Standley

5. _____ Wilhelm von Osten

6. _____ Oskar Pfungst

7. _____ Clever Hans

a. Clever Hans' owner, who thought Clever Hans could count

b. owner of two seizure alert dogs

c. dogs that have been trained to help people once their seizures have started

d. dogs that are able to predict seizures before they happen and warn their owners

e. horse that apparently could count and answer questions

f. dogs that use their sense of smell to find contraband such as drugs or explosives

g. psychologist who proved that Clever Hans wasn't really counting

2 Look at your notes and at your answers in Preview. How did they help you understand the article?

Inferring the Use of Hedging

Sometimes authors employ cautious language, called hedging, when they are not entirely sure that their information is supported by facts. This caution can be denoted by verb choice (*seem, look like, say, indicate, suggest, think, believe*), the use of modals (*might, may, could*), adverbs (*really, sometimes, possibly, perhaps, apparently*), quantifiers (*most, some, sometimes*), or certain phrases (*to my knowledge, as far as I'm concerned*). These words alone do not always indicate hedging. You must look at the context the author uses them in to understand if he or she is using them to hedge.

In addition to this specific vocabulary, authors also hedge by stating that an idea is the opinion of someone else, emphasizing that something is a belief rather than a fact, or indicating that something is controversial.

Look at the example and read the explanation.

Look at the excerpt from paragraph 2. What cautious language does Temple Grandin use to show that the information may not be factual?

> The seizure alert dogs are an example of an animal using advanced perceptual abilities to solve a problem no dog was born knowing how to solve. Seizure alert dogs are dogs who, their owners say, can predict a seizure before it starts.

She doesn't say that seizure alert dogs *can* predict seizures, but rather that *their owners say* that they can.

Why does she include the phrase "their owners say"? She does not have scientific proof but only anecdotal evidence.[1]

It is important to recognize hedging language, as it indicates that the author is not 100 percent certain of the information he or she writes.

_____

[1] **anecdotal evidence:** evidence collected in a casual or informal manner, relying heavily on personal stories

1 **Look at the indicated paragraphs in Reading One and write the words or phrases used that indicate hedging and the reason that hedging language is used.**

	Hedging language	Reason hedging language used
Paragraph 4		
Paragraph 5		
Paragraph 6		
Paragraph 8		
Paragraph 9		

2 **Discuss your answers with a partner. Point out the sentences, words, or phrases in the paragraphs that helped you find your answer.**

USE YOUR NOTES

Use your notes to support your answers with information from the reading.

Work in a small group. Choose one of the questions. Discuss your ideas. Then choose one person in your group to report the ideas to the class.

1. Oskar Pfungst proved that Clever Hans wasn't able to solve mathematical problems. Do you believe that Hans showed intelligence by learning to "read" the movements of his questioners and audience members?

2. Temple Grandin feels that seizure alert dogs are showing signs of high intelligence. Others may say that what they do is just an example of animals reacting based on instinct. Do you agree with Temple Grandin? Why or why not? Explain using evidence from the text.

3. How do Temple Grandin's ideas change or expand on your own observations of animal intelligence discussed at the beginning of this unit?

🅚 Go to **MyEnglishLab** to give your opinion about another question.

READING TWO | How Smart Are Animals?

PREVIEW

Reading Two talks about why it is difficult to judge animal intelligence. One problem is that we often use human standards to evaluate animal intelligence.

1 Look at the title of the reading and the pictures. Write two questions that you think will be answered in the reading.

_____

_____

2 Look at the boldfaced words in the reading. Which words do you know the meanings of?

1 Read the article about animal intelligence. As you read, guess the meanings of the words that are new to you. Remember to take notes on main ideas and details.

How Smart Are Animals?

By Gita Simonsen

How intelligent are animals?

1 We think that crows are smart, but what do we really know? Intelligence takes on diverse meanings for different species, and researchers think we are too prone to use human standards.

2 We've all heard talk of animal intelligence. We speak of crafty crows, clever foxes, discerning dolphins, and brilliant squids, but can we really use the word intelligence with regard to animals?

3 Researchers are concerned with learning mechanisms and other cognitive abilities— thinking, acquiring knowledge, **sensory** perception, memory, and language. These are the thought processes which form the basis for what we experience and comprehend of the world around us.

4 The problem is that we often look for human traits when we study animal behavior. But what may be clever for us needn't be a **viable** attribute in other members of the animal kingdom.

5 "Animals are often given tasks based on human behavior, such as the use of tools," says Peter Bøckman, a zoologist at the Natural History Museum in Oslo.

6 "If you turn it around and visualise a flock[1] of screaming chimpanzees hauling you up into a treetop and **confronting** you with a complicated problem involving nuts, how intelligently do you think you would perform?" he asks.

7 Indeed, we can easily fail to notice animal intelligence if we only look for human qualities, says Bjarne Braastad, an animal behaviorist at the Norwegian University of Life Sciences.

8 "It can be limiting if your point of departure is human traits. Animals have other abilities and can have elements of intelligence that humans lack," he says.

IQ by the kilo

9 We often measure intelligence, particularly in mammals, in accordance with how much the brain weighs in relation to total body weight. Humans lead by a long shot on this list, and the animal right behind us is not one of the apes—it's the dolphin.

10 Dolphins can thus be said to have the potential for very high intelligence, but we can't measure this optimally. Dolphins come from a completely different world, in a way, and have a language we can't fathom[2]. Communication is definitely a great barrier in the understanding of animal behavior.

11 "Human intelligence is strongly linked to the language we use to communicate with one another," says Bøckman. "As long as we can't communicate with animals, it's really hard to decide how smart they are."

12 "Language is such an integral part of being human, and that makes it hard to avoid using human traits as a framework for considering the intelligence of animals."

---

[1] **flock:** group of some types of animals, including chimpanzees, birds, and sheep
[2] **fathom:** to understand what something means after thinking about it carefully

continued on next page

Bees smarter than babies?

13 A group of scientists from Queen Mary University in London examined studies of animal intelligence to find out what scientists currently think about comparable cognition in different species.

14 They found that concepts and terms used to calculate the intelligence of animals are often borrowed from studies of human psychology.

15 One recent study charting the learning speed of bees, human infants, birds, and fish ended with the bees on top and our offspring[3] at bottom. So the researchers behind the experiment concluded that learning speed couldn't be used to measure intelligence—because humans weren't first across the finish line[4].

16 The British scientists point out that the bees beat the babies in a learning test because the lab tested characteristics that bees have been perfecting during aeons[5] of evolutionary development.

17 In comparisons of intelligence among species, it's hard to avoid dealing trump cards to[6] one species or another.

18 "It's difficult to **discern** between reasoning, learned reflexes, and pure instincts. This makes it challenging for humans to create tests that don't remind animals of their natural behavior," says Bøckman.

Bottom-up

19 The British scientists suggest what they term a bottom-up method. This differs from what they regard as top-bottom studies in animal behavior research. In these, researchers pick out a cognitive trait and investigate how the animal's nerve system guides this **trait**.

20 With more emphasis on a bottom-up method, they would study the species' neural networks in attempts to perceive what uses these networks can have.

21 "The advantage of the bottom-up methods is that we can find traits that we didn't know existed in animals," says Braastad.

22 Bøckman comments that one of the challenges of this method is the extreme difficulty of investigating tiny neural circuitry in minuscule brains, such as in small insects.

Better tools required

23 There are now numerous studies that compare the cognitive capabilities of various species through investigations of their brains' neural circuitry. This has contributed toward answering questions about whether some of our human qualities can also exist in other species and help lay the groundwork for better comparisons.

24 For instance, multiple studies have been conducted with regard to facial recognition, imitation, social behavior, and empathy, and these can be found among many of our animal cousins.

25 "If the neural paths that are active in animals are the same ones acting in humans, we could have kindred[7] abilities," says Bøckman.

26 Gro Amdam conducts research on bees and what happens to their brains as they age. She is a professor at Arizona State University, and a researcher at the Norwegian University of Life Sciences.

27 "Scientists need to develop better tools, methods, and theories for comparing the brain skills in different species, but we are well on our way," she says.

---

[3] **offspring:** someone's child or children; an animal's baby or babies
[4] **first across the finish line:** the winner
[5] **aeons [also spelled *eons*]:** extremely long periods of time
[6] **dealing trump cards to:** giving an advantage to
[7] **kindred:** of the same family

2 Compare your notes on main ideas and details with a partner's. How can you improve your notes next time?

🔖 Go to the **Pearson Practice English App** or **MyEnglishLab** for more vocabulary practice.

Taking Notes with Outlining

When you outline a text, you summarize it in shortened form. In readings with a lot of information, it is often helpful to create an outline. Outlining sections of the text will help you better understand how main ideas and details and examples are connected.

Outlines are arranged with the main ideas on the left side of the paper and supporting details and examples are indented to the right.

A formal outline uses roman numerals and letters and numbers, while an informal outline may just use bullets or indentation. Indents and sub-indents show the relationship of ideas.

Look at the outline of paragraphs 1–8.

Formal Outline

I. How intelligent are animals?
   a. Different animals have different types of intelligence
   b. Researchers judge animals by human standards
      i. Concerned with learning and cognitive abilities
         1. Thinking
         2. Acquiring knowledge
         3. Sensory perception
         4. Memory
         5. Language
      ii. Human traits not useful for animals
         1. Researchers give animals tasks based on human behavior
            a. Tools
      iii. When judged by animal standards, humans not intelligent
         1. chimpanzee nut problem in treetops
      iv. If researchers focus on human qualities, will not see animal's intelligence

Informal Outline

How intelligent are animals?

   Different animals have different types of intelligence

   Researchers judge animals by human standards
   • Concerned with learning and cognitive abilities
         Thinking
         Acquiring knowledge
         Sensory perception
         Memory
         Language
   • Human traits not useful for animals
         Researchers give animals tasks based on human behavior
            Tools
   • When judged by animal standards, humans not intelligent
         chimpanzee nut problem in treetops
   • If researchers focus on human qualities, will not see animal's intelligence

Reading Two is broken up into sections, each with its own subheading. Choose either *IQ by the kilo* or *Bees smarter than babies?* and write an outline for the section. Find a partner who outlined the same section. Share and discuss your outlines.

🔊 Go to **MyEnglishLab** for more note-taking practice.

1 **Two of the three answers for each question are correct. Circle the two correct answers and cross out the incorrect answer. Use your notes from Reading Two to help you. Discuss your answers with a partner.**

1. It is difficult to define animal intelligence because

   a. animals have extreme sensory perception.

   b. intelligence has different meanings depending on the species of animal.

   c. what is intelligent for one species may not be for another.

2. The presence of human traits in animal behavior may not be a good indicator of animal intelligence because

   a. an animal's ability to imitate human behavior may have no value in its own life.

   b. animals may have other types of intelligence that humans lack.

   c. animals are given tasks based on human behavior.

3. Despite the fact that dolphins apparently are very intelligent based on their brain size, we cannot optimally measure their intelligence because

   a. we cannot use language to communicate.

   b. the concepts and terms used to calculate animal intelligence are often borrowed from human psychology.

   c. they live in a very different environment.

4. If animals do better than humans in intelligence tests, then researchers assume that

   a. it is due to comparable cognition in different species.

   b. there is something wrong with the assessment.

   c. the test must have been similar to the animal's, and not the human's, natural environment.

5. A new way of assessing animal intelligence, the bottom-up method, involves finding a cognitive trait and investigating how the neural system guides this trait. An advantage of this method is that

   a. many animals have minuscule brains.

   b. researchers can find traits they didn't even know existed in animals.

   c. it allows researchers to understand the use of neural networks.

6. For scientists to eventually be able to effectively assess animal intelligence, they need to

   a. develop better tools and methods.

   b. develop new theories.

   c. develop facial recognition.

2 **Review the boldfaced words from the reading with a partner. Use a dictionary or ask your teacher for any meanings you still do not know.**

1 Look at paragraphs 6–8 of Reading Two. The author uses a quotation in paragraph 8 to support a point she has made previously in the article. Which point is she supporting?

Recognizing the Role of Quoted Speech

One way that authors use quotations is to support a point they want to make. By doing this, they are giving the reader an example of why their assertion is correct. Seeing how the quotation is related to an author's point helps the reader to understand the author's point and its importance.

In paragraph 11, the author quotes Peter Bøckman, a zoologist, who says, "As long as we can't communicate with animals [dolphins], it's really hard to decide how smart they are."

Which of the author's points does this quotation support?

Look at paragraph 10:

> Dolphins can thus be said to have the potential for very high intelligence, but we can't measure this optimally. Dolphins come from a completely different world, in a way, and have a language we can't fathom. Communication is definitely a great barrier in the understanding of animal behavior.

The author's assertion that the quotation supports is "Communication is definitely a great barrier in the understanding of animal behavior."

In fact, this statement is a paraphrase of the quotation that the author included for support. Seeing the connection between an author's point and another person's quotation will give you a deeper understanding of the ideas the author is presenting.

2 In Reading Two, Gita Simonsen often makes statements about animal intelligence and then supports them with an appropriate quotation. Look at the quotations, and then look at the preceding paragraph(s). Underline the author's words that the quotations support.

1. "If you turn it around and visualise a flock of screaming chimpanzees hauling you up into a treetop and confronting you with a complicated problem involving nuts, how intelligently do you think you would perform?" (*paragraph 6*)

2. "It's difficult to discern between reasoning, learned reflexes, and pure instincts. This makes it challenging for humans to create tests that don't remind animals of their natural behaviour." (*paragraph 18*)

3. "The advantage of the bottom-up methods is that we can find traits that we didn't know existed in animals." (*paragraph 21*)

4. "If the neural paths that are active in animals are the same ones acting in humans, we could have kindred abilities." (*paragraph 25*)

🔊 Go to **MyEnglishLab** for more skill practice.

CONNECT THE READINGS 🔍

ORGANIZE

Both Reading One (R1) and Reading Two (R2) explore what intelligence is for animals, how it differs from instinct and learned reflexes, and the problems associated with assessing animal intelligence. Complete the chart with examples from each reading. Use the information in the box.

USE YOUR NOTES

Review your notes from Reading One and Two. Use the information in your notes to complete the chart.

For humans, intelligence is linked to language, but we can't understand animal language (e.g., dolphins).

Looking for human traits and qualities (e.g., the use of tools)

Diverse meanings for different species

Extreme perception

Using extreme perception to invent jobs (recognizing something and then deciding to act)

Instinct

Using human standards (Clever Hans can count → he is smart; He is not really counting → he is a dumb animal.)

Learned reflexes

Brain weight of mammals

	R1	R2
What is intelligence?	1.	1.
Problems with assessing animal intelligence	1.	1. 2. 3.
Other abilities vs. intelligence	1. Forensic Dogs: 2. Clever Hans:	1. Bees:

SYNTHESIZE

Read the interview with students responsible for the material in Reading One and Reading Two. Complete the interview using information from Organize and from the readings.

PROFESSOR: Today, I am talking with two students who have extensively studied the work of Temple Grandin and Gita Simonsen. They are both especially interested in the question of animal intelligence. How would Temple Grandin and Gita Simonsen define animal intelligence?

STUDENT 1 (TEMPLE GRANDIN EXPERT): She might start by saying that many people confuse extreme perception with intelligence. Many animals have extreme perception, at least compared to humans, but that alone _____ .

She believes that seizure alert dogs are a good example of animal intelligence because

_____ .

This is not something they need to do or have been taught to do, but something that

_____ .

This is what she thinks shows intelligence.

STUDENT 2 (GITA SIMONSEN EXPERT): Ms. Simonsen would definitely agree that seizure alert dogs are showing intelligence, but, in her opinion, what can be considered intelligence in animals

_____ .

PROFESSOR: How do they believe animal intelligence can be assessed?

STUDENT 1 (TEMPLE GRANDIN EXPERT): Ms. Grandin feels that one problem in assessing animal intelligence is that _____ .

STUDENT 2 (GITA SIMONSEN EXPERT): Yes, Ms. Simonsen would agree with that. For example,

_____ .

STUDENT 1 (TEMPLE GRANDIN EXPERT): In the case of the "counting" horse, Clever Hans, many people judged him to be intelligent when _____ .

However, as soon as they realized that he was getting unconscious cues from the audience, then _____ .

Temple Grandin wouldn't agree with them. She would think Clever Hans was showing intelligence because _____ .

STUDENT 2 (GITA SIMONSEN EXPERT): That's a good point. However, let me explain one more thing Gita Simonsen has noted about the problems with assessing animal intelligence. Because for humans, intelligence is so linked to language, the fact that we don't understand animal language _____ .

PROFESSOR: Are all of these apparently amazing things that animals are capable of doing really a sign of intelligence, or are there other explanations for their actions?

STUDENT 1 (TEMPLE GRANDIN EXPERT): Temple Grandin believes there are sometimes other explanations. For example, she feels forensic dogs that work at airports looking for explosives or illegal drugs _____

_____ .

STUDENT 2 (GITA SIMONSEN EXPERT): Yes, similarly, a recent test of intelligence across species (including humans) found bees to be smarter than all other species including humans. However, for Ms. Simonsen, the explanation might not be intelligence, but rather

_____ .

PROFESSOR: Thank you both very much. I am afraid we have run out of time. I see that you have learned a lot about these two women and their ideas on animal intelligence. Thanks again.

Go to **MyEnglishLab** to check what you learned.

VOCABULARY

REVIEW

Two of the three words in each row have similar meanings to the boldfaced word from the reading. Circle the two words with similar meanings and cross out the word with a different meaning. If you need help, use a dictionary.

READING ONE

1. **achieve**	assess	accomplish	attain
2. **acquire**	obtain	need	gain
3. **apparently**	seemingly	allegedly	visually
4. **approach**	method	attempt	procedure
5. **behavior**	ability	action	conduct
6. **category**	section	group	aspect
7. **cognition**	understanding	instinct	intelligence
8. **controversy**	consensus	disagreement	debate
9. **obvious**	clear	evident	possible
10. **perception**	thought	awareness	observation
11. **unconscious**	cautious	involuntary	unintentional
12. **unique**	singular	normal	solitary

READING TWO

13. **confront**	remind	challenge	present
14. **discern**	differentiate	figure out	dislike
15. **sensory**	auditory	visual	habitual
16. **trait**	characteristic	path	feature
17. **viable**	usable	applicable	achievable

EXPAND

Many academic words, especially those used in the sciences, have Latin or Greek roots. For example, the word *psychologist* comes from the Greek root, *psych*, meaning *mind*. A **psych**ologist is someone who is trained to study the mind and how it works.

Complete the chart. If you need more space, use your notebook.

1. **For each root (column 1), find a word with that root in the reading(s) and paragraph(s) listed.**
2. **Write the word in column 4.**
3. **Guess the meaning of the word using the meaning of the root and the context of the sentence in which you found the word. Write the meaning in column 5.**
4. **In the last column, write other words you can think of with the same root. If you need help, use a dictionary.**

1 ROOT	2 MEANING	3 READING and PARAGRAPH(S)	4 WORD	5 MEANING	6 OTHER WORDS WITH THE SAME ROOT
1. psych-	mind	R1–6	*psychologist*	*someone who is trained to study the mind*	*psychic*
2. cogni-	know / learn	R1–2, 10			
		R2–3, 13			
3. dict-	say / tell	R1–2			
4. act-	do	R1–10			
		R2–25			
5. cept-	taken	R1–2			
		R2–14			
6. numer-	number	R2–23			
7. nov-	new	R1–2			
8. sens-	feeling	R1–4			
		R2–3			
9. cent-	one hundred	R1–3			
10. sci-	know	R1–6			
		R2–7			
11. neur-	nerve	R2–20			

CREATE

APPLY Write five questions about Clever Hans. Use at least one word from Review or Expand in each question. Then exchange questions with a partner and answer the questions.

⬆ Go to the **Pearson Practice English App** or **MyEnglishLab** for more vocabulary practice.

GRAMMAR FOR WRITING

1 Read the sentences and answer the questions that follow.

a. Animals have other abilities and can have elements of intelligence **that humans lack**.

b. No human being can look at someone **who is about to have a seizure** and see (or hear, smell, or feel) what's coming.

c. Oskar Pfungst thought back proudly on the afternoon **when he was finally able to figure out how Clever Hans was able to answer the questions**.

1. In sentence *a*, what elements of intelligence is the writer describing?

2. In sentence *b*, what type of person does the writer say no human being can look at and see what's coming?

3. In sentence *c*, which afternoon is the writer describing?

4. What words begin the boldfaced phrases? Are the words that come just before these phrases verbs, adjectives, nouns, or adverbs?

Adjective Clauses

1. **Identifying adjective clauses**, sometimes called restrictive relative clauses, are groups of words (phrases) that act as adjectives to describe or identify a noun. These phrases come directly after the nouns they describe and begin with relative pronouns that refer to the noun. Sentences with adjective clauses can be seen as a combination of two shorter sentences about the same noun.

> **He** had **a horse**. + **The horse** could answer mathematical questions.
>
> = He had **a horse that could answer mathematical questions**.
>
> Clever Hans lived in **a small town**. + **The small town** was in Germany.
>
> = **The small town where Clever Hans lived** was in Germany.

2. Identifying adjective clauses begin with a **relative pronoun**. The noun that the clause describes determines the choice of pronoun.

> *who* = person or people (and sometimes animals)
>
> *which* = thing or things
>
> *that* = thing, things, person, or people (less formal than *which* or *who*)
>
> *when* = a time or times
>
> *where* or *in which* = a place or places
>
> *whose* = possession

3. Remember that the relative pronoun replaces the noun it describes; the noun is not repeated.

> I saw **the horse**. + The scientist was testing **the horse**.
>
> = I saw **the horse** *that* the scientist was testing.
>
> INCORRECT: I saw **the horse** *that* the scientist was testing **the horse**.

2 **Read the sentences and circle *Correct* or *Incorrect* for the underlined relative pronouns. If the pronoun is correct, add an alternative, or other, pronoun that could also be used. If the pronoun is incorrect, write one or two pronouns that could be used.**

1. The scientist <u>which</u> observed Clever Hans wrote a book.

   Correct   Alternative: _____

   (Incorrect)   Correction(s): *The scientist who / that observed Clever Hans wrote a book.*

2. The museum <u>where</u> Peter Bøckman works is in Oslo, Norway.

   Correct   Alternative: _____

   Incorrect   Correction(s): _____

3. Seizure alert dogs are dogs <u>whose</u> can predict a seizure before it starts.

   Correct   Alternative: _____

   Incorrect   Correction(s): _____

4. Hans was the world-famous horse <u>which</u> owner, Wilhelm von Osten, was a retired school teacher.

   Correct   Alternative: _____

   Incorrect   Correction(s): _____

5. On the day <u>when</u> Oskar Pfungst discovered Clever Hans's secret, Wilhelm von Osten was visiting his sister.

    Correct   Alternative: _____

    Incorrect   Correction(s): _____

6. Zoologists are now developing tests <u>that</u> assess animal intelligence more accurately.

    Correct   Alternative: _____

    Incorrect   Correction(s): _____

7. Many people <u>when</u> study animals are convinced that they are able to understand some human language.

    Correct   Alternative: _____

    Incorrect   Correction(s): _____

8. Oskar Pfungst put the questioners in a place <u>which</u> they could not be seen by Clever Hans.

    Correct   Alternative: _____

    Incorrect   Correction(s): _____

3 Combine each pair of sentences into one sentence using an identifying adjective clause.

1. a. Clever Hans was trained by a retired school teacher.

    b. The school teacher had taught science for many years.

       Clever Hans was trained by a retired school teacher who had taught science for many years.

2. a. The afternoon was cold and rainy.

    b. That afternoon Clever Hans was ready to perform in front of an audience.

       The afternoon when Clever Hans was ready to perform in front of an audience was cold and rainy.

3. a. Binti the gorilla is best known for an amazing incident.

    b. The incident occurred on August 16, 1996.

       _____

       _____

4. a. I spoke with a man.

    b. The man had trained dolphins and killer whales.

       _____

       _____

5. a. Psychologists study many animals.

    b. Animals live in zoos.

       _____

       _____

6. a. I saw my friend.

   b. Her dog could predict seizures before they started.

   _____

   _____

7. a. We saw the dolphin.

   b. The dolphin performed some spectacular feats.

   _____

   _____

8. a. The psychologist had studied at the University of Berlin.

   b. The psychologist developed a new test of animal intelligence.

   _____

   _____

9. a. The morning was sunny and hot.

   b. That morning the dogs saved Ms. Standley.

   _____

   _____

10. a. The contraband was in an old brown suitcase.

    b. The contraband was discovered by the forensic dog.

    _____

    _____

⬆ Go to the **Pearson Practice English App** or **MyEnglishLab** for more grammar practice. Check what you learned in **MyEnglishLab**.

FINAL WRITING TASK: A Summary in Journalistic Style 🔍 APPLY

In this unit, you read two passages on animal intelligence. How would you summarize the important information from one of the readings?

You are going to *write a summary of Reading One in the journalistic style found in newspapers and magazines.*

For an alternative writing topic, see page 115.

PREPARE TO WRITE: Asking and Answering *Wh-* Questions

Many writers, especially journalists, use the *Wh-* questions when they are writing a summary of an important story or news event. To help you to plan your summary of Reading One, you will ask and answer the *Wh-* questions *Who, What, Where, When, Why,* and *How.*

Write one or two questions for each *Wh-* question. Share your questions with a partner and answer them.

Q: **What:** *What is the main idea (paragraph) or thesis (essay or longer article)? What does the person have to say? What issues are discussed?* _____

A: _____

Q: **Who:** *Who wrote the article or passage?* _____

A: _____

Q: **When:** _____

_____

A: _____

Q: **Where:** _____

_____

A: _____

Q: **Why:** _____

_____

A: _____

Q: **How:** _____

_____

A: _____

WRITE

Writing a Summary in Journalistic Style

A **summary** is a shortened version of a text that focuses on the thesis or main idea. Summaries do not include many details or examples. They also do not include personal opinions. Here are some important points about summaries:

1. **Read and reread the text.** As you read, think about the *Wh-* questions. Make sure you understand the text.

2. **Highlight or underline the thesis.** To find the thesis, think about the reason the author wrote the text. What is the author's main idea?

3. **Rewrite the thesis in one sentence.** Use your own words.

4. **Continue reading.** Highlight the main idea and key words and phrases for each paragraph. Write one-sentence summaries in your own words for each paragraph.

5. **Check your sentences against the text.** Remember to use your own wording.

6. **Make sure you have not included irrelevant examples or your own opinion.**

7. **Write your summary.**

8. **Look at your summary later and check it again** with fresh eyes.

9. **Polish the summary for flow.** It needs to read well.

1 Read the summary of Reading Two. Then answer the questions.

In *How Smart Are Animals?*, author Gita Simonsen discusses the problems scientists face in assessing animal intelligence. The first problem is defining animal intelligence. Too often, our tests of animal intelligence are based on how well animals can imitate human behavior. This method does not recognize other elements of intelligence that animals use in their own lives that humans may not possess.

Another method that scientists use with mammals is brain weight as a proportion of total weight. This measurement finds dolphins high in intelligence. However, since human intelligence is linked to language, and we can't communicate with dolphins, or other animals, it is not possible to fully assess their intelligence.

A further problem of animal intelligence testing, especially when comparing intelligence across species, is the assumption that humans must be smarter than any other animal. In a study where bees outperformed human babies, scientists reassessed the test itself. They concluded that the test must have been flawed and that the bees came out on top because of instinct, not intelligence.

A new method of assessment involves studying animals' neural networks and trying to figure out what traits they are designed to allow. This helps scientists to identify traits they had not even thought about. Nevertheless, the minuscule size of some animal brains makes this method very challenging.

Simonsen concludes by quoting Gro Amdam, a professor at Arizona State University, who states, "Scientists need to develop better tools, methods, and theories for comparing the brain skills in different species, but we are well on our way."

1. Who is the author? What is the title of the article?

_____

_____

2. What is the thesis?

_____

_____

3. What are some of the problems of testing an animal's intelligence?

_____

_____

_____

4. What is the author's conclusion about testing animal intelligence?

_____

_____

_____

2 **Before you write your summary of Reading One, practice by summarizing sections of it. For paragraphs 1–7, choose the sentence that best describes the main idea. For paragraphs 8–10, write the one-sentence summary.**

1. Read paragraph 1 of Reading One. Which statement best describes the main idea of the paragraph?

   a. Animals that display a deep understanding of the world around them are plentiful.

   b. There are some dogs that can sniff out dangerous materials at a very successful rate.

   c. Some forensic dogs are so good at their jobs that they are much better than x-ray machines.

2. Read paragraph 2. Which statement best describes the main idea of the paragraph?

   a. Some seizure response dogs have trained themselves to be seizure alert dogs.

   b. Dogs who are truly intelligent will apply their thinking skills to new situations.

   c. Seizure response dogs are trained to save their owners' lives.

3. Read paragraphs 3 and 4. Which statement best describes the main idea of the paragraphs?

   a. Connie Standley's dogs predict her seizures before they happen.

   b. No one knows how seizure response dogs read signs given off by humans before a seizure.

   c. Some seizure response dogs have become seizure alert dogs without any training.

4. Read paragraphs 5, 6, and 7. Which statement best describes the main idea of the paragraphs?

   a. Clever Hans was not really counting but was able to detect and understand human signs that even humans could not see, just as seizure alert dogs can.

   b. Oskar Pfungst, a psychologist, eventually proved that Clever Hans was not really counting.

   c. Clever Hans looked like he was counting but was really just tapping his foot until he knew to stop.

5. Read paragraph 8. Write a one-sentence summary of the main idea.

   _____

   _____

6. Read paragraphs 9 and 10. Write a one-sentence summary of the main idea.

   _____

   _____

3 **Use the information from Prepare to Write and Write on page 110 to plan your summary of Reading One.**

• Make sure you state the thesis and eliminate any unimportant details.

• Be sure to use correct relative pronouns in identifying adjective clauses.

REVISE: Paraphrasing

Paraphrasing is restating an author's ideas in your own words. When paraphrasing, first think of the main idea or what the author is trying to tell you. Then think of ways to say the same thing using your own words. Do not just replace words in a sentence with synonyms.

1 Choose the best paraphrase. Explain why you think it is the better choice.

<u>Original</u>

Many animals have extreme perception.

<u>Paraphrase</u>

a. Many animals have excellent awareness.

b. Animals that display a deep understanding of their world are common.

Paraphrasing

Summary writing often requires the writer to restate an author's ideas. It is very important to restate the author's ideas in your own words while keeping true to the author's ideas. This is called **paraphrasing**.

Author's Own Words

"A group of scientists from Queen Mary University in London examined studies of animal intelligence to find out what scientists currently think about comparable cognition in different species. One recent study charting the learning speed of bees, human infants, birds, and fish ended with the bees on top and our offspring at bottom. So the researchers behind the experiment concluded that learning speed couldn't be used to measure intelligence—because humans weren't first across the finish line. The British scientists point out that the bees beat the babies in a learning test because the lab tested characteristics that bees have been perfecting during aeons of evolutionary development."

When using a direct quote, use these punctuation rules:

1. Lift the quote directly as is from the text. Do not change the capitalization or punctuation.

2. Place a comma before the first quotation mark and the final punctuation mark at the end of the sentence before the final quotation mark: Simonsen concludes by quoting Gro Amdam who states**,** "Scientists need to develop better tools, methods, and theories for comparing the brain skills in different species, but we are well on our way."

Paraphrased Text

A further problem of animal intelligence testing is comparing intelligence across species. Scientists from Queen Mary University in London recently studied the learning speed of different species. When bees outperformed all the other species, including human babies, scientists reassessed the test itself. They concluded that the test must have been flawed and the bees came out on top because of instincts they had developed over millions of years, not intelligence.

When paraphrasing or quoting, use a variety of reporting verbs to introduce an author's ideas:

says	*states*	*thinks*
tells	*explains*	*writes*
acknowledges	*notes*	*believes*
concedes	*mentions*	*concludes*

When paraphrasing, first think of the main idea or what the author is trying to tell you. Think of ways to say the same thing using your own words. Do not just replace words in a sentence with synonyms.

continued on next page

Rules for Paraphrasing

1. Read the original text. Make sure you understand it. Highlight the main idea and key words or phrases.

2. Read the text again. Put the text aside.

3. Write the idea in your own words without looking at the text. Try to use different words than the text.

4. Try to reorder the ideas in the sentence. Start with the middle or the end. Put the paraphrased text aside for a while.

5. With fresh eyes, check your paraphrased sentence against the original. Make sure it is not too close to the original.

Original	Correct Paraphrase
Many animals have extreme perception.	Animals that display a deep understanding of their world are common.

2 Paraphrase the sentences from Reading Two in your own words.

1. The problem is that we often look for human traits when we study animal behaviour. But what may be clever for us needn't be a viable attribute in other members of the animal kingdom.

   _____

   _____

2. "Human intelligence is strongly linked to the language we use to communicate with one another," says Bøckman. "As long as we can't communicate with animals, it's really hard to decide how smart they are."

   _____

   _____

3. There are now numerous studies that compare the cognitive capabilities of various species through investigations of their brains' neural circuitry. This has contributed toward answering questions about whether some of our human qualities can also exist in other species and help lay the groundwork for better comparisons.

   _____

   _____

3 Now go back to the first draft of your summary.

- Make sure you have paraphrased the author of Reading One using your own words. Check against the original text and make any changes necessary. Add a quote if you think it will be effective. Make sure you use correct punctuation with the quote!

- Try to use the grammar and some of the vocabulary from the unit.

🅝 Go to **MyEnglishLab** for more skill practice.

EDIT: Writing the Final Draft

APPLY Write the final draft of your summary and submit it to your teacher. Carefully edit it for grammatical and mechanical errors, such as spelling, capitalization, and punctuation. Consider how to apply the vocabulary, grammar, and writing skills from the unit. Use the checklist to help you.

FINAL DRAFT CHECKLIST

☐ Does the summary include the author's name and the title of the reading?

☐ Does the summary include a thesis statement?

☐ Does the summary answer some of the *Wh-* questions?

☐ Is the summary in your own words?

☐ Did you use a variety of reporting verbs?

☐ If you are using quotes, are they properly punctuated?

☐ Do you use identifying adjective clauses?

☐ Do you use vocabulary from the unit?

ALTERNATIVE WRITING TOPIC

APPLY Noted animal intelligence expert Dorothy Hinshaw believes, "The things that are important to animals can be different than those that matter to humans. When studying animals, we must test them in situations that have meaning for their lives, not ours, and not just look to see how much they resemble us." Think of a specific animal or group of animals. What situations would have meaning for them? Why? How could you test them in these situations? Use the grammar and vocabulary from the unit.

CHECK WHAT YOU'VE LEARNED

Check (✔) the outcomes you've met and vocabulary you've learned. Put an X next to the skills and vocabulary you still need to practice.

Learning Outcomes

☐ **Infer the use of hedging**
☐ **Take notes with outlining**
☐ **Recognize the role of quoted speech**
☐ **Use adjective clauses**
☐ **Paraphrase**
☐ **Write a summary in journalistic style**

Vocabulary

☐ **achieve** AWL
☐ **acquire** AWL
☐ **apparently** AWL
☐ **approach** (*n.*) AWL
☐ **behavior**
☐ **category** AWL
☐ **cognition**
☐ **confront**
☐ **controversy** AWL

☐ **discern**
☐ **obvious** AWL
☐ **perception** AWL
☐ **sensory**
☐ **trait**
☐ **unconscious**
☐ **unique** AWL
☐ **viable**

⬥ Go to **MyEnglishLab** to watch a video about talking to animals, access the Unit Project, and take the Unit 4 Achievement Test.

LEARNING OUTCOMES

> Infer attitudes and feelings
> Take notes with signposts
> Use titles and headings to identify main ideas

> Contrast simple past, present perfect, and present perfect progressive
> Use figurative language
> Write a descriptive essay

🔍 Go to **MyEnglishLab** to check what you know.

Too Much of a Good Thing?

1 FOCUS ON THE TOPIC

1. It has been projected that by the year 2050, the average lifespan will reach 125, and by 2087 it will be 150! Is living longer a good thing? Why or why not?

2. How would issues such as relationships, marriage, family structure, living situations, and career be affected by people's having very long lifespans?

READING ONE | Death Do Us Part

VOCABULARY

Reading One is a story about Marilisa and her husband, Leo. Read the message Marilisa wrote to a friend about Leo. Then choose the correct definition for each boldfaced word.

1. a. mean
   b. energetic
   c. lazy

2. a. on time
   b. well dressed
   c. considerately

3. a. understandably
   b. incredibly
   c. to some extent

4. a. difficult
   b. fascinating
   c. different

5. a. disturbing
   b. confusing
   c. very interesting

6. a. complicated
   b. impressive
   c. terrible

7. a. doing things slowly after much thinking
   b. doing things because somebody said to
   c. doing things quickly without thinking

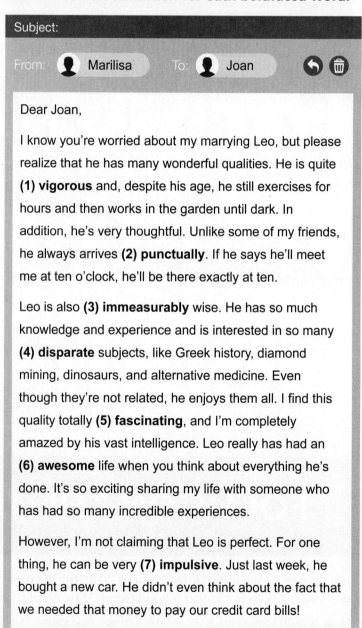

Subject:

From: Marilisa   To: Joan

Dear Joan,

I know you're worried about my marrying Leo, but please realize that he has many wonderful qualities. He is quite **(1) vigorous** and, despite his age, he still exercises for hours and then works in the garden until dark. In addition, he's very thoughtful. Unlike some of my friends, he always arrives **(2) punctually**. If he says he'll meet me at ten o'clock, he'll be there exactly at ten.

Leo is also **(3) immeasurably** wise. He has so much knowledge and experience and is interested in so many **(4) disparate** subjects, like Greek history, diamond mining, dinosaurs, and alternative medicine. Even though they're not related, he enjoys them all. I find this quality totally **(5) fascinating**, and I'm completely amazed by his vast intelligence. Leo really has had an **(6) awesome** life when you think about everything he's done. It's so exciting sharing my life with someone who has had so many incredible experiences.

However, I'm not claiming that Leo is perfect. For one thing, he can be very **(7) impulsive**. Just last week, he bought a new car. He didn't even think about the fact that we needed that money to pay our credit card bills!

continued on next page

8. a. annoying

   b. friendly

   c. interesting

9. a. pleasant

   b. unfriendly

   c. unhappy

10. a. rude or arrogant

   b. modest or shy

   c. admired or respected

11. a. intermittently

   b. truly

   c. continually

12. a. maybe

   b. currently

   c. in the end

Furthermore, at times, he can be **(8) insufferable**. I was trying to watch television last night, and he was constantly interrupting me to ask questions. Couldn't he understand that I was trying to concentrate on the show?

His family is another problem. Take his ex-wife, Katrin, for example. I don't understand why he ever married her. Leo, of course, is very nice and friendly to everyone. She, however, always seems very **(9) chilly**, especially toward me. Also, one of his sons from a previous marriage can be very **(10) presumptuous**. He expects me to do things for him (like his laundry!) just because I am now married to his father . . . even though I barely know him! His daughter, however, is lovely. I am **(11) genuinely** fond of her. I think you would really like her, too.

Despite my complaints, I know that Leo is **(12) ultimately** the best first husband I could ever wish for, so don't worry. I'm sure we'll be very happy together.

Joan, I hope all is well with you.

Love,

Marilisa

Go to the **Pearson Practice English App** or **MyEnglishLab** for more vocabulary practice.

PREVIEW

You are going to read a science fiction story. Science fiction is a genre of writing that describes imaginary future developments in science and technology and their effects on people. Science fiction often includes elements that seem familiar to our lives today, making the story seem "real." Read the first two paragraphs of *Death Do Us Part*. Answer the questions.

1. What do you think was "her first, his seventh"?

2. What is happening with Marilisa and Leo?

3. Where and when do you think this story takes place?

4. What seems real?

5. What seems unreal?

6. What do you think the "Process" is?

Read the story *Death Do Us Part*. Create a chart like the one below to take notes.

TAKE NOTES

Main Ideas	Details
Leo and Marilisa	M – 1st marriage, age 32
	L – 7th marriage, age 363
Marriage and Process	Friend's shocked, L 10x older
	L – multiple marriages, each 30–40 years
	L – sweet, kind, loving
	– looks young
	– faithful to Process

Go to **MyEnglishLab** to view example notes.

Death Do Us Part

By Robert Silverberg

1   It was her first, his seventh. She was thirty-two, he was three hundred and sixty-three: the good old May / December[1] number. They honeymooned in Venice, Nairobi, the Malaysia Pleasure Dome, and one of the posh[2] L-5 resorts, a shimmering, glassy sphere with round-the-clock sunlight and waterfalls that tumbled like cascades of diamonds, and then they came home to his lovely sky-house suspended on tremulous guy-wires[3] a thousand meters above the Pacific to begin the everyday part of their life together.

2   Her friends couldn't get over it. "He's ten times your age!" they would exclaim. "How could you possibly want anybody that old?" Marilisa admitted that marrying Leo was more of a lark[4] for her than anything else. An **impulsive** thing: a sudden impetuous leap. Marriages weren't forever, after all—just thirty or forty years and then you moved along. But Leo was sweet and kind and actually quite sexy. And he had wanted her so much. He **genuinely** did seem to love her. Why should his age be an issue? He didn't appear to be any older than thirty-five or so. These days you could look as young as you like. Leo did his Process[5] faithfully and **punctually**, twice each decade, and it kept him as dashing and **vigorous** as a boy.

---

[1] **May / December:** term used to describe a romantic relationship where there is a big difference in the ages of the two people
[2] **posh:** expensive and used by rich people
[3] **tremulous guy-wires:** shaking cables (metal ropes)
[4] **lark:** something you do to amuse yourself or as a joke
[5] **Process:** a fictional procedure that allows people to live forever

continued on next page

3 There were little drawbacks, of course. Once upon a time, long, long ago, he had been a friend of Marilisa's great-grandmother: They might have even been lovers. She wasn't going to ask. Such things sometimes happened, and you simply had to work your way around them. And then also he had an ex-wife on the scene, Number Three, Katrin, two hundred and forty-seven years old and not looking a day over thirty. She was constantly hovering[6] about. Leo still had warm feelings for her. "A wonderfully dear woman, a good and loyal friend," he would say. "When you get to know her, you'll be as fond of her as I am." That one was hard, all right. What was almost as bad, he had children three times Marilisa's age and more. One of them—the next-to-youngest, Fyodor—had an **insufferable** and **presumptuous** way of winking[7] and sniggering[8] at her. "I want you to meet our father's newest toy," Fyodor said of her once, when yet another of Leo's centenarian sons, previously unsuspected by Marilisa, turned up. Someday Marilisa was going to pay him back[9] for that.

4 Still and all, she had no serious complaints. Leo was an ideal first husband: wise, warm, loving, attentive, and generous. She felt nothing but the greatest tenderness for him. And then too he was so **immeasurably** experienced in the ways of the world. If being married to him was a little like being married to Abraham Lincoln or Augustus Caesar, well, so be it: They had been great men, and so was Leo. He was endlessly **fascinating**. He was like seven husbands rolled into one. She had no regrets, none at all, not really.

5 In the spring of eighty-seven they go to Capri for their first anniversary. Their hotel is a reconstructed Roman villa on the southern slope of Monte Tiberio: alabaster wall frescoed in black and red, a brilliantly colored mosaic of sea creatures in the marble bathtub, a broad travertine terrace that looks out over the sea. They stand together in the darkness, staring at the **awesome** sparkle of the stars. A crescent moon slashes across the night. His arm is around her; her head rests against his breast. Though she is a tall woman, Marilisa is barely heart-high to him.

6 "Tomorrow at sunrise," he says, "we'll see the Blue Grotto[10]. And then in the afternoon we'll hike down below here to the Cave of the Mater Magna. I always get a shiver when I'm there. Thinking about the ancient islanders who worshipped their goddess under that cliff, somewhere back in the Pleistocene. Their rites and rituals, the offerings they made to her."

7 "Is that when you first came here?" she asks, keeping it light and sly. "Somewhere in the Pleistocene?"

8 "A little later than that, really. The Renaissance, I think it was. Leonardo and I traveled down together from Florence . . ."

9 "You and Leonardo, you were like *that*?"

10 "Like that, yes. But not like *that*, if you take my meaning."

11 "And Cosimo di'Medici. Another one from the good old days. Cosimo gave such great parties, right?"

12 "That was Lorenzo," he says. "Lorenzo the Magnificent, Cosimo's grandson. Much more fun than the old man. You would have adored him."

Blue Grotto

---

[6] **hovering:** staying in the same place especially because you are waiting for something
[7] **winking:** closing and opening one eye quickly, usually to show that you are joking, being friendly, or telling a secret
[8] **sniggering:** laughing quietly in a way that is not nice
[9] **pay (someone) back:** to do something unpleasant to someone as a punishment because that person has done something unpleasant to you
[10] **Blue Grotto:** a famous sea cove on the coast of the Italian island of Capri

continued on next page

13 "I almost think you're serious when you talk like that."

14 "I'm always serious. Even when I'm not." His arm tightens around her. He leans forward and down, and buries a kiss in her thick dark hair. "I love you," he whispers.

15 "I love you," she says. "You're the best first husband a girl could want."

16 "You're the finest last wife a man could ever desire."

17 The words skewer[11] her. Last wife? Is he expecting to die in the next ten or twenty or thirty years? He is old—ancient—but nobody has any idea yet where the limits of the Process lie. Five hundred years? A thousand? Who can say? No one able to afford the treatments has died a natural death yet, in the four hundred years since the Process was invented. Why then does he speak so knowingly of her as his last wife? He may live long enough to have seven, ten, fifty wives after her.

18 Marilisa is silent a long while.

19 Then she asks him, quietly, uncertainly. "I don't understand why you said that."

20 "Said what?"

21 "The thing about my being your last wife."

22 He hesitates[12] a moment. "But why would I ever want another, now that I have you?"

23 "Am I so utterly[13] perfect?"

24 "I love you."

25 "You loved Tedesca and Thane and Lavilda, too," she says. "And Miaule and Katrin." She is counting on her fingers in the darkness. One wife is missing from the list. "And . . . Syantha. See, I know all their names. You must have loved them, but the marriage ended anyway. They have to end. No matter how much you love a person, you can't keep a marriage going forever."

26 "How do you know that?"

27 "I just do. Everybody knows it."

28 "I would like this marriage never to end," he tells her. "I'd like it to go on and on and on. To continue to the end of time. Is that all right? Is such a sentiment[14] permissible, do you think?"

29 "What a romantic you are, Leo!"

30 "What else can I be but romantic, tonight? This place, the spring night, the moon, the stars, the sea, the fragrance of the flowers in the air. Our anniversary. I love you. Nothing will ever end for us. Nothing."

31 "Can that really be so?" she asks.

32 "Of course. Forever and ever, as it is this moment."

33 She thinks from time to time of the men she will marry after she and Leo have gone their separate ways. For she knows that she will. Perhaps she'll stay with Leo for ten years, perhaps for fifty; but **ultimately**, despite all his assurances to the contrary[15], one or the other of them will want to move on. No one stays married forever. Fifteen, twenty years, that's the usual. Sixty or seventy tops.

---

[11] **skewer:** to hurt
[12] **hesitates:** pauses before doing or saying something because of uncertainty
[13] **utterly:** completely, absolutely
[14] **sentiment:** an opinion or feeling that you have about something
[15] **to the contrary:** showing that the opposite is true

continued on next page

34 She'll marry a great athlete, next, she decides. And then a philosopher; and a political leader; and then stay single for a few decades, just to clear her palate, so to speak, an intermezzo[16] in her life; and when she wearies of that she'll find someone entirely different, a simple rugged man who likes to hunt, to work in the fields with his hands; and then a yachtsman with whom she'll sail the world; and then maybe when she's about three hundred she'll marry a boy, an innocent of eighteen or nineteen who hasn't even had his first Prep[17] yet; and then—then a childish game. It always brings her to tears, eventually. The unknown husbands that wait for her in the misty future are vague, **chilly** phantoms, fantasies, frightening, and inimical.[18] They are like swords that will inevitably fall between her and Leo, and she hates them for that.

35 The thought of having the same husband for all the vast expanse[19] of time that is the rest of her life, is a little disturbing—it gives her a sense of walls closing in, and closing and closing and closing—but the thought of leaving Leo is even worse. Or of his leaving her. Maybe she isn't truly in love with him, at any rate not as she imagines love at its deepest to be, but she is happy with him. She wants to stay with him. She can't really envision parting with him and moving on to someone else.

36 But of course she knows that she will. Everybody does in the fullness of time. *Everybody.*

37 Leo is a sand-painter. Sand-painting is his fifteenth or twentieth career. He has been an architect, an archeologist, a space-habitats developer, a professional gambler, an astronomer, and a number of other **disparate** and dazzling things. He reinvents himself every decade or two. That's as necessary to him as the Process itself. Making money is never an issue, since he lives on the compounding interest of investments set aside centuries ago. But the fresh challenge—ah, yes, always the fresh challenge.

38 Marilisa hasn't entered on any career path yet. It's much too soon. She is, after all, still in her first life, too young for the Process, merely in the Prep stage yet. Just a child, really. She has dabbled[20] in ceramics, written some poetry, composed a little music. Lately she has begun to think about studying economics or perhaps Spanish literature. No doubt her actual choice of a path to follow will be very far from any of these. But there's time to decide. Oh, is there ever time.

---

[16] **intermezzo:** a short period of time between two longer periods
[17] **Prep:** short for preparation, what is needed before you undergo the "Process"
[18] **inimical:** harmful
[19] **vast expanse:** large, wide area
[20] **dabbled:** did something in a way that wasn't very serious

MAIN IDEAS

Reading One discusses Marilisa's and Leo's views on marriage, family structure and relationships, careers, and longevity. Write sentences about how their views are different from some of the present-day society views described.

1. **Marriage**

   Present-day society: Marriage is seen as a lifelong commitment, although in some societies divorce is common. Some people may have more than one or two marriages.

   "Death Do Us Part": _____

   _____

   _____

2. Family structure / Relationships

Present-day society: Three generations of a family living at the same time is common.

"Death Do Us Part": _____

_____

_____

3. Careers

Present-day society: Although many people have different jobs throughout their lives, they usually continue working in the same career.

"Death Do Us Part": _____

_____

_____

4. Longevity

Present-day society: The average lifespan varies around the world, but in developed countries the average lifespan is mid-seventies.

"Death Do Us Part": _____

_____

_____

DETAILS

1 Marilisa and Leo have different perspectives on the topics in the chart. Complete the chart with examples of their differing views.

TOPIC	MARILISA	LEO
Marriage	*first marriage – assumes she'll be married again to a variety of men*	
Family Structure / Relationships		
Careers		
Longevity		

2 Look at your notes and at your answers in Preview. How did they help you to understand the story?

MAKE INFERENCES 🔍

Inferring Attitudes and Feelings

Writers sometimes suggest relationships between characters in a story without directly stating what the relationships are. We use inference to understand characters' attitudes and feelings on a deeper level.

Look at the question and read the explanation.

How does Marilisa feel about Leo? *(paragraph 2)*

a. He is too old for her.

b. He is a joke.

c. He is youthful.

The best answer is c.

Evidence: In paragraph 2, we learn that Marilisa's friends are concerned about Leo's age. Marilisa doesn't seem concerned because she believes that marriages aren't forever. We also learn that her marriage "was more of a lark," but she doesn't say that Leo himself is a joke. He is "sweet, kind, and actually quite sexy." This makes him appear youthful to Marilisa.

After reading the text closely, we can infer that Marilisa's strongest feeling about Leo is that he is youthful.

1 Choose the correct answer. Look back at the paragraph in parentheses. Cite the evidence from the story that supports your answer.

1. How does Marilisa feel about Katrin? (*paragraph 3*)

   a. warm

   b. loyal

   c. jealous

   Evidence: _____

   _____

   _____

2. How does Fyodor feel toward Marilisa? (*paragraph 3*)

   a. playful

   b. disrespectful

   c. bored

   Evidence: _____

   _____

   _____

3. How does Leo feel about his marriage with Marilisa? (*paragraphs 23–32*)

    a. tired

    b. unclear

    c. secure

    Evidence: _____

    _____

    _____

4. How does Marilisa feel about her marriage to Leo? (*paragraphs 29–34*)

    a. It's romantic.

    b. She wants it to be permanent.

    c. She sadly accepts that it will end.

    Evidence: _____

    _____

    _____

5. Which word best describes Marilisa's feeling about her marriage to Leo? (*paragraph 35*)

    a. conflicted

    b. committed

    c. insecure

    Evidence: _____

    _____

    _____

2 **Discuss your answers with a partner. Point out sentences, words, or phrases in the paragraphs that helped you find the answers.**

DISCUSS 🔍

Work in a small group. Choose one of the questions. Discuss your ideas. Then choose one person in your group to report the ideas to the class.

USE YOUR NOTES

Use your notes to support your answers with information from the reading.

1. It appears that in the story, societal expectations are that everyone has multiple marriages. At this point in Leo's life, he has a different idea about the ideal length of a marriage. Why does he want Marilisa to be his last wife while she is still looking forward to multiple future marriages?

2. The story talks about problems Marilisa experiences because many generations of family and ex-wives are all alive at the same time. Why does she find this a problem? Do you think it would be a problem for you? Why or why not?

3. Leo has had many different careers. "He reinvents himself every decade or two. That's as necessary to him as the Process itself." Why do you think he changes careers so often?

↩ Go to **MyEnglishLab** to give your opinion about another question.

PREVIEW

Scientific understanding of aging at the cellular and molecular level may be the key to a longer lifespan. More and more scientists now believe that the human lifespan could be increased to 140 years or more in the future. This may be achieved through genetic manipulation or caloric restriction (eating less). These strategies have proved effective with worms, flies, and mice. Maybe someday they will work on humans.

1 Look at the title of the reading and the picture. Write two questions that you think will be answered in the reading.

_____

_____

2 Look at the boldfaced words in the reading. Which words do you know the meanings of?

READ

1 Read *Toward Immortality: The Social Burden of Longer Lives.* As you read, guess the meanings of the words that are new to you. Remember to take notes on main ideas and details.

TOWARD IMMORTALITY:
The Social Burden of Longer Lives
By Ker Than   LiveScience Staff Writer

A doubled lifespan

1 If scientists could create a pill that let you live twice as long while remaining free of infirmities[1], would you take it?

2 If one considers only the personal benefits that longer life would bring, the answer might seem like a no-brainer[2]: People could spend more quality time with loved ones, watch future generations grow up, learn new languages, master new musical instruments, try different careers, or travel the world.

3 But what about society as a whole? Would it be better off if lifespans were doubled? The question is one of growing relevance, and serious debate about it goes back at least a few years to the Kronos Conference on Longevity Health Sciences in Arizona. Gregory Stock, director of the Program on Medicine, Technology, and Society at UCLA's School of Public Health, answered the question with an **emphatic** "Yes." A doubled lifespan, Stock said, would "give us a chance to recover from our mistakes, lead us towards longer-term thinking and reduce health care costs by delaying the onset of expensive diseases of aging. It would also raise productivity by adding to our prime years."

---

[1] **infirmities:** sicknesses, diseases
[2] **no-brainer:** something that you do not have to think about because it is easy to understand   *continued on next page*

4 Bioethicist Daniel Callahan, a cofounder of the Hastings Center in New York, didn't share Stock's enthusiasm. Callahan's objections were practical ones. For one thing, he said, doubling lifespans won't solve any of our current social problems. "We have war, poverty, all sorts of issues around, and I don't think any of them would be at all helped by having people live longer," Callahan said in a recent telephone interview. "The question is, 'What will we get as a society?' I suspect it won't be a better society."

5 Others point out that a doubling of the human lifespan will affect society at every level. Notions about marriage, family, and work will change in fundamental ways, they say, as will attitudes toward the young and the old.

Marriage and family

6 Richard Kalish, a psychologist who considered the social effects of life extension technologies, thinks a longer lifespan will **radically** change how we view marriage.

7 In today's world, for example, a couple in their 60s who are stuck in a loveless but **tolerable** marriage might decide to stay together for the remaining 15 to 20 years of their lives out of inertia[3] or familiarity. But if that same couple knew they might have to suffer each other's company for another 60 or 80 years, their choice might be different. Kalish predicted that as lifespans increase, there will be a shift in emphasis from marriage as a lifelong union to marriage as a long-term commitment. Multiple, brief marriages could become common.

8 A doubled lifespan will reshape notions of family life in other ways, too, says Chris Hackler, head of the Division of Medical Humanities at the University of Arkansas. If multiple marriages become the norm as Kalish predicts, and each marriage produces children, then half-siblings will become more common, Hackler points out. And if couples continue the current trend of having children beginning in their 20s and 30s, then eight or even ten generations might be alive **simultaneously**, Hackler said. Furthermore, if life extension also increases a woman's period of fertility, siblings could be born 40 or 50 years apart. Such a large age difference would radically change the way siblings or parents and their children interact with one another.

9 "If we were 100 years younger than our parents or 60 years apart from our siblings, that would certainly create a different set of social relationships," Hackler told LiveScience.

The workplace

10 For most people, living longer will **inevitably** mean more time spent working. Careers will necessarily become longer, and the retirement age will have to be pushed back, not only so individuals can support themselves, but to avoid overtaxing a nation's social security system.

11 Advocates of anti-aging research say that working longer might not be such a bad thing. With skilled workers remaining in the workforce longer, economic productivity would go up. And if people got bored with their jobs, they could switch careers.

12 But such changes would carry their own set of dangers, critics say. Competition for jobs would become fiercer as "mid-life re-trainees" beginning new careers vie with young workers for a limited number of entry-level positions. Especially **worrisome** is the problem of workplace mobility, Callahan said. "If you have people staying in their jobs for 100 years, that is going to make it really tough for young people to move in and get ahead," Callahan explained.

13 Callahan also worries that corporations and universities could become dominated by a few individuals if executives, managers, and tenured professors refuse to give up their posts[4]. Without a constant infusion of youthful talent and ideas, these institutions could stagnate[5].

Time to act

14 While opinions differ wildly about what the ramifications for society will be if the human lifespan is extended, most ethicists agree that the issue should be discussed now, since it might be impossible to stop or control the technology once it's developed. "If this could ever happen, then we'd better ask what kind of society we want to get," Callahan said. "We had better not go anywhere near it until we have figured those problems out."

---

[3] **inertia:** the feeling that you do not want to do anything at all
[4] **give up their posts:** leave their jobs
[5] **stagnate:** to stop developing or improving

2 Compare your notes on main ideas and details with a partner's. How can you improve your notes next time?

🔊 Go to the **Pearson Practice English App** or **MyEnglishLab** for more vocabulary practice.

Taking Notes with Signposts

When you use signposts (visual markings or indicators) to mark a text, you are identifying groups of similar ideas. This will help you understand the text more easily. In Reading Two, the author asks the reader to analyze a controversial issue. In a reading of this type, the author presents two sides of a question and leaves it to the readers to decide which side they agree with. It can be helpful to mark paragraphs or sections of the text with **+, −,** or **Ø** to indicate which side of the question the paragraph / section supports. This marking can be done directly in the margins of the text or on post-it notes. The question the author asks the reader in Reading Two is whether you would want an extended lifespan if it were possible.

Look at Paragraph 2. Would you mark this paragraph with a **+** (positive aspect(s) of longer life), a **−** (negative aspect(s) of longer life), or **Ø** (neutral − neither positive nor negative)?

> If one considers only the personal benefits that longer life would bring, the answer might seem like a no-brainer: People could spend more quality time with loved ones; watch future generations grow up, learn new languages, master new musical instruments, try different careers, or travel the world.

You probably marked it with a *+*. Why? Because you like the idea of having more time to spend with loved ones and more time to learn and do new exciting things.

Go through the rest of Reading Two and mark each paragraph with a *+, −,* or *θ* to indicate which side of the question the paragraph / section supports. When you are finished, compare and discuss your markings with a partner. You may have different markings than your partner. If so, explain your thinking.

⬆ Go to **MyEnglishLab** for more note-taking practice.

COMPREHENSION

1 **Answer the questions. Use your notes from Reading Two to help you. Discuss your answers with a partner.**

   1. One example from Reading Two of why a longer lifespan is a good thing for society is that it will "raise productivity by adding to our prime years." What does this mean? What are some other reasons given that are in favor of a longer lifespan?

   2. How will longer lifespans affect how individuals and families socialize? Are these changes negative or positive?

2 **Review the boldfaced words from the reading with a partner. Use a dictionary or ask your teacher for any meanings you still do not know.**

1 **Look at Reading Two again. You looked at the title before you read. Did it help you understand the article? Why or why not? You may also have looked at the headings before you read. If so, did they help you understand the article? Why or why not?**

Using Titles and Headings to Identify Main Ideas

The title of a reading and the headings within the reading give the reader important information. Good readers use the clues provided by titles and headings to help them predict the content of the whole reading and the individual sections in the reading. Based on the title and headings, readers can ask themselves questions they think the reading or section will answer.

Think about the title, *Toward Immortality: The Social Burden of Longer Lives.* What questions would you expect this article to answer? Two of the choices are correct.

a. How long will people live in the future?

b. Why will there be fewer diseases in the future?

c. What problems may longer lives cause for society?

The best answers are *a* and *c*. Answer *a* is correct because the words "immortality" and "longer lives" are in the title. Therefore, we know that the author will probably mention how long people will live. Answer *c* is also correct because the words "social burden" suggest there will be problems or issues with longer lives. Answer *b* is not a good choice because there is no indication in the title that the article will discuss medical issues associated with longer lives.

Just as with titles, headings and subheadings also provide clues about what readers can expect to find in those sections of the text. Predicting content from headings will improve your reading comprehension.

2 **Imagine that you are looking at the headings from Reading Two for the first time. For each heading, write two questions you might ask.**

1. A doubled lifespan _____

   _____

   _____

2. Marriage and family _____

   _____

   _____

3. The workplace _____

   _____

   _____

Go to **MyEnglishLab** for more skill practice.

CONNECT THE READINGS 🔍

ORGANIZE

Reading One (R1) and Reading Two (R2) discuss both
positive and negative effects of longer lifespans.
Complete the diagram with information from the readings.

USE YOUR NOTES

Review your notes from
Reading One and Two. Use
the information in your
notes to complete the chart.

CAUSE: Prolonged Lifespan

↓

EFFECTS

Marriage Positive Effect	Marriage Negative Effect
R1	R1
R2	R2

Careers Positive Effect	Careers Negative Effect
R1	R1 *NO NEGATIVE EFFECTS*
R2	R2

Family Structure Positive Effect	Family Structure Negative Effect
R1 *NO POSITIVE EFFECTS*	R1
R2	R2

SYNTHESIZE

In Reading Two, bioethicist Daniel Callahan stated, when talking about the potential for
doubled lifespans, "'What will we get as a society?' I suspect it won't be a better society."
Write a paragraph about whether you agree or disagree with his statement. Support your
answer with at least three pieces of information from Organize.

▶ Go to **MyEnglishLab** to check what you learned.

Too Much of a Good Thing?   **131**

REVIEW

Look at the adjectives and adverbs in the box. Decide if the words give you positive, negative, or neutral feelings. Then write the words in the chart. Note that some words can be interpreted in more than one way. Compare your answers with a partner's. If your answers are different, discuss why.

awesome	emphatic	immeasurably	insufferable	radically	ultimately
chilly	fascinating	impulsive	presumptuous	simultaneously	vigorous
disparate	genuinely	inevitably	punctually	tolerable	worrisome

POSITIVE	NEGATIVE	NEUTRAL

EXPAND

Many adjectives are formed by combining a base / root word with a suffix. (*vigor + ous = vigorous*). Look at the boldfaced adjectives in the excerpts from the readings.

- They stand together in the darkness, staring at the **awesome** sparkle of the stars.

- A couple in their 60s who are stuck in a loveless but **tolerable** marriage might decide to stay together.

- Fyodor had a **presumptuous** way of winking and sniggering at her.

Suffixes can sometimes change the meaning of the base word.

- love → loveless (without love)

- care → careful (with care)

- tolerate → tolerable (able to be tolerated)

In addition, suffixes always change the form of the word.

- vigor (noun) → vigorous (adjective)

Common Adjective Suffixes						
-able	-ar	-en	-ful	-ic	-ish	-ous
-al	-ary	-ent	-ial	-ical	-ive	-some
-ant	-ed	-ese	-ible	-ing	-less	-y

Adjective suffixes can be added to nouns or verbs.

- adventure (n.) → adventurous
- care (n.) or (v.) → careful
- fascinate (v.) → fascinating

Sometimes there are spelling changes when a suffix is added.

- Leave out the final *e*.
  measure → measurable
- Double the final consonant.
  sun → sunny
- Leave out the final *s* before *-al*.
  politics → political

Complete the chart with synonyms from Reading One (R1) and Reading Two (R2) that have the suffixes listed. Then think of your own example of an adjective with the same suffix.

DEATH DO US PART (R1)			
SUFFIXES	EXAMPLE FROM TEXT	DEFINITION OR SYNONYM	EXAMPLE OF A NEW ADJECTIVE WITH THE SAME SUFFIX
Paragraphs 1–2			
-ing		sparkling	
-ive	*impulsive*	impetuous	*active*
Paragraphs 3–5			
-able		intolerable	
-al		perfect	
Paragraphs 6–15			
-ent		very old	
-ous		sincere	
Paragraphs 26–33			
-ible		allowable	
-ic		passionate	
Paragraphs 34–38			
-y		foggy	

TOWARD IMMORTALITY (R2)			
SUFFIXES	EXAMPLE FROM TEXT	DEFINITION OR SYNONYM	EXAMPLE OF A NEW ADJECTIVE WITH THE SAME SUFFIX
Paragraphs 1–2			
-al		individual	
Paragraphs 3–4			
-ic		forceful	
-ical		sensible	
Paragraphs 5–7			
-less		without love	
-ing		still left	
Paragraphs 10–13			
-ly		without doubt	
-ed		restricted	
-some		troublesome	
-ant		steady	
-ful		young	

CREATE

APPLY Write five questions you have for the bioethicist Daniel Callahan, Gregory Stock of UCLA's School of Public Health, or Leo from Reading One. Use at least one word from Review or Expand in each question. Then exchange questions with a partner and answer the questions as you believe the individual from the readings would answer. Use evidence from the readings to support your answers. Write the questions and answers in your notebook if more space is needed.

Go to the **Pearson Practice English App** or **MyEnglishLab** for more vocabulary practice.

1 Read the sentences and answer the questions.

a. Marilisa and Leo **went** to Nairobi and Venice on their honeymoon three years ago.

b. Leo **has been** an architect, an archeologist, a space-habitats developer, a professional gambler, an astronomer, and a number of other disparate and dazzling things.

c. People **have been searching** for the "fountain of youth" since the beginning of recorded history.

1. In sentence *a*, is Leo and Marilisa's honeymoon over? How do you know?

2. In sentence *b*, is Leo still an architect, an archeologist . . . ? How do you know?

3. In sentence *c*, are people still searching for the fountain of youth? How do you know? When did people start searching?

4. What verb forms are used in sentences *a*, *b*, and *c*?

Contrasting Simple Past, Present Perfect, and Present Perfect Progressive

Simple Past

1. Use the simple past for things that happened in the past and were completed.	Leo **watched** the movie. *(Leo is no longer watching the movie. He finished watching the movie.)*
2. Use past time expressions such as: *last, ago, in, on, at, yesterday, when* . . . to indicate that an action or event was completed at a definite time in the past.	Leo **watched** the movie **yesterday**. *(Leo is no longer watching the movie. He finished watching the movie yesterday.)*

Present Perfect

3. Use the present perfect for completed actions that happened at an indefinite time in the past.	Marilisa **has eaten** breakfast. *(She has finished her breakfast, but we don't know exactly when she ate it, or it is not important.)*
4. You can also use the present perfect for repeated actions that were completed in the past, but that may happen again in the future.	Leo **has visited** Paris six times. *(Those six visits are finished. However, he may visit Paris again in the future.)*
5. Use the present perfect with *for* or *since* for actions that began in the past. These actions were not completed, have continued up to the present, and may continue into the future. • *For* is followed by a length of time, for example, *six years*. • *Since* is followed by a specific point in time, for example, *2099*. • Use *for* or *since* for this meaning, especially with non-action verbs, such as *be, feel,* and *know*.	Leo **has been** a sand-painter **for** six years. *(Leo became a sand-painter six years ago. He is still a sand-painter today and may continue to be a sand-painter in the future.)* Leo **has been** a sand-painter **since** 2099. *(Leo became a sand-painter in 2099. He is still a sand-painter today and may continue to be a sand-painter in the future.)*

continued on next page

6. Compare the present perfect without *for* or *since*.	Leo **has been** a sand-painter. *(Leo was a sand-painter at some time in the past, but he is not anymore. We don't know exactly when he was, or it is not important.)*

Present Perfect Progressive

7. Use the present perfect progressive for actions that began in the past. These actions were not completed, have continued up to the present, and may continue into the future. The use of *for* or *since* with the present perfect progressive is optional. Using *for* or *since* gives additional information about when the action began or how long it has been in progress, but it does not change the meaning of the verb.	Daniel Callahan **has been studying** about the ramifications of increasing human lifespans. *(Daniel Callahan began studying sometime in the past. He is still studying and will probably continue to study in the future.)*
8. Non-action (stative) verbs are not usually used in the progressive. Use the present perfect with *for* or *since* for this meaning with a non-action verb.	Callahan **has been** at the Hastings Center **for** many years. Callahan **has been** at the Hastings Center **since** 1969.

A present perfect sentence with *for / since* and a present perfect progressive sentence often have the same meaning and can be used interchangeably. But if the verb is stative or short action (meaning that the verb is used to express actions that begin and end quickly) the verb can't be progressive.

Stative Verbs (Partial List)			Short Action Verbs (Partial List)		
admire	dislike	need	arrive	depart	meet
agree	have (possession)	see	break	drop	open
be	know	suppose	close	finish	start
contain	like	want	crash	leave	turn off / on

2 Choose the correct forms of the verbs to complete each conversation.

Conversation 1

REPORTER: Our readers may already know about the "fountain of youth," but can you give us some historical perspective? Also, do you think scientific advancements will turn out to be a "fountain of youth," allowing people to live forever?

STUDENT OF DANIEL CALLAHAN: People **(1) have been searching / searched** for the "fountain of youth" since the beginning of recorded history. People believed that drinking from this fountain would allow them to be healthy and vigorous forever. They would never get sick and would be full of energy. So far, the "fountain" **(2) has been / was** impossible to find.

People **(3) have not been / were not** able to truly achieve eternal life. Human lifespans have been increasing, but we are still far from reaching immortality. Even considering the scientific advancements that **(4) have taken / took** place in the twentieth century, I, as a scientist, believe that ultimately the limit of human life will be no more than 150 years.

Conversation 2

STUDENT OF DR. KALISH: I know you have been very busy attending conferences this month. I believe you recently attended a conference on longevity. Did you learn a lot?

STUDENT OF DR. GREGORY STOCK: What a month! The conference on longevity I **(5) attended / have been attending** last week did not begin very punctually. It was supposed to begin at 9:00 a.m. but **(6) didn't actually start / hasn't actually started** until 9:45! On top of that, the first speaker was insufferable. He finished every sentence with, "you know." Luckily, I **(7) have gone / have been going** to three other conferences this month that had awesome speakers who provided us with lots of interesting facts and ideas about longevity. At the first conference, the speaker **(8) discussed / has been discussing** how restricting the amount of food eaten may increase lifespans. At the next conference, I learned about some ongoing research that Dr. Clynes **(9) did / has been doing** with mice that has ramifications for human longevity.

Conversation 3

MARILISA'S FRIEND, JOAN: Leo has such a large family. Now that you are married, how are you getting along with them?

MARILISA: Not as well as I would like, but I suppose the problems I am having are quite normal for a newlywed. I **(10) have had / had** problems with Leo's son, Fyodor, since the first time I met him, but I am willing to tolerate him for Leo's sake. Other than Fyodor and one or two of Leo's ex-wives, I **(11) have enjoyed / enjoyed** getting to know Leo's family. I really like Leo's brother, Max. Max is a writer and scientist who **(12) has completed / completed** a book on "the Process" two years ago. Ever since that was published, he **(13) worked / has been working** on his autobiography.

3 **Complete the sentences with the verb in the correct tense: simple past, present perfect, or present perfect progressive.**

1. Leo (**meet**) _____ many important historical figures during his life, and he looks forward to meeting many more.

2. Marilisa and Leo (**visit**) _____ Capri in 1987 on their first anniversary.

3. Leo (**have**) _____ at least ten different careers so far.

4. Marilisa (**talk**) _____ to Fyodor for at least thirty minutes. Do you think they will be done soon?

5. Leo (**meet**) _____ Leonardo da Vinci over 500 years ago.

6. Doctors at the Hastings Center (**study**) _____ longevity for many years and plan to continue for many more years.

7. Daniel Callahan doesn't believe that scientists should continue working on extending lifespans. Once they (**figure**) _____ out the effects longer lives will have on society, then they can start to work on this again.

8. The conference that Dr. Kalish (**attend**) _____ last August dealt with the future of marriage in a society with prolonged lifespans.

9. Dr. Chris Hackler (**do**) _____ research concerning family relationships of siblings born forty to fifty years apart. He expects to finish his research next year.

10. Although it is only March, Gregory Stock (**write**) _____ four papers on how increased lifespans can decrease healthcare costs. He is expecting to write at least two more papers before the end of the year.

➤ Go to the **Pearson Practice English App** or **MyEnglishLab** for more grammar practice. Check what you learned in **MyEnglishLab.**

FINAL WRITING TASK: A Descriptive Essay 🔍 APPLY

In this unit, you read about immortal life in the future. Imagine that scientists have discovered a way to make you immortal, and it is now the year 2175.

You are going to ***write a descriptive essay about the positive and negative aspects of your life in 2175.*** You may want to consider these questions as you write:

What is your life like? What jobs have you had? What relationships have you had? Are you married? If so, to whom? What is your family like? What have been the advantages of living so long? What have been the disadvantages?

For an alternative writing topic, see page 143.

PREPARE TO WRITE: Using an Idea Web

An **idea web** helps you see how different topics are related to one central theme.

Imagine your life in the year 2175. Look at the topics in the idea web. Close your eyes and try to create a mental picture of yourself and your life. Think about the topics in the circles as they relate to your life. Write your ideas about each topic in the circles. Be sure to include details and adjectives.

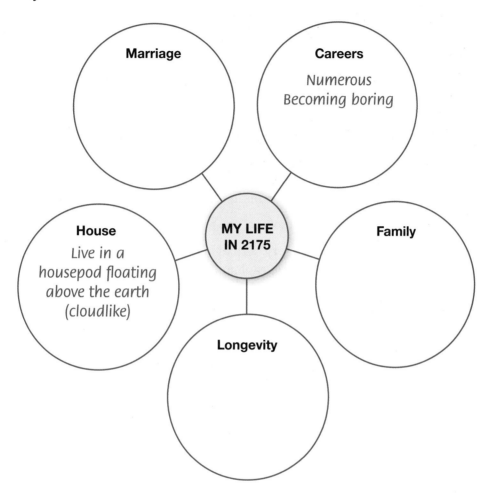

WRITE

Writing a Descriptive Essay

A **descriptive essay** describes a place, person, or situation. The writer uses such vivid or descriptive language that the reader can create a clear mental picture of the description. Here are some important points to keep in mind:

1. **Have an introduction.** Capture the reader's attention by telling an interesting anecdote or story. Be sure to include the main idea of the essay in the introduction.

2. **Use strong imagery.** Create mental pictures for your reader by using descriptive adjectives and details.

3. **Rely on sensory details.** Create strong sensory images by describing smells, sights, sounds, tastes, and senses of touch.

4. **Have a conclusion.** Bring the ideas of the essay to a close by providing final thoughts or predictions.

1 **Read the introductory paragraph from a descriptive essay about life in the future. Then discuss the questions with a partner.**

> I sleepily open my eyes as my alarm robot vigorously shakes me awake. I can smell the usual insufferable morning smells: bitter coffee made with sour milk and burnt toast. I haven't had time to reprogram my breakfast robot since the electric meteor shower last week blew out its motherboard with a loud crack that sounded as if my housepod had split in half. It's during these times that I fondly remember the simple days decades ago when I made my own breakfast and lived on Earth, not floating above it like a lonely cloud. No matter. I'll glide through a convenient coffee shop's hovercraft window on the way to work. Work. I used to be so punctual. "As utterly dependable as a Swiss watch," my bosses always said, even with a half a world commute every day. After more than 150 years of work, it's hard to get excited. But I am getting ahead of myself. In the past 200 years, I have had numerous marriages, careers, countless children, and awesome experiences. My life has been an endless roller coaster ride filled with immeasurable happiness and sadness.

1. Underline the sentence that contains the main idea of the paragraph.

2. Based on the main idea, what do you expect the next paragraphs of the essay will be about?

3. Descriptive essays often include sensory details and create mental imagery. What are some examples of sensory details in the paragraph above?

TOUCH	SMELL	SIGHT	TASTE	SOUND

4. What mental picture does this paragraph create? Underline the words or sentences that create these images for you.

2 **Use your notes from Prepare to Write on page 139 to write the first draft of your descriptive essay.**

• Make sure you have multiple paragraphs.

• Be sure to use verb forms correctly to show when events took place.

• Be sure to use descriptive language that includes adjectives and sensory details.

REVISE: Using Figurative Language

1 Read the sentences. Which sentence is more interesting? Why?

His smile was very nice.

His smile was as bright as the sun.

Figurative Language

Many descriptive essays and stories include **figurative language**, such as **similes**, **metaphors**, and **personification**, to add depth and imagery.

A **simile** is a comparison of two things using the connecting words *like* or *as*. The comparison is usually between things that are normally unrelated to each other but that share a similar quality or characteristic.

Simile: The snow was like a blanket.

Explanation: The subject, snow, is being compared to a blanket because it covers the ground in the same way a blanket covers a bed.

A **metaphor** is another kind of comparison between two things that are normally unrelated. However, unlike a simile, a metaphor does not use the connecting words *like* or *as.* It directly states the comparison, saying that one thing "is" another. For example:

Metaphor: The setting sun is a red ball of fire falling into the sea.

Explanation: The sun is not *like* a red ball of fire, it *is* a red ball of fire.

Personification gives human qualities to animals or objects. This helps the reader better connect with the image.

Without Personification	With Personification
The leaves blew around in the wind.	The leaves **danced** in the wind.
The sun was shining in the sky.	The sun **sang** its happy summer song.

2 Look at the introductory paragraph in Write on page 140. Find the two similes and complete the information.

_____ is being compared to _____ because _____

_____

_____ is being compared to _____ because _____

_____

3 Look at Reading One. Find the similes and complete the information.

Paragraph 1: _____ is/are being compared to _____

because _____

Paragraph 2: _____ is/are being compared to _____

because _____

Paragraph 34: _____ is/are being compared to _____

because _____

4 Look at Reading One, paragraph 34. What metaphor does Marilisa use to describe her unknown future husbands? Why does she use this metaphor?

_____

_____

5 Look at Reading One, paragraph 17. Find an example of personification. With a partner, discuss how personification helps the description come alive.

_____

_____

6 Now go back and look at the first draft of your essay.

• Make sure your descriptions are clear and they create vivid mental images.

• Add at least one simile, one metaphor, or one example of personification.

• Try to use the grammar and some of the vocabulary from the unit.

 Go to **MyEnglishLab** for more skill practice.

EDIT: Writing the Final Draft

APPLY Write the final draft of your essay and submit it to your teacher. Carefully edit it for grammatical and mechanical errors, such as spelling, capitalization, and punctuation. Consider how to apply the vocabulary, grammar, and writing skills from the unit. Use the checklist to help you.

FINAL DRAFT CHECKLIST

☐ Does your essay have an interesting introduction?

☐ Does your essay have multiple paragraphs?

☐ Does your essay include clear descriptive language including lots of adjectives?

☐ Does your essay contain vivid mental imagery, including sensory details and a simile, a metaphor, or an example of personification?

☐ Does your essay have a conclusion?

☐ Do you use verb forms correctly?

☐ Do you use new vocabulary from the unit?

ALTERNATIVE WRITING TOPIC

APPLY If scientists created a pill that would allow you to live twice as long while remaining free of infirmities, would you take it? Why or why not? Use the grammar and vocabulary from the unit.

CHECK WHAT YOU'VE LEARNED

Check (✔) the outcomes you've met and vocabulary you've learned. Put an X next to the skills and vocabulary you still need to practice.

Learning Outcomes

☐ Infer attitudes and feelings

☐ Take notes with signposts

☐ Use titles and headings to identify main ideas

☐ Contrast simple past, present perfect, and present perfect progressive

☐ Use figurative language

☐ Write a descriptive essay

Vocabulary

☐ awesome

☐ chilly

☐ disparate

☐ emphatic AWL

☐ fascinating (*adj.*)

☐ genuinely

☐ immeasurably

☐ impulsive

☐ inevitably AWL

☐ insufferable

☐ presumptuous AWL

☐ punctually

☐ radically AWL

☐ simultaneously

☐ tolerable

☐ ultimately AWL

☐ vigorous

☐ worrisome

⬥ Go to **MyEnglishLab** to watch a video about the long lives of the residents of Acciaroli, access the Unit Project, and take the Unit 5 Achievement Test.

LEARNING OUTCOMES

> Infer people's reactions
> Take compare and contrast notes with a T-chart
> Recognize persuasive language

> Use concessions
> Write introductions and thesis statements
> Write a persuasive essay

 Go to **MyEnglishLab** to check what you know.

Making a Difference

1 FOCUS ON THE TOPIC

1. Volunteering is a way of helping people in need without being paid. What can people learn from volunteering?

2. What are some different ways that people volunteer their time to help others? Why do they do this?

READING ONE | Justin Lebo

VOCABULARY

1 Two of the three words in each row have meanings similar to the boldfaced word. Cross out the word with a different meaning. If you need help, use a dictionary.

1. **passion**	enthusiasm	~~decision~~	interest
2. **proudly**	modestly	self-satisfyingly	contentedly
3. **challenge**	pride	test	demand
4. **satisfaction**	happiness	pleasure	amusement
5. **determined**	insistent	stubborn	uncertain
6. **proposal**	suggestion	order	recommendation
7. **donate**	contribute	give	sell
8. **admiring**	complimentary	approving	boring
9. **devote**	dedicate	appreciate	commit
10. **inspired**	saddened	encouraged	motivated
11. **manage**	handle	cope with	respond
12. **thrilled**	happy	scared	excited

2 Members of organizations (corporate, educational, religious, and governmental) and individuals volunteer for many different reasons: some for political or religious reasons; some for personal or social reasons. Others volunteer, or participate in what is called community service, because it's mandatory as part of a school's curriculum or as a requirement for graduation.

Read what five people say about volunteering. Complete each statement with the words in the boxes. Then write the reasons you think they volunteer. (Note: Not all words are used, and some people may have more than one reason.)

Reasons for and Types of Volunteering			
care of the elderly	mandatory	personal	religious
environmental	medical research	political	tutoring

1. Matt Olsen, age 65: raised $2,000 for AIDS research in the annual Boston-to-New York AIDS bicycle ride

admiring	challenge	donate	manage

"I'm trying to raise money for AIDS research in memory of my brother. I'm hoping to _____ more than $2,000 this year. Maybe this way what happened to him won't happen to others. The ride is certainly a physical _____ , especially since I hurt my leg last weekend. However, I still think I can _____ to finish the ride. In any case, I enjoy biking, and this way I can combine my favorite sport with a good cause."

Reasons: _personal and medical research_ _____

2. Steve Hooley, age 36: donates his time as a Boy Scout leader

inspired	manage	passion	thrilled

"I've always loved the outdoors and camping. In fact, preserving the environment is a _____ for me. Therefore, I'm _____ to be a Scout leader. By being a Scout leader, I can do something I like and share my love of nature with the next generation. If they are _____ to care about nature, maybe they'll take better care of the environment than our generation has."

Reasons: _____

3. Hannah Bullard, age 22: volunteers in a shelter for homeless women

inspired	passion	proudly	satisfaction

"I've always been taught that we should help those who are less fortunate than we are. Reverend Woodson spoke at church last Sunday about all the good work being done here. He spoke with such _____ that I knew I wanted to participate. It gives me a lot of _____ to work with these women. Some of them have been through so much: alcoholism, drug addiction, and in many cases, abuse. I am very _____ by how far some of them have come. Despite their many problems, many of these women have now taken back control of their lives."

Reasons: _____

4. Louisa Deering, age 17: spends three hours a week playing guitar for senior citizens in a nursing home

determined	devoting	proposal	satisfaction

"I started coming here last year because it was a school requirement. After I completed my requirement, I didn't want to stop. In order to continue volunteering, I made a _____ to the director of the program—I asked him if I could come back again this year after school and on weekends because I really have a good time with the people. I want to continue _____ time to them because I truly enjoy being with them and I think they like to listen to my music, too. In fact, this experience has inspired me to study music therapy in college."

Reasons: _____

5. Ted Sirota, age 23: spends five hours a week volunteering at a politician's office

admiring	determined	donate	inspire

"I feel that this person is the best candidate. I find her truly amazing. She's someone I can really look up to and want to be like. However, I'm not just one of her many _____ supporters. I also volunteer for her. By volunteering, I can do more than just vote. I am _____ to help her get elected. That way I can be more involved in the whole political process."

Reasons: _____

🔾 Go to the **Pearson Practice English App** or **MyEnglishLab** for more vocabulary practice.

PREVIEW

You are going to read an article about Justin Lebo, a boy who volunteers his time and energy to help others in a unique way. Read the first two paragraphs of *Justin Lebo.* Answer the questions.

1. What condition is the bicycle in?

2. Why do you think Justin would be interested in a bike in that condition?

3. What do you think Justin will do with the bicycle?

READ

Read the article about a charitable boy named Justin Lebo on the next page. Create a chart like the one below to take notes.

TAKE NOTES

Main Ideas	Details
Justin likes bikes.	• buying them • fixing them • racing them has a bike shop in his garage
He has too many bikes to use.	made 2 bikes for Kilbarchan Home wants to make 19 more so all kids have a bike

🔾 Go to **MyEnglishLab** to view example notes.

JUSTIN LEBO

BY PHILLIP HOOSE (from *It's Our World, Too*)

1 Something about the battered old bicycle at the garage sale[1] caught ten-year-old Justin Lebo's eye. What a wreck! It was like looking at a few big bones in the dust and trying to figure out what kind of dinosaur they had once belonged to.

2 It was a BMX bike with a twenty-inch frame. Its original color was buried beneath five or six coats of gunky paint. Everything—the grips, the pedals, the brakes, the seat, the spokes—was bent or broken, twisted and rusted. Justin stood back as if he were inspecting a painting for sale at an auction. Then he made his final judgment: perfect.

3 Justin talked the owner down to $6.50 and asked his mother, Diane, to help load the bike into the back of their car.

4 When he got it home, he wheeled the junker into the garage and showed it **proudly** to his father. "Will you help me fix it up?" he asked. Justin's hobby was bike racing, a **passion** the two of them shared. Their garage barely had room for the car anymore. It was more like a bike shop. Tires and frames hung from hooks on the ceiling, and bike wrenches dangled from the walls.

5 Now Justin and his father cleared out a work space in the garage and put the old junker up on a rack. They poured alcohol on the frame and rubbed until the old paint began to yield, layer by layer. They replaced the broken pedal, tightened down a new seat, and restored the grips. In about a week, it looked brand new.

6 Soon, he forgot about the bike. But the very next week, he bought another junker at a yard sale[2] and fixed it up, too. After a while, it bothered him that he wasn't really using either bike. Then he realized that what he loved about the old bikes wasn't riding them: It was the **challenge** of making something new and useful out of something old and broken.

7 Justin wondered what he should do with them. They were just taking up space in the garage. He remembered that when he was younger, he used to live near a large brick building called the Kilbarchan Home for Boys. It was a place for boys whose parents couldn't care for them for one reason or another.

8 He found "Kilbarchan" in the phone book and called the director, who said the boys would be **thrilled** to get two bicycles. The next day when Justin and his mother unloaded the bikes at the home, two boys raced out to greet them. They leapt aboard the bikes and started tooling around the semicircular driveway, doing wheelies and pirouettes[3], laughing and shouting.

9 The Lebos watched them for a while, then started to climb into their car to go home. The boys cried after them, "Wait a minute! You forgot your bikes!" Justin explained that the bikes were for them to keep. "They were so happy," Justin remembers. "It was like they couldn't believe it. It made me feel good just to see them happy."

10 On the way home, Justin was silent. His mother assumed he was lost in a feeling of **satisfaction**. But he was thinking about what would happen once those bikes got wheeled inside and everybody saw them. How could all those kids decide who got the bikes? Two bikes could cause more trouble than they would solve. Actually, they hadn't been that hard to build. It was fun. Maybe he could do more. . . .

11 "Mom," Justin said as they turned onto their street, "I've got an idea. I'm going to make a bike for every boy at Kilbarchan for Christmas." Diane Lebo looked at Justin out of the corner of her eye. She had rarely seen him so **determined**.

12 When they got home, Justin called Kilbarchan to find out how many boys lived there. There were twenty-one. It was already June. He had six months to make nineteen bikes. That was almost a bike a week. Justin called the home back to tell them of his plan. "I could tell they didn't think I could do it," Justin remembers. "I knew I could."

---

[1] **garage sale:** a sale of used furniture, clothes, toys, etc. that are no longer wanted, usually held in a home's garage
[2] **yard sale:** another phrase for garage sale
[3] **wheelies and pirouettes:** tricks done on a bicycle

continued on next page

13 Justin knew his best chance to build bikes was almost the way General Motors or Ford builds cars: in an assembly line. He figured it would take three or four junkers to produce enough parts to make one good bike. That meant sixty to eighty bikes. Where would he get them?

14 Garage sales seemed to be the only hope. It was June, and there would be garage sales all summer long. But even if he could find that many bikes, how could he ever pay for them? That was hundreds of dollars.

15 He went to his parents with a **proposal**. "When Justin was younger, say five or six," says his mother, "he used to give away some of his allowance[4] to help others in need. His father and I would **donate** a dollar for every dollar Justin donated. So, he asked us if it could be like the old days, if we'd match every dollar he put into buying old bikes. We said yes."

16 Justin and his mother spent most of June and July hunting for cheap bikes at garage sales and thrift shops[5]. They would haul the bikes home, and Justin would start stripping them down in the yard.

17 But by the beginning of August, he had **managed** to make only ten bikes. Summer vacation was almost over, and school and homework would soon cut into his time. Garage sales would dry up when it got colder, and Justin was out of money. Still he was determined to find a way.

18 At the end of August, Justin got a break. A neighbor wrote a letter to the local newspaper describing Justin's project, and an editor thought it would make a good story. In her **admiring** article about a boy who was **devoting** his summer to help kids he didn't even know, she said Justin needed bikes and money, and she printed his home phone number.

19 Overnight, everything changed. "There must have been a hundred calls," Justin says. "People would call me up and ask me to come over and pick up their old bike. Or I'd be working in the garage, and a station wagon would pull up. The driver would leave a couple of bikes by the curb. It just snowballed[6]."

20 The week before Christmas Justin delivered the last of the twenty-one bikes to Kilbarchan. Once again, the boys poured out of the home and leapt aboard the bikes, tearing around in the snow.

21 And once again, their joy **inspired** Justin. They reminded him how important bikes were to him. Wheels meant freedom. He thought about how much more the freedom to ride must mean to boys like these who had so little freedom in their lives. He decided to keep on building.

22 "First I made eleven bikes for the children in a foster home[7] my mother told me about. Then I made bikes for all the women in a women's shelter. Then I made ten little bikes and tricycles for children with AIDS. Then I made twenty-three bikes for the Paterson Housing Coalition."

23 In the four years since he started, Justin Lebo has made between 150 and 200 bikes and given them all away. He has been careful to leave time for his homework, his friends, his coin collection, his new interest in marine biology, and of course, his own bikes.

24 Reporters and interviewers have asked Justin Lebo the same question over and over: "Why do you do it?" The question seems to make him uncomfortable. It's as if they want him to say what a great person he is. Their stories always make him seem like a saint, which he knows he isn't. "Sure, it's nice of me to make the bikes," he says, "because I don't have to. But I want to. In part, I do it for myself. I don't think you can ever really do anything to help anybody else if it doesn't make you happy."

25 "Once I overheard a kid who got one of my bikes say, 'A bike is like a book; it opens up a whole new world.' That's how I feel, too. It made me happy to know that kid felt that way. That's why I do it."

---

[4] **allowance:** money you are given regularly or for a special reason
[5] **thrift shops:** stores that sell used goods, especially furniture, clothes, and toys, often in order to raise money for a charity
[6] **snowballed:** got bigger quickly or got harder to control
[7] **foster home:** a home where a child is taken care of for a period of time by someone who is not a parent or legal guardian

MAIN IDEAS

Read the statements and check the three that represent the main ideas of Reading One. Discuss the reasons for your choices with a partner.

☐ Justin paid $6.50 for the first bike he fixed up.

☐ Justin needed to find a way to get a lot of used bikes.

☐ Justin was able to fix up and donate hundreds of bikes because of the support of his parents and community.

☐ Justin's hobby was bike racing.

☐ Justin is a special boy because he likes to help others.

☐ After the newspaper article, people called Justin and offered him their old bikes.

DETAILS

1 The chart lists some benefits of doing community service. Complete the chart with examples of how Justin Lebo benefited from his experience.

THE BENEFITS OF COMMUNITY SERVICE	EXAMPLES OF JUSTIN LEBO
Encourages people to use their free time constructively	Justin spent his free time in the summer making bicycles for the children at the Kilbarchan Home for Boys.
Gives a sense of satisfaction; builds self-esteem	
Opens volunteers' eyes to the great variety of people in need by providing opportunities to meet new and different types of people	
One successful community service experience leads to performing other services.	
Volunteers learn they can help solve real social problems and needs.	
Helps people to find out who they are, what their interests are, and what they are good at	

2 Look at your notes and at your answers in Preview. How did they help you understand the article?

Inferring People's Reactions

Paying attention to how different people in a story react to an event, a situation or a person's decisions will help the reader to better understand a story.

Look at the example and read the explanation.

> He [Justin] went to his parents with a proposal. "When Justin was younger, say five or six," says his mother, "he used to give away some of his allowance to help others in need. His father and I would donate a dollar for every dollar Justin donated. So, he asked us if it could be like the old days, if we'd match every dollar he put into buying old bikes. We said yes."

How would you describe the reaction of Justin's parents to his proposal?

a. excited   b. skeptical[1]   c. supportive

The correct answer is *c*. Answer *a* is not correct because his parents are not expressing their happiness with the project at this moment. Answer *b* is not correct because his parents were not doubtful or questioning of his proposal. Answer *c* is correct because by saying "yes" to his proposal, his parents agreed to help Justin buy more old bikes. They supported him by deciding to give him money.

---

[1] **skeptical:** doubting or not believing something to be true.

1 **Work with a partner. Think about the people mentioned in Reading One. How do they react to Justin and his ideas? Read the questions and the paragraphs noted. Then choose the best answer.**

1. What was the Kilbarchan boys' first reaction when Justin started to leave without taking his bikes? *(paragraph 9)*

    a. confused   b. admiring   c. appreciative

2. How do you think Justin's mother felt about his idea to build one bike for every boy at Kilbarchan? *(paragraph 11)*

    a. excited   b. unsure   c. appreciative

3. How would you characterize the Kilbarchan director's reaction to Justin's proposal to build a bike for every boy at Kilbarchan? *(paragraph 12)*

    a. confused   b. helpful   c. skeptical

4. How did the people who called and left bikes react to the letter in the newspaper? *(paragraph 19)*

    a. stubbornly   b. enthusiastically   c. resentfully

5. How do you think the kid who Justin overheard felt about getting a bike? *(paragraph 25)*

    a. proud   b. surprised   c. appreciative

2 **Discuss your answers with a partner. Point out sentences, words, or phrases that helped you find the answers.**

Work in a small group. Choose one of the questions. Discuss your ideas. Then choose one person in your group to report the ideas to the class.

USE YOUR NOTES

Use your notes to support your answers with information from the reading.

1. Justin was able to combine something he loved to do with volunteer work. How did Justin show that it is important to have a passion for your volunteer work?

2. Who received more joy from Justin's work: Justin or the people who received the bikes? Explain.

3. No one forced Justin to do what he did. What makes Justin an exceptional young man? Explain.

↘ Go to **MyEnglishLab** to give your opinion about another question.

READING TWO | Some Take the Time Gladly Problems with Mandatory Volunteering

PREVIEW

Many high schools in the United States require students to devote a certain number of hours outside of the classroom to community service in order to graduate. Supporters of mandatory volunteering believe that the school's role should include both preparing children to be academically successful and helping them to be responsible citizens who are active participants in their communities.

However, not everybody believes that mandatory volunteering is a good idea. Those opposed to the requirement believe that the term "mandatory volunteering" is an oxymoron, a contradiction. They believe that volunteering should be something you do of your own free will. It is not something that is forced on you.

1 Look at the titles of the readings and the picture. Write two questions that you think will be answered in this reading.

_____

_____

2 Look at the boldfaced words in the readings. Which words do you know the meanings of?

1 Read the two opinions about mandatory volunteering. As you read, guess the meanings of the words that are new to you. Remember to take notes on main ideas and details.

HOME

CONTACT

SOME TAKE THE TIME GLADLY
By Mensah Dean (from the *Washington Times*)

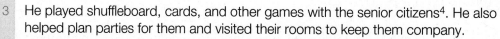
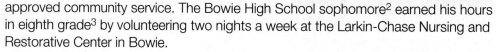

1   Mandatory volunteering made many students at Bowie High School in Maryland grumble with **indignation**.

2   Future seniors[1], however, probably won't be as resistant now that the program has been broken in. Some, like John Maloney, already have completed their required hours of approved community service. The Bowie High School sophomore[2] earned his hours in eighth grade[3] by volunteering two nights a week at the Larkin-Chase Nursing and Restorative Center in Bowie.

3   He played shuffleboard, cards, and other games with the senior citizens[4]. He also helped plan parties for them and visited their rooms to keep them company.

4   John, fifteen, is not finished volunteering. Once a week he videotapes animals at the Prince George County animal shelter in Forestville. His footage is shown on the Bowie public access television channel in hopes of finding homes for the animals.

5   "Volunteering is better than just sitting around," says John, "and I like animals; I don't want to see them put to sleep[5]."

6   He's not the only volunteer in his family. His sister, Melissa, an eighth grader, has completed her hours also volunteering at Larkin-Chase.

7   "It is a good idea to have kids go out into the community, but it's frustrating to have to write essays about the work," she said. "It makes you feel like you're doing it for the requirement and not for yourself."

8   The high school's service learning office, run by Beth Ansley, provides information on organizations seeking volunteers so that students will have an easier time **fulfilling** their hours.

9   "It's ridiculous that people are opposing the requirements," said Amy Rouse, who this summer has worked at the Ronald McDonald House[6] and has helped to rebuild a church in Clinton.

10 "So many people won't do the service unless it's mandatory," Rouse said, "but once they start doing it, they'll really like it and hopefully it will become a part of their lives—like it has become a part of mine."

[1] **seniors:** students in the last year of high school, approximately 17–18 years old
[2] **sophomore:** a student in the second year of high school, approximately 15–16 years old
[3] **eighth grade:** The United States public school system begins with kindergarten and continues with grades 1–12. A student in eighth grade is approximately 13–14 years old.
[4] **senior citizens:** people over the age of 65
[5] **put to sleep:** to give a very sick animal drugs so that it dies without pain
[6] **Ronald McDonald House:** a residence, usually near a hospital, which provides a home and other support services for the families of children who require a lot of time in the hospital because of serious illness

continued on next page

PROBLEMS WITH MANDATORY VOLUNTEERING

By Jeonghoon Lee

1   I think the school board's plan to implement a mandatory volunteering program is a terrible idea.

2   First of all, let me say that I am already a volunteer and proud of it. In fact, I do volunteer work at my local library, as well as tutor elementary school kids at my church's after-school program. I believe that, at least in part, the reason that I enjoy volunteering and am effective at it is that I am not being forced to do it. In addition, I can choose to volunteer with people and organizations that interest me; that is not always the case with mandatory volunteering.

3   I am a new transfer student in this district and am very happy that we currently do not have a mandatory volunteering program here; however, my last school did, and for many students it was not a good experience. Imagine how new students must feel when they are told that to graduate, they will have to volunteer hundreds of hours! They are already overwhelmed by schoolwork and so often end up just completing their hours, but not putting in any effort. As a result, the quality of their volunteer work is much worse than the work done by volunteers who actually choose to volunteer. In addition, students who are told they must volunteer may become **resentful** and do not want to volunteer in the future. Volunteering becomes a negative experience. On the other hand, many students do already volunteer, and those who choose to do so make a real difference.

4   Another problem is that many students have busy after-school schedules: they have family, work, and athletic responsibilities. For example, many students need to be able to work after school in order to help out their families or to save money for college. Some have to take care of younger siblings or grandparents, and still others use this time to participate in athletics. School starts and ends at set times, and any school-related activity after those times is extracurricular, such as the football team or science club. To participate in these activities is a personal choice, just as volunteering should be. Nothing should be required of a student after school except homework.

5   Finally, the term 'mandatory volunteering' is an **oxymoron**. Volunteering is something you do of your own free will. If it is mandatory, it is not volunteering. For all these reasons, I am totally **opposed** to our school implementing a mandatory volunteering program and suggest that volunteering be left as a personal choice. It should not be made mandatory.

2   Compare your notes on main ideas and details with a partner's. How can you improve your notes next time?

> Go to the **Pearson Practice English App** or **MyEnglishLab** for more vocabulary practice.

Taking Compare and Contrast Notes with a T-chart

When comparing and contrasting two readings with opposing viewpoints, use a T-chart to clarify the writers' ideas. A T-chart will help you compare the reasons for each viewpoint and decide which viewpoint you agree with.

Reading Two, *Some Take the Time Gladly* and *Problems with Mandatory Volunteering,* contains two opposing opinion editorials. In *Problems with Mandatory Volunteering,* one of the first reasons the writer gives is that volunteering is a personal choice and should not be made mandatory. Complete the T-chart with reasons for and against mandatory volunteering from Reading Two.

For Mandatory Volunteering	Against Mandatory Volunteering
1.	1. Volunteering is a personal choice.
2.	2.
3.	3.
	4.
	5.
	6.

2 Look at Reading Two again. Mark the information that you think is most important.

Go to **MyEnglishLab** for more note-taking practice.

COMPREHENSION

1 **Answer the questions. Use your notes from Reading Two to help you. Discuss your answers with a partner.**

1. Amy Rouse supports mandatory volunteering by saying, "Once they start doing it, they'll really like it and hopefully it will become a part of their lives—like it has become a part of mine."

   How would a student opposed to mandatory volunteering respond to this?

2. The writer who opposes mandatory volunteering worries that students often just complete their hours, but don't put in any effort. What would be the reaction of someone in favor of mandatory volunteering?

3. John Maloney states, "Volunteering is better than just sitting around." How would someone opposed to mandatory volunteering respond?

2 **Review the boldfaced words from the reading with a partner. Use a dictionary or ask your teacher for any meanings you still do not know.**

READING SKILL

1 **Look at the two opinions in Reading Two again. What words do the writers use to show that the opposing point of view is unreasonable or doesn't make sense? Why do they choose to use these words?**

Recognizing Persuasive Language

When trying to convince a reader to agree with their ideas, writers use persuasive language. These words or phrases add structure and depth to writers' ideas. Writers use persuasive language to support their own points of view and also to oppose ideas they are trying to refute or disprove. In many cases, persuasive language evokes strong emotions.

Look at this quote from paragraph 9 of *Some Take the Time Gladly*. What words does the writer use to persuade the reader that his point of view is the only sensible way to think?

> "It's ridiculous that people are opposing the requirements," said Amy Rouse, who this summer has worked at the Ronald McDonald House and has helped to rebuild a church in Clinton.

He uses a quotation that connects the words *ridiculous* and *opposing* to support his point of view and dismiss those who don't agree with him. The writer could have stated the same idea without evoking such strong emotions. For example, instead of using that quotation, he could have written, "It *doesn't make sense* that people *don't like* the requirements," but that would not be as persuasive.

The word *ridiculous* suggests that it is impossible to take people's reactions seriously; they make no sense. With *opposing,* the writer shows that it is not just that people don't like the idea of mandatory volunteering but that they are actively trying to stop it. This choice of words is strong and creates a clear difference in attitudes toward mandatory volunteering.

2 Look at Reading Two again and find the persuasive words that describe the opposing point of view in the paragraphs noted.

SOME TAKE THE TIME GLADLY

Paragraph and number of words or phrases	Persuasive words that evoke negative emotions
Paragraph 1 (2)	
Paragraph 2 (1)	
Paragraph 7 (1)	
Paragraph 9 (2)	*ridiculous* *opposing*

PROBLEMS WITH MANDATORY VOLUNTEERING

Paragraph and number of words or phrases	Persuasive words that evoke negative emotions
Paragraph 1 (1)	
Paragraph 3 (5)	
Paragraph 5 (2)	

3 With a partner, look at the words and phrases you selected and discuss the questions.

1. How do these words influence your thinking about the topic of mandatory volunteering?

2. Do these words make you agree more or less with the writers' opinions?

3. Which two words from each article were most effective in making you agree with the writers?

⬤ Go to **MyEnglishLab** for more skill practice.

ORGANIZE

The readings in this unit address four issues relating to volunteering.

- Personal enrichment
- Personal choice
- Time commitment
- Dedication to work

USE YOUR NOTES

Review your notes from Reading One and Two. Use the information in your notes to complete the chart.

Go back to the paragraphs noted and find quotes or statements that relate—either positively or negatively—to one or more of the issues. Underline the passages in the text. Then write the issue(s) next to the correct paragraph number in the chart. You may use some issues more than once.

JUSTIN LEBO (R1)	
Paragraph	**Issue**
22	Dedication to work
23	
24	

SOME TAKE THE TIME GLADLY (R2)	
Paragraph	**Issue**
2	
5	

PROBLEMS WITH MANDATORY VOLUNTEERING (R2)	
Paragraph	**Issue**
2	
3	
4	

SYNTHESIZE

You have read two opposing views of mandatory volunteering in Reading Two. Write a letter to the author of the editorial in Reading Two with whose opinion you disagree. Be sure to clearly state your opinion about mandatory volunteering. Use Justin's experience as a volunteer and / or examples from Reading Two to **disagree** with the position stated in the editorial and explain why. Use the quotes or statements that you underlined in Organize.

🔾 Go to **MyEnglishLab** to check what you learned.

REVIEW

1 Look at the word forms chart. The vocabulary from the unit is boldfaced.

NOUN	VERB	ADJECTIVE	ADVERB
admiration	admire	**admiring**	admiringly
challenge	challenge	challenging	X
determination	determine	**determined**	X
devotion	**devote**	devoted	devotedly
donation	**donate**	donated	X
fulfillment	fulfill	fulfilled **fulfilling**	X
indignation	X	indignant	indignantly
inspiration	**inspire**	inspired inspiring inspirational	inspirationally inspiringly
management	**manage**	manageable	manageably
opposition	**oppose**	opposite opposing	X
oxymoron	X	oxymoronic	X
passion	X	passionate	passionately
pride	X	proud	**proudly**
proposal	propose	proposed	X
resentment	resent	**resentful**	resentfully
ridicule	ridicule	**ridiculous**	ridiculously
satisfaction	satisfy	satisfied satisfying satisfactory	satisfactorily
thrill	thrill	**thrilled** thrilling	thrillingly

2 **Complete the sentences using the correct form of the word in parentheses. Pay attention to verb tense and subject verb agreement. Use the chart in Review to help you.**

1. Justin had to rely on _____ (*donate*) from people in order to complete the bicycles for the children at Kilbarchan.

2. Justin felt _____ (*inspire*) when he saw how the boys enjoyed the first two bicycles he had made.

3. People hope that after experiencing mandatory volunteering, students will become _____ (*passion*) about volunteering in general.

4. Justin met the _____ (*challenge*) of making a bike for each boy at Kilbarchan.

5. When Justin _____ (*proposal*) that his parents give a dollar for every dollar he donated, they agreed.

6. Critics worry that students who are forced to volunteer and have a bad experience may _____ (*resent*) their experience and never volunteer again.

7. Although many people support mandatory volunteering, there is still a lot of _____ (*oppose*) to it.

8. Justin feels a lot of _____ (*proudly*) in the fact that he was able to donate so many bikes.

9. Justin's neighbor _____ (*admiring*) his accomplishments.

10. In many schools, students are not able to graduate without having _____ (*fulfilling*) the volunteering requirement.

11. Mandatory volunteering is an emotionally charged issue. Many critics are _____ (*indignation*) that volunteering is not left up to the individual.

EXPAND

A **phrasal verb** consists of a verb and a particle (an adverb or preposition). The combination often has a meaning that is different from the meaning of the separate parts. Phrasal verbs are often used in everyday communication.

Phrasal verbs (also called two-part or two-word verbs) combine a verb with a **particle**.

Verb	+	Particle	=	Meaning
go	+	back	=	return
let	+	down	=	disappoint

Some phrasal verbs (also called three-part or three-word verbs) combine with a **preposition**.

Phrasal Verb	+	Preposition	=	Meaning
come up	+	with	=	imagine or invent
think back	+	on	=	remember

Some phrasal verbs are **transitive**. They take a direct object. Many (two-word) transitive phrasal verbs are **separable**. This means the verb and the particle can be separated by the direct object.

She didn't want to **let down** the other volunteers.
   [verb][particle]   [object]

She didn't want to **let** the other volunteers **down**.
   [verb]   [object]   [particle]

Some phrasal verbs are **intransitive**. They do not take a direct object. Intransitive phrasal verbs are always **inseparable**. This means that the verb and particle are never separated.

I liked volunteering at the animal shelter. I want to **go back** there next week.
               [verb][particle]

Work in a small group. Read the sentences. Choose the correct definition for each underlined phrasal verb.

1. Supporters of mandatory volunteering say doing community service is time better spent than <u>sitting around</u> watching television or playing computer games.

   a. doing nothing special or useful

   b. sitting with friends in a circle

   c. not taking part in something

2. Justin Lebo has <u>fixed up</u> between 150 and 200 bikes and has given them all away.

   a. arranged a date for someone

   b. repaired or restored something to working order

   c. bought at a low price

3. Supporters of mandatory volunteering hope that students will <u>keep on</u> volunteering after they have fulfilled their requirement.

   a. hold

   b. consider

   c. continue

4. At first, Justin could not <u>figure out</u> what to do with his two bikes.

   a. satisfy

   b. understand

   c. take part in

5. Justin had so many bikes that he had to <u>clear out</u> his basement and start building them there.

   a. make room on a table

   b. paint an area or place

   c. empty an area or place

6. When the students <u>found out</u> the new graduation requirements, they were indignant and completely opposed to them.

    a. created something

    b. discovered something that had been lost

    c. learned new information about something

7. After the newspaper article was published, many people <u>called</u> Justin <u>up</u> and offered him their old bikes.

    a. discussed a situation

    b. spoke disrespectfully to someone

    c. contacted by phone

8. Some worry that if students do not do community service, they will <u>end up</u> being uncaring people.

    a. complete a project

    b. be in a situation without planning it

    c. stop something

9. The community center's staff will <u>pick up</u> clothing donations from anywhere in town.

    a. start to increase

    b. clean something

    c. collect something

10. Justin was afraid that the garage sales would <u>dry up</u> by the end of the summer.

    a. be dull and uninteresting

    b. slowly come to an end

    c. become useless

CREATE

APPLY Imagine you are a reporter interviewing the people below. How would they respond to the questions? Write answers using the words given. Change the word form if necessary.

1. | devote | determined | keep on | proudly |
   |---|---|---|---|

   REPORTER: Your neighbor, Justin, is quite remarkable, isn't he?

   JUSTIN LEBO'S NEIGHBOR: _Yes, he is. After Justin saw the boys having so much fun on their_ _bicycles, he became devoted to the project. He was determined to get every boy on a_ _bicycle, so he kept on working hard. I'm very proud of him._

2. | challenge | inspired | passion | sit around |
   |---|---|---|---|

   REPORTER: After fixing the first bike, did you ever think Justin would end up repairing and donating over 150 more?

   JUSTIN LEBO'S FRIEND: _____

   _____

   _____

   _____

3. | donate | end up | manage | proposal |
   |---|---|---|---|

   REPORTER: What do you think the director thought when Justin first told him he was planning on building a bicycle for every boy at Kilbarchan?

   BOY AT THE KILBARCHAN SCHOOL: _____

   _____

   _____

   _____

4. | donate | figure out | fulfilling | proudly |
   |---|---|---|---|

   REPORTER: Why do you support mandatory volunteering?

   STUDENT SUPPORTING _____

   _____

   _____

   _____

| 5. | find out | indignant | manage | oxymoron |

Reporter: Why are you opposed to mandatory volunteering?

Student Opposing Mandatory Volunteering: _____

_____

_____

_____

↖ Go to the **Pearson Practice English App** or **MyEnglishLab** for more vocabulary practice.

GRAMMAR FOR WRITING

1 Read the sentences and answer the questions.

a. <u>**Even though** Justin was not required by his school to volunteer</u>, he chose to work on bikes and donate them.

b. <u>**Despite the fact that** many students initially don't want to volunteer</u>, they learn to love it and continue after the school requirements are fulfilled.

c. It is a good idea to get students to go out into the community **although** <u>it can be frustrating to have to write about it.</u>

1. Each sentence is composed of two clauses.[1] What are the clauses in each sentence?

2. Do the clauses that begin with the concessions *although*, *even though*, and *despite the fact that* introduce a positive or negative opinion of mandatory volunteering?

3. Do the three sentences have the same punctuation? If not, why not?

4. Which clauses express the writer's main idea: the clauses with the concessions *although*, *even though*, and *despite the fact that* . . . or the other clauses?

---

[1] **clause:** a group of words containing a subject and verb that forms part of a sentence. Clauses can be dependent or independent.

Concessions

1. Use **concessions** in a situation where you are expressing an opinion that you need to support, but at the same time, need to recognize and describe the opposing opinion. Presenting similarities and differences in contrasting points of view makes your argument stronger.

2. Use these words to concede or acknowledge similarities or differences between two contrasting ideas.

although	even though	despite the fact that
though	in spite of the fact that	

Note that these words do not introduce a complete thought; they introduce **dependent clauses.** A dependent clause cannot stand alone as a sentence. It must be joined to an independent (main) clause.

continued on next page

3. The **main clause** usually describes the point that is more important.

   a. Even though Justin was not required by his school to volunteer, **he chose to work on bikes and donate them**.

      <u>Writer's opinion</u>: Justin's school had no requirement for volunteering, but he still wanted to use his time to help others.

      <u>Acknowledging the opposing opinion</u>: You would expect Justin not to volunteer unless he was forced to.

   b. **It is a good idea to get students to go out into the community** although it can be frustrating to have to write about it.

      <u>Writer's opinion</u>: There may be problems with assignments relating to mandatory volunteering, but students should still be required to go out into the community.

      <u>Acknowledging the opposite view</u>: Being forced to write about your volunteering takes away from any benefit you may receive from it.

4. When a sentence begins with a dependent clause, use a comma to separate it from the main clause.

   Even though garage sales had dried up by the end of August, Justin got enough old bikes as the result of a letter to the newspaper.

5. When a sentence begins with an independent clause, do not use a comma.

   Justin got enough old bikes as the result of a letter to the newspaper **even though garage sales had dried up by the end of August**.

2 **Combine each pair of sentences using the words in parentheses. Does your new sentence support mandatory volunteering or oppose mandatory volunteering?**

1. Supporters of mandatory volunteering say that it is a good way for students to get valuable work experience. Critics say students should be paid if they are doing work. (even though)

   Supporters of mandatory volunteering say it is a good way for students to get valuable

   experience even though they are not paid.

   (supports mandatory volunteering)/ opposes mandatory volunteering

2. Critics of mandatory volunteering maintain that a school should not require a student to do anything after school except homework. Supporters of mandatory volunteering say that volunteering is better than just sitting around watching TV or playing video games. (though)

   _____

   _____

   supports mandatory volunteering / opposes mandatory volunteering

3. Opponents argue that volunteering is a personal choice, and so it shouldn't be mandatory. Supporters note that schools have many required classes that may not be a student's personal choice. (although)

   _____

   _____

   supports mandatory volunteering / opposes mandatory volunteering

4. Critics worry that a bad volunteering experience will stop people from volunteering again in the future. Supporters maintain that most student volunteers have successful experiences, and many continue to volunteer later in life. (in spite of the fact that)

_____

_____

supports mandatory volunteering / opposes mandatory volunteering

5. Supporters believe that mandatory volunteering can benefit the community. Critics feel that mandatory volunteers may do a bad job and, therefore, cause more harm than good. (despite the fact that)

_____

_____

supports mandatory volunteering / opposes mandatory volunteering

3 **APPLY** Write sentences expressing your opinion about each educational issue related to volunteering. Use the concession words in the box. Write *S* on the line if your sentence supports mandatory volunteering. Write *O* if it opposes it.

although	despite the fact that	even though	in spite of the fact that	though

1. busy after-school schedules ___S___

   Although many students do have busy after-school schedules, with planning, most should be able to find some time to volunteer either after school or during free class periods.

2. personal choice _____

   _____

   _____

   _____

3. good to get students out into the community _____

   _____

   _____

   _____

4. volunteers may do a bad job _____

   _____

   _____

   _____

5. builds self-esteem _____

   _____

   _____

   _____

Go to the **Pearson Practice English App** or **MyEnglishLab** for more grammar practice.
Check what you learned in **MyEnglishLab.**

In this unit, you read about the pros and cons of mandatory volunteering, also called community service. What is your opinion about schools that require community service as a graduation requirement?

You are going to *write a persuasive essay explaining your opinion about mandatory volunteering programs*.

For an alternative writing topic, see page 175.

PREPARE TO WRITE: Using a T-Chart

A **T-chart** is a prewriting tool that helps you examine two aspects of a topic, such as the pros and cons associated with it. When you want to persuade someone to agree with your point of view, you need to have strong reasons to support your opinion (pros). You also need to acknowledge and address possible arguments against your opinion (cons). The arguments against your opinion are called counterarguments.

1   **Complete a T-chart like the one below with reasons to support a mandatory community service program (pros) and reasons against it (cons). Share your ideas with the class.**

Pros	Cons

2   **Use your T-chart to decide if these programs should be implemented or not. Write a thesis statement stating your opinion. The thesis statement is a sentence that includes the topic of your essay (mandatory volunteering) and the position you are taking or the point you are making (for or against).**

WRITE

Writing a Persuasive Essay

In a **persuasive essay,** your goal is to convince the reader to agree with your position. Here are some important points:

1. **State your position in the thesis statement.** The reader must know how you feel at the start of the essay. All of your points will support the position of your thesis statement.

2. **Present strong arguments to support your position.**

3. **Present strong support for your arguments.** Provide detailed examples, anecdotes, quotes, and statistics.

4. **Acknowledge the counterarguments presented by the opposing side.** Then refute the counterarguments by showing why they are weak. This will make your argument stronger.

1 Read the persuasive essay and answer the questions with a partner.

Cutting Our Sports Teams Is Not a Healthy Decision

Obesity rates are escalating! Students are more stressed than ever before! These are just a couple of recent news headlines. At the same time, ironically, our school administration has recently proposed eliminating all sports teams, citing a decrease in team participation, low attendance, and the overall high cost of maintaining these teams. While cutting team sports from the budget would save money, the immediate and long-term negative results would not be worth the money saved.

First, though it is true that many teams have not had high numbers of participants, this is not a reason to cut all teams. A few teams still do have high participation rates and very dedicated players. One solution is to keep one or two high participation sports per season, for example, fall football, winter basketball and swimming, and spring track and baseball.

Second, the school is concerned about poor audience attendance at the games and uses this argument to support the idea that there is a decreasing interest in our teams. Although there may be lower audience numbers than in the past, the students who do go are loyal fans. Moreover, this devoted fan base has helped build a community that promotes school spirit across the campus. This school spirit affects all students whether or not they attend each game. For example, after last year's baseball finals, more baseball hats were sold in the campus store than ever before even though most of the students wearing the hats had not attended one game! Adam Deering, a student, stated, "Even though I don't go to all of the games, I am still supportive of my school and proud of it. School can be really stressful, and the teams help reduce that stress and give students something else to focus on and bring them together besides academics."

Finally, the administration states that the cost of keeping team sports is just too high. Though the cost of sports teams may be high, the price paid for cutting the teams in the long term is even higher. Sports teams are a daily reminder of the importance of maintaining a balanced, healthy lifestyle. School sports help promote life-long healthy habits. With this in mind, shouldn't the school be putting more money into sports rather than taking it away?

1. What is the student's main position in regards to cutting school sports?

_____

2. What are the three main arguments the school uses to support cutting school sports? Complete the left side of the chart.

3. What are the counterarguments the student presents? Complete the right side of the chart.

ARGUMENTS TO CUT SCHOOL SPORTS	COUNTERARGUMENTS

4. Do you think the counterarguments are convincing? Why or why not?

_____

_____

5. What examples are used to strengthen the student's argument? Underline them.

2 Start planning your essay by looking at your list of pros and cons in Prepare to Write. Choose three of the strongest arguments you will use to support your position and write them in sections 2–4 below. Add details on the lettered lines to support your arguments. You will add the introduction and conclusion paragraphs later.

1. Introduction (including Thesis Statement)

2.

a. _____

_____

b. _____

_____

c. _____

_____

3.

a. _____

_____

b. _____

_____

c. _____

_____

4.

a. _____

_____

b. _____

_____

c. _____

_____

5. Conclusion

3 Look at the arguments in support of your position in Exercise 2. Write them in the left column below. What are the possible counterarguments? Write them in the middle column. Why are those counterarguments weak? Write the reasons in the right column. You will acknowledge the counterarguments in your essay using a concession clause and then refute or disprove them.

ARGUMENTS FOR / AGAINST COMMUNITY SERVICE PROGRAMS	COUNTERARGUMENTS	REFUTATION (REASONS WHY THE COUNTERARGUMENT IS WEAK)

4 Look at the information in Prepare to Write on page 168 and Exercise 2 to plan your essay. Now write the first draft of your persuasive essay.

- Include an introductory and a concluding paragraph.

- In the body, be sure to acknowledge the counterarguments by using a concession clause.

REVISE: Writing Introductions and Thesis Statements

1 Choose the sentence that better states the main idea and focus of an opinion essay about mandatory volunteering. Explain your choice.

a. Mandatory volunteering is a terrible idea, and in this essay I will explain the reasons why I think it is a bad idea.

b. Mandatory volunteering is a terrible idea for several reasons, including a fake external motivation to do good, an unreasonable time commitment, and competition with other after-school commitments.

Introductions and Thesis Statements

The **introduction** to an essay has several functions. First, it presents the thesis statement. The thesis statement is a sentence that states the main idea and focus of the essay. The introduction also provides necessary background information to help the reader's understanding.

The Thesis Statement

The thesis statement is a sentence that communicates the main idea or the claim of the essay. It is more than just the topic, as it includes the writer's opinion, point of view, or judgment on the topic. It guides the writing and provides a focus for the writer. Look at the examples of weak and strong thesis statements.

Mandatory volunteering is a requirement of graduation in many high schools.	This is not a strong thesis statement for a persuasive essay. It states a fact but has no point of view or opinion.
Mandatory volunteering is a terrible idea, and in this essay I will explain the reasons why I think it is a bad idea.	This is not a strong thesis statement. It gives the writer's opinion but there is no focus. Why is it a bad idea?
Mandatory volunteering is a terrible idea for several reasons, including a fake external motivation to do good, an unreasonable time commitment, and competition with other after-school commitments.	This is a strong thesis statement. It explains why the writer believes mandatory volunteering is wrong. It also presents how the claims will be presented in the body paragraphs. 1. External motivation is fake. 2. Expecting students to dedicate hours of time after school is unrealistic. 3. Students have equally important after-school commitments.

Engaging the Reader's Interest

One of the most important functions of a well-written introduction is to engage the reader's interest and make the reader want to continue reading.

Here are three common techniques (called *hooks*) used in introductions:

1. State why the topic is important.

2. Ask a provocative question.

3. Tell a relevant story or anecdote.

2 Evaluate the thesis statements. Put a check next to the strong thesis statements.

_____ 1. I volunteered at the hospital to fulfill my community service hours in high school.

_____ 2. From doing community service at the hospital, I learned the values of commitment, cooperation, and caring.

_____ 3. In this essay, I will discuss the positive experiences I had doing my community service at the hospital.

_____ 4. Without my community service experience, I would be a different person.

_____ 5. It is important to have community service experiences as it enhances our relationships with friends, family members, and community members.

3 Read the three introductions. Underline the thesis statements. Then label each introduction with the number of the technique from the presentation box used.

Introduction 1   Technique: _____

Society today is obsessed with commercialism. People think only about making money and buying more and more possessions. Many college students choose their majors by deciding which careers will pay the most money. Young people today are not learning enough about the nonfinancial rewards in life. They are not learning about the joy and fulfillment of helping others. This is a very serious problem with education today. It is important to support the proposal for a mandatory community service program so that young people will learn the value of giving to others.

Introduction 2   Technique: _____

When I was in high school, I was required to take part in a community service project. At first, I really didn't want to do it. I thought it would be boring and a waste of time. The school let us choose our project, and I decided to work at an animal shelter. I like animals and I thought the work wouldn't be too difficult. I worked all semester helping the veterinarian take care of sick and abandoned animals. I was surprised to find that by the end of the semester, I really liked my community service job. In fact, it was my favorite part of the week, and I signed up to work another semester. So, I am a perfect illustration of the benefits of mandatory community service programs in school. This is why I support a program of mandatory community service in our university.

Introduction 3   Technique: _____

We all want to live in a better world, don't we? Poor children do not get enough to eat. The school system is not educating our kids. The environment is getting more and more polluted. What would happen if we all did something to solve the problems around us? Well, we can do something, and we should. A mandatory community service program in our school will give students a valuable experience and also help solve important problems in our community.

4 Practice revising your introduction. Choose two techniques and revise your introduction using them. Be sure to include your thesis statement. Identify the technique used.

Technique: _____

_____

_____

_____

_____

Technique: _____

_____

_____

_____

_____

5 Now go back to the first draft of your essay.

- Make sure your thesis statement communicates the main idea or the claim of the essay.

- Choose one of your introductions and use it in your essay.

- Try to use the grammar and some of the vocabulary from the unit.

⬆ Go to **MyEnglishLab** for more skill practice.

EDIT: Writing the Final Draft

APPLY Write the final draft of your essay and submit it to your teacher. Carefully edit it for grammatical and mechanical errors, such as spelling, capitalization, and punctuation. Consider how to apply the vocabulary, grammar, and writing skills from the unit. Use the checklist to help you.

FINAL DRAFT CHECKLIST

☐ Does your essay have an introduction, three body paragraphs, and a conclusion?

☐ Does the introduction include a thesis statement? Does it engage the interest of the reader?

☐ Does each body paragraph have a topic sentence? Do all the topic sentences support the thesis statement?

☐ Do the body paragraphs present your arguments for or against mandatory volunteering? Do you acknowledge and then refute possible counterarguments?

☐ Did you use concessions to introduce the counterargument?

☐ Does the conclusion restate the thesis and offer final thoughts?

☐ Do you use the vocabulary from the unit?

ALTERNATIVE WRITING TOPIC

APPLY Imagine you are responsible for setting up a community service program in your city. What kind of program would you start? Who would it serve? Would there be volunteers? Who would they be? What would you hope to accomplish? Be specific. Use the grammar and vocabulary from the unit.

CHECK WHAT YOU'VE LEARNED

Check (✔) the outcomes you've met and vocabulary you've learned. Put an X next to the skills and vocabulary you still need to practice.

Learning Outcomes

☐ **Infer people's reactions**

☐ **Take compare and contrast notes with a T-chart**

☐ **Recognize persuasive language**

☐ **Use concessions**

☐ **Write introductions and thesis statements**

☐ **Write a persuasive essay**

Vocabulary

☐ **admiring (*adj.*)**

☐ **challenge (*n.*)** AWL

☐ **determined**

☐ **devote** AWL

☐ **donate**

☐ **fulfill**

☐ **indignation**

☐ **inspire**

☐ **manage**

☐ **oppose**

☐ **oxymoron**

☐ **passion**

☐ **proposal**

☐ **proudly**

☐ **resentful**

☐ **satisfaction**

☐ **thrilled**

▶ Go to **MyEnglishLab** to watch a video about philanthropy, access the Unit Project, and take the Unit 6 Achievement Test.

LEARNING OUTCOMES

> Infer the author's point of view and possible bias
> Take notes on pros and cons
> Create headings based on main ideas

> Use transitions and subordinators
> Write conclusions
> Write a problem-solution essay

 Go to **MyEnglishLab** to check what you know.

An Ocean
of Problems

1 FOCUS ON THE TOPIC

1. What do you see in the photo? Where do you think this is?
2. What do you think the problem is, and how did it happen?
3. Do you think the problem has gotten worse? If so, why?

READING ONE | Sea Unworthy: A Personal Journey Into the Pacific Garbage Patch

1 Look at the diagram and read the summary about the Great Pacific Garbage Patch. Pay attention to the boldfaced words.

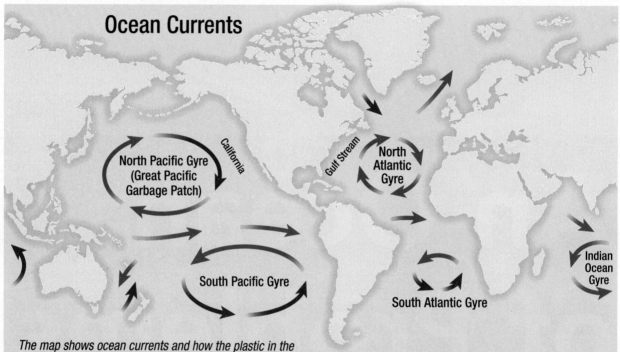

Ocean Currents

The map shows ocean currents and how the plastic in the ocean is contained in the gyres or vortexes. It also shows where the Great Pacific Garbage Patch is located.

Between California and Hawaii, in the middle of the Pacific Ocean, is an area called the Great Pacific Garbage Patch. It has been **portrayed** as an island or a mass so large and deep that one could walk on it. It isn't really a patch or an island at all; rather it is a **robust**, moving area of the ocean filled with **debris**, such as fishing nets, electronics, toys, bottles, and millions of pieces of plastic. The plastic and debris **accumulate** in the gyres or vortexes that are formed by ocean currents. The Great Pacific Garbage Patch is about four times the size of California and it is growing daily. It is hard to **quantify** the actual amount of plastic in the patch. However, some researchers **estimate** that it contains 87,000 tons of plastic.

And the plastic does not go away. Instead, the plastic simply breaks down into smaller and smaller pieces called microplastics. Small fish **consume** the microplastics, and then larger fish eat the small fish, which results in the microplastic working its way into the food chain. The microplastics are so **pervasive** that they have now been **detected** in many land and ocean animals, and even in humans. Microplastics are also very **toxic**; scientists **hypothesize** that they are changing animal behaviors, as well as their physical characteristics. Cleaning up this mess **entails** a great amount of research and work, but a number of marine biologists and other scientists are dedicated to just that mission. Perhaps this clean-up will come down to us, as well. **Bans** on plastics such as shopping bags and straws are already happening around the world. Whatever the solutions may be, it is clear that cleaning our oceans is imperative.

2 Match each word with its definition.

_____ 1. portrayed

_____ 2. robust

_____ 3. debris

_____ 4. accumulate

_____ 5. quantify

_____ 6. estimate

_____ 7. consume

_____ 8. pervasive

_____ 9. detected

_____ 10. toxic

_____ 11. hypothesize

_____ 12. entail

_____ 13. ban

a. to gradually increase in size

b. poisonous or very dangerous

c. to make an assumption or explanation based on limited research

d. something that is prohibited, especially by law

e. something that is large and powerful

f. involve or demand

g. found or discovered

h. calculate a rough (not exact) number or value

i. litter or trash

j. to express something by measuring or counting

k. to eat or ingest

l. found in every part of something

m. described or shown as something

⬆ Go to the **Pearson Practice English App** or **MyEnglishLab** for more vocabulary practice.

PREVIEW

You are going to read a scientific article about the Great Pacific Garbage Patch. Read the title, headings, and first two paragraphs of the article. Write three questions that you think will be answered in the reading.

1. _____ ?

2. _____ ?

3. _____ ?

Read the article about the Great Pacific Garbage Patch. Create a chart like the one below to take notes.

TAKE NOTES

Main Ideas	Details
the GPCP – area of the ocean filled with toxic plastic	– between CA and HI – plastics all sizes – microplastics=tiny pieces of plastic – mp gets into food chain by big fish → eat small fish

Go to **MyEnglishLab** to view example notes.

Sea Unworthy:
A Personal Journey Into the Pacific Garbage Patch

Erica Cirino

The Patch Close Up

1 It's about four o'clock in the afternoon on a clear day last November onboard the S/Y *Christianshavn*, a 54-foot Danish steel sailboat, which is bound for Honolulu from Los Angeles, across the most famous plastic-clogged place on Earth: the Great Pacific Garbage Patch.

2 As on most days during the 23-day journey, I spend my free time in the cockpit on the lookout for trash. Every once in a while, I see disturbingly familiar plastic items float by—a pink dustpan, a punctured green condiment bottle, a barnacle-covered Tupperware lid, a white Styrofoam packing wedge. Then I notice a cloudy white blob floating on the water's surface—hundreds of white plastic pieces, some tiny confetti-like bits and some **robust**, rugged chunks that look like peeled paint chips.

3 I stick my head over the ship's railing for a closer look. Near the floating mass of white plastic there is something else in the water—something small, finned. Something alive. I watch as a quarter-size blue-green larval fish swims to the surface, opens its mouth and swallows a bit of plastic the size of a pencil eraser. Within moments, the fish and plastic have floated away. "You just got a firsthand look at how plastic gets into the food chain," Kristian Syberg tells me a few minutes later. Syberg is an associate professor of environmental risk at Roskilde University in Denmark and one of two resident scientists onboard the vessel, which has set out to measure the smallest, most **toxic** pieces of plastic in the ocean, called "microplastic." Prior to this voyage scientists have never before searched for plastic deep in

continued on next page

the Pacific Ocean water column. "It's the smallest fish that eat the most plastic and become toxic. Then the middle-sized fish eat those smallest fish and become a little more toxic. Then the larger fish eat those middle-sized fish and become even more toxic. And then we eat the largest fish," he notes.

plastic

4   Suddenly, I think twice about **consuming** the mahi-mahi we've caught for dinner that night.

A Growing Problem

5   Plastic can be **detected** in the bodies of more than 50 percent of the world's sea turtles. Scientists **estimate** 90 percent of all seabirds have ingested plastic at some time in their lives. Fish, too, contain plastic and appear to consume it in large quantities when it is available.

6   Although there is a huge amount of plastic trash that has **accumulated** on land, much of the world's plastic resides in the oceans, where it is deposited after being whisked there by the wind from land, being dumped at sea or on the shore, or being carried there in runoff from rivers and streams. Scientists predict that by 2050 there will be more plastic in the oceans than fish.

7   Current estimates put the oceans' total plastic load at 165 million tons. But that is just based on plastic samples collected from surface trawling[1]. More microplastic found at greater depths in the oceans means scientists might be greatly underestimating the total amount of plastic in the ocean—and its total effect.

8   Syberg's expedition **entails** collecting water samples and trawling this famous stretch of ocean for evidence of microplastic. His group's previous research in the Atlantic Ocean revealed that microplastic exists at a greater depth than previously believed. What is more, a 2016 study found that seafloor animals like lobsters, sea cucumbers, and hermit crabs, which can live at depths of up to 6,000 feet (1,800 meters), have consumed the stuff.

Pervasive Plastics

9   Plastic is so **pervasive** in the natural environment that if you took a look inside the body of any animal—on land or at sea—you would likely find at least a trace of plastic, Syberg says. That includes inside us humans. "Unfortunately," he adds, "to date no systematic studies can confirm plastic is present in people on a wide scale. Not enough money or attention has been allotted to address this issue."

10 Although the garbage patch is typically **portrayed** as "a floating island of plastic trash the size of Texas," in actuality it only contains the occasional large piece of trash or fishing gear and is mostly a large soup of microscopic plastic bits, many of which are too small to see with the naked eye. That is because plastic breaks up over time, but never fully breaks down.

11 When plastic is exposed to UV radiation from the sun and mechanical movement of waves, it breaks into little pieces. As I saw firsthand, fish tend to eat small pieces of plastic, mistaking it for plankton, their preferred food source. Research reveals consuming plastics can increase fish mortality by causing behavioral and physical abnormalities, such as slowed reaction time and reduced size. Scientists **hypothesize** these problems are caused by the man-made chemicals that plastic absorbs from seawater. The worry now is that these tiny toxic pieces of plastic may affect more than just fish—possibly causing cancer in humans, altering our

[1] **trawling:** method of fishing in which a large net is dragged through the water from the back of a boat

continued on next page

hormones, and maybe even killing us. "In a little more than sixty years, we know we've littered more than 150 million tons of plastic into the oceans," says Henrik Beha Pedersen, founder and president of the Danish nonprofit Plastic Change. "Where does it all end up? Is it in the fish? Is it in the birds? Is it on the beaches? Is it on the deep-sea floor? Where has all the plastic gone? Is it in us, us humans?"

Research and Change

12 Over the course of the expedition, Syberg and Malene Møhl, an advisor on chemicals to The Danish Ecological Council and Plastic Change volunteer, trawl for plastic, and additionally gather water at 200 meters (650 feet) down in the water column, flesh samples from fish, and bits of seaweed. Back in Denmark it will be Syberg's responsibility to process the samples, estimating how much microplastic is in the Pacific. He will also test for chemicals in the plastic, fish, and seaweed, which will help him determine to what degree plastic acts as a "vector," soaking up and delivering toxic chemicals in the bodies of living things.

13 It is research that is most helpful in combating our plastic problem, according to National Oceanic and Atmospheric Administration agent Mark Manuel, regional coordinator of NOAA's Pacific Islands Marine Debris Program, whom I meet up with in Honolulu a few weeks after *Christianshavn's* journey ended in Kewalo Basin Harbor. He says with government environmental agencies—including his own—strapped for cash and staff, it is largely up to nonprofits like Plastic Change to gather data that, when analyzed and published, can push plastic-curbing policies like plastic bag, microbead, and Styrofoam **bans**, which he says appear effective in curbing plastic use and reducing pollution. For example, San Jose, Calif. officials found a 2012 ban on plastic bags in their city helped reduce plastic litter in streets by 59 percent, storm drains by 89 percent, and creeks by 60 percent, as well as increased consumer use of reusable shopping bags.

14 In the future, Syberg hopes he and other researchers will be able to get the funding they need to pursue studies on the effects plastic has on human health—the last big question remaining after the total amount of plastic in the world's oceans is properly **quantified**. As of now, a substantial portion of the research effort comes from the nonprofit sphere— organizations currently collaborating with scientists to study plastic include 5 Gyres Institute, Mission Blue, and Greenpeace.

15 NOAA currently provides grants to nonprofits for plastic education, clean-up, pollution prevention and research projects—such as trash surveys—in the Pacific and in coastal regions across the United States. Manuel says he has found one of the biggest challenges to getting more data on marine **debris** and microplastic is garnering enough volunteer help.

16 "Changing behaviors can be hard, but we've seen how nonprofits' research can help get policies passed," says Manuel, a Big Island native and father of two young sons. "It can be hard to incentivize spending hours counting and cleaning up trash on a beach, for free. Yet the more people that get involved, that help to get the science done, the closer we get to cleaning up this mess."

1 Look at your predictions from Preview on page 179 again. How did your answers to the questions help you understand the story?

2 Reading One is divided into four sections, each of which has a heading. The headings are the main ideas of each section. Choose the sentence that gives the best summary of each section.

1. **The Patch Close Up**

   a. Plastics of all sizes can be found in the Garbage Patch, but the most toxic are the microplastics.

   b. The microplastics are getting into the food chain, and eventually humans may be eating them.

2. **A Growing Problem**

   a. Humans are using more and more plastic, and this is the cause of plastic pollution in the ocean.

   b. More and more plastic is ending up in the ocean and is found at all depths of the ocean, not just on the surface.

3. **Pervasive Plastics**

   a. Plastics can be found in many living things on both land and in the sea.

   b. UV light and the motion of the waves breaks up plastic into microplastics.

4. **Research and Change**

   a. More government research is the best solution to the problem.

   b. Government research is severely underfunded, but nonprofits and volunteers can help the cause immensely.

1 Choose the correct answer.

1. Why are microplastics more dangerous than other types of trash found in the ocean?

 a. Fish that eat microplastics become sick and die, so there are fewer fish in the ocean.

 b. Humans eat fish that have eaten microplastics, so humans are exposed to toxicity.

 c. Microplastics are found in the deepest part of the ocean, and it is a risky place for scientists to explore.

2. Where are microplastics most commonly found in the ocean?

 a. on the ocean's surface

 b. in the deepest parts of the ocean

 c. both on the surface of and deep in the ocean

3. What is the best way to describe the Great Pacific Garbage Patch?

 a. a mixture of many small pieces of plastic, many of which we cannot see

 b. a mixture of both small and large pieces of plastic

 c. large pieces of plastic that break up and fully break down after many years

4. What causes large pieces of plastic to break into smaller pieces?

 a. radiation from the sun and the movement of the waves

 b. large fish trying to eat the plastic and radiation from the sun

 c. the movement of the waves and the chemicals from the plastic

5. Which of the following has been an effective tool for combatting the plastics problem?

 a. getting money from government agencies to fund research projects

 b. checking fish to make sure they have not eaten plastic before allowing people to eat them

 c. encouraging government policies that limit use of plastics

6. What has been a major challenge in the fight against plastics?

 a. many people's lack of interest in trying to help the environment

 b. getting people to volunteer since governments often do not have the money to help

 c. dangerous conditions prevent researchers from going into the deeper areas of the ocean

2 Look at your notes and at your questions in Preview. How did they help you understand the article?

MAKE INFERENCES 🔍

Inferring the Author's Point of View and Possible Bias

Writers show their point of view, or bias, toward a topic by their language and word choice, choice of expert testimony and quotes, and use of evidence. Bias in writing occurs when an author presents only one side of a story or only presents information that supports his or her opinion on the subject. Authors usually try to find strong evidence that is proven with quotes from experts or data. However, they may choose to also include weak evidence if it supports their opinion. Being able to infer an author's point of view and analyze text for any bias is a critical reading skill. If weak evidence is included in a reading, it may be a sign that the author's bias is included in a reading and that all sides of the story may not be included.

What is the point of view of the author of Reading One about the topic of ocean pollution?

continued on next page

Some of the author's evidence and support for the danger and degree of plastic pollution is strong, while other evidence is weaker and uses hypothetical rather than factual information.

Look at the excerpts from Reading One. In which excerpt does the author use language that shows complete certainty or strong evidence, such as firsthand knowledge, research, or data? In which excerpt is the evidence less strong or not yet proven to be true? The underlined words or phrases indicate the author's level of certainty.

> Scientists <u>hypothesize</u> these problems are caused by the man-made chemicals that plastic absorbs from seawater. The worry now is that these tiny toxic pieces of plastic <u>may</u> affect more than just fish—<u>possibly</u> causing cancer in humans, altering our hormones, and <u>maybe</u> even killing us.

This is weak evidence. The author uses words such as *hypothesize, may, possibly,* and *maybe.* She does this because this information supports her point of view and she wants to include it even though it has not yet been scientifically proven.

> <u>I watch</u> as a quarter-size blue-green larval fish swims to the surface, opens its mouth and swallows a bit of plastic the size of a pencil eraser. Within moments, the fish and plastic have floated away.

This is strong evidence. The author saw the fish swallow the plastic herself. This evidence cannot be disputed, and it is not a hypothesis.

1 **Read the excerpts. Write *S* if the evidence is strong. Write *W* if the evidence is weak. Underline the words or phrases that show certainty or uncertainty.**

1. <u>W</u> Plastic is so pervasive in the natural environment that if you took a look inside the body of any animal—on land or at sea—you <u>would likely</u> find <u>at least</u> a trace of plastic, Syberg says.

2. _____ "It's the smallest fish that eat the most plastic and become toxic. Then the middle-sized fish eat those smallest fish and become a little more toxic. Then the larger fish eat those middle-sized fish and become even more toxic. And then we eat the largest fish," he [Syberg] notes.

3. _____ Current estimates put the oceans' total plastic load at 165 million tons.

4. _____ But that is just based on plastic samples collected from surface trawling. More microplastic found at greater depths in the oceans means scientists might be greatly underestimating the total amount of plastic in the ocean—and its total effect.

5. _____ "Unfortunately," he [Syberg] adds, "to date no systematic studies can confirm plastic is present in people on a wide scale. Not enough money or attention has been allotted to address this issue."

6. _____ "In a little more than sixty years, we know we've littered more than 150 million tons of plastic into the oceans," says Henrik Beha Pedersen, founder and president of the Danish nonprofit Plastic Change.

2 **Discuss your answers with a partner. Point out sentences, words, or phrases in the paragraphs that helped you find the answers.**

USE YOUR NOTES

Use your notes to support your answers with information from the reading.

Work in a small group. Choose one of the questions. Discuss your ideas. Then choose one person in your group to report the ideas to the class.

1. What information surprised you the most in this text? Give examples.

2. What are some other environmental problems in the world today? What are some solutions you know of that have been proposed to help solve these problems?

🔵 Go to **MyEnglishLab** to give your opinion about another question.

READING TWO | Two Proposals to Clean Up Our Oceans of Garbage: Will Either Work?

PREVIEW

1 Look at the title of the reading and the picture. What two proposals do you think will be discussed?

_____

_____

2 Look at the boldfaced words in the reading. Which words do you know the meanings of?

1 **Read the article about two proposals to clean up the oceans. As you read, guess the meanings of the words that are new to you. Remember to take notes on main ideas and details.**

Two Proposals to Clean Up Our Oceans of Garbage: Will Either Work?

By David Leveille | From *PRI's The World*

A boom trapping garbage

1 By now, most everyone knows this dirty truth about our oceans: Tons and tons of plastic waste in the form of bottles, bags, fishing nets, Styrofoam, and a myriad of other containers are routinely **discarded** into the sea. Marine scientists estimate that over 5 trillion pieces of plastic currently litter the oceans.

2 So is there any way to clean up that mess, and how **feasible** is it?

3 "In the past, people have **proposed** to clean up these areas using boats and nets, but of course these areas are very large, many times the size of Texas, so if you were to do that it would take many thousands of years and billions of dollars to clean up just one of those areas," says Boyan Slat, the young man behind an **ambitious** strategy called The Ocean Cleanup.

4 Slat was a teenager in the Netherlands in 2013 when he first proposed a technological solution to the problem of plastic pollution. It's focused particularly in the region located between Hawaii and California known as the Great Pacific Garbage Patch. It's considered the largest of five ocean garbage patches where ocean currents act like a gyre[1] to concentrate the floating plastic debris.

5 "But then I thought this plastic is actually moving around, it doesn't stay in one spot. So, why would you go after the plastic when the plastic can come to you?" says Slat. "So, we came up with this passive system that uses very long floating screens floating around to concentrate the plastic like an artificial coastline."

6 Despite much hype, Slat's solution is still in the prototype stage. But the plan is that, within a year, the first Ocean Cleanup system will be towed out into the Pacific and will get to work[2]. Basically, a floating U-shaped screen is weighed down and moves more slowly in the current than the floating plastic, so the trash gets snagged by the screen. Once gathered, the waste can be collected and stored more easily before it's shipped to land for recycling.

7 Many questions have been raised about the **viability** of the Ocean Cleanup. Some critics call the elaborate environmental scheme a boondoggle[3].

8 For example, can the technology withstand fierce ocean storms? Slat and his team did test out floating screen technology in harsh North Sea conditions, and it seemed to pass with flying colors, according to Slat. Also, what about the huge amounts of plastic litter **entrapped** by the floating screens? How does Slat propose to efficiently collect and retrieve vast amounts of plastic waste?

---

[1] **gyre:** an area of the ocean where the ocean currents move in circular currents
[2] After a successful trial, the first system is being towed out to the Great Pacific Garbage Patch.
[3] **boondoggle:** a project that is considered a waste of time or money

continued on next page

9 "Basically I have a fleet of clean-up systems floating around, up to fifty that we plan on deploying. Once a month, a vessel comes and basically goes from clean-up system to clean-up system, like a garbage truck of the ocean. With this we basically calculated that we should be able to clean up about 50 percent of this Great Pacific Garbage Patch in just five years' time," he says.

10 But the bottom line is this: Ocean Cleanup hasn't yet been actually deployed. It's still in development and could come online sometime in the coming year. So, stay tuned.

11 In the meantime, other marine scientists, including Marcus Eriksen, founder of the 5 Gyres Institute in California, are working on an entirely different and global approach to ridding the world's oceans of plastic litter. Eriksen believes that a **prevention** model and changing the systems that create the problems in the first place are the best way forward.

12 "That's where a lot of the hard work is happening," says Eriksen. "It's far upstream trying to stop this flow of trash to sea. If you pick up what's out there, you're not stopping the problem continuing far into the future. You've got to stop the source."

13 Eriksen points to what he calls a "rising tide of activism[4] to fight plastic pollution." Many cities around the world, for example, are installing booms in their rivers and estuaries to capture plastic trash before it washes to sea. Plastic recovery centers are starting to appear in Southeast Asia, which Eriksen says are "getting really good at sourcing where plastic trash is coming from and separating what can be recycled and composted. Any plastic trash left over, they're working with local companies to deal with it and to redesign excessive plastic packaging."

14 That's the kind of hard work that is required, Eriksen says, to stop the flow of plastic into the ocean. He insists, "That's where it's happening."

15 As for Slat's big floating screens to be installed in the Pacific Ocean to be serviced by "ocean garbage trucks"?

16 Eriksen responds: "I'm sorry to say, but I think these downstream mitigations[5] out in the middle of the ocean are a distraction from the work that almost all environmental organizations are focused on."

---

[4] **activism:** the act of mobilizing people to push for social or political change
[5] **mitigation:** the act of making something less severe or dangerous

2 **Compare your notes on main ideas and details with a partner's. How can you improve your notes next time?**

➤ Go to the **Pearson Practice English App** or **MyEnglishLab** for more vocabulary practice.

Taking Notes with Pros and Cons

Analyzing solutions to a complex problem is an important reading skill, especially when evaluating a scientific article. In addition, thinking critically about the positive and negative aspects of a proposal or solution helps to form an educated opinion. Reading Two features two solutions, or models, for cleaning up the ocean. Both solutions have their pros (positive aspects) and cons (negative aspects). Find the pros and cons of each model using the information in the article.

Read the excerpt from Reading Two. Is this a positive aspect (pro) or a negative aspect (con)?

> In the past people have proposed to clean up these areas using boats and nets, but of course these areas are very large, many times the size of Texas, so if you were to do that it would take many thousands of years and billions of dollars to clean up just one of those areas.

This is a positive aspect of Slat's plan.

Slat states that the proposal of using boats and nets would take a long time and cost lots of money. His clean up may be less expensive.

Complete the chart with information about the pros and cons of each model.

CLEAN UP MODEL - Boyan Slat	PREVENTION MODEL - Markus Eriksen
Pros: *Will take much less time and will be less expensive than using boats and nets.*	Pros:
Cons:	Cons:

🔾 Go to **MyEnglishLab** for more note-taking practice.

COMPREHENSION

1 Use your notes to help you answer the questions.

1. How is Boyan Slat's proposal different from other people's proposals to use boats and nets to clean up the ocean?

2. How does Boyan Slat use the currents in the gyre in his system?

3. How much of the Great Pacific Garbage Patch does Slat think he will clean up in five years?

4. Eriksen refers to his proposal as a prevention model. What does he mean by this?

2 Review the boldfaced words from the reading with a partner. Use a dictionary or ask your teacher for any meanings you still do not know.

1 **Look at Reading Two again. There are sixteen paragraphs. Group paragraphs together that share common ideas. How would you label or categorize the groups?**

Creating Headings Based on Main Ideas

Recognizing how paragraphs of a text are connected helps you to identify the main ideas in a reading and notice when an author moves to a new idea. This type of close reading helps you analyze the text and understand the reading more thoroughly. Notice how in Reading One, the paragraphs were grouped into four sections. The heading for each section represented the main idea. Reading Two does not have headings

Think about a possible heading for Reading Two, paragraphs 1 and 2. Note that a heading is not usually a full sentence. Instead, it is similar to a title, using only the most important words.

These two paragraphs can be grouped together because all the information in paragraph 1 is about the problem. Paragraph 2 presents the guiding question of the article, how can this mess be cleaned up? These two paragraphs are like the introduction. A possible heading for these paragraphs is, "A Dirty Problem."

2 **Look at the paragraph groupings. Choose the main ideas that would make a good heading. Share and discuss with a partner.**

  1. Paragraphs 3–6

     a. About the Garbage Patch

     b. All About Boyan Slat

     c. Cleaning Up the Garbage Patch

  2. Paragraphs 7–10

     a. Answers to Questions

     b. Floating Screens

     c. Garbage Trucks of the Ocean

3 **Now write headings for these groups of paragraphs. Share and discuss with a partner.**

  a. Paragraphs 11–12

     Heading: _____

  b. Paragraphs 13–16

     Heading: _____

 Go to **MyEnglishLab** for more skill practice.

CONNECT THE READINGS

ORGANIZE

Reading One (R1) and Reading Two (R2) describe both the problems of ocean pollution and possible solutions. Complete the chart with information from both readings. An X means there is no information for the box.

USE YOUR NOTES

Review your notes from Reading One and Two. Use the information in your notes to complete the chart.

	Sea Unworthy: A Personal Journey Into the Pacific Garbage Patch (R1)	*Two Proposals to Clean Up Our Oceans of Garbage (R2)*
Sources of plastics in the ocean		
Dangers of microplastics		X
Responses and solutions		
Challenges ahead		

SYNTHESIZE

Complete the summary paragraph using information from Organize.

There are many reasons why our oceans are filled with plastic including ______________________ and ______________________. Plastics in the ocean are a problem to all living things. These plastics break down into smaller pieces called ______________________, which never disappear. The problem with microplastics is ______________________. There have been several responses and solutions to this problem including ______________________ and ______________________. Even with these proposals and responses, there are still challenges ahead. For example, ______________________ and ______________________.

Go to **MyEnglishLab** to check what you learned.

VOCABULARY

REVIEW

Complete the crossword puzzle. Read the clues and choose words from the box.

accumulate	discard	estimate	pervasive	robust
ambitious	discover	feasible	portray	toxic
ban	entail	hypothesize	prevent	viability
debris	entrap	ingest	propose	

ACROSS

2. to prohibit the use of something

7. to show or represent

8. to present a possible solution to a problem

12. possible or reasonable

14. to detect or find

15. to make an educated guess

17. to involve or require

18. to consume or eat

DOWN

1. to catch something

3. an approximate number

4. the ability for something to work successfully

5. to gather something

6. motivated, with a strong desire to succeed

7. something widely spread and found in many areas

9. large and powerful

10. poisonous or harmful

11. to throw away or get rid of

13. litter or trash

16. to stop or not allow

EXPAND

1 Complete the chart with the correct word forms. Some categories can have more than one form. Use a dictionary if necessary. An X indicates that you do not need to put a form in that category.

NOUN	VERB	ADJECTIVE	ADVERB
	accumulate		X
	X	ambitious	
ban			X
1. 2.	consume		X
debris	X	X	X
1. 2. 3.	detect		X
	discard	1. 2.	X
	entail	X	X
	entrap		X
1. 2.	estimate		X
	X	feasible	
	hypothesize		X
		pervasive	
1. 2.	portray		X
1. 2.	prevent		X
1. 2.	propose		X
quantity quantifier			X
	X	robust	
1. 2.	X	toxic	
viability	X		

2 Complete the sentences with the correct form of the word.

1. **consume**

   a. Scientists believe that the _____ of microplastics has caused abnormalities in land and sea animals.

   b. The food chain is contaminated because of larger fish _____ smaller fish which have eaten microplastics.

   c. Our _____ society is at least in part responsible for the amount of plastic pollution in the ocean.

2. **ambitious**

   a. Many activists have _____ plans to clean up the waters.

   b. Boyan Slat's _____ to clean up the ocean grew out of his disgust with the plastics he saw on the beaches while on vacation in Greece.

3. **estimate**

   a. Scientists _____ that people are responsible for there being more than 150 million tons of plastic in the oceans.

   b. This _____ may be low, as it does not include the amount of plastic below the ocean's surface.

   c. The _____ amount of plastic in the ocean seems to be growing each year as scientists find more sophisticated research methods.

4. **prevent**

   a. Eriksen believes that a _____ model and changing the systems that create the problems in the first place are the best way forward.

   b. Banning plastic bags is one way to _____ plastic from reaching the sea through runoff from rivers.

   c. Ocean pollution caused by garbage should be _____ with education and the changing of people's habits.

5. **feasible**

   a. The _____ of asking people to change their daily behaviors is always in question.

   b. Are the solutions to the microplastics pollution problem _____ ?

6. **proposal**

   a. Many communities have made _____ to impose plastic bag bans.

   b. Many scientists were skeptical when Boyan Slat _____ his ideas for the Ocean Cleanup.

   c. Boyan Slat's _____ plan involves using the ocean's current to entrap the plastic and garbage in the buoys.

CREATE

APPLY After reading about the problems and possible solutions to the issue of microplastics in the ocean, what questions do you still have about the problem and the proposals? Focus the content of your questions on the people from the readings.

Write two questions for each person. Use at least one word from Review or Expand in each question.

1. Erica Cirino (author and voyager, R1)

   a. _____

   b. _____

2. Boyan Slat (founder of Ocean Cleanup, R2)

   a. _____

   b. _____

3. Marcus Eriksen (founder of the 5 Gyres Institute, R2)

   a. _____

   b. _____

🔵 Go to the **Pearson Practice English App** or **MyEnglishLab** for more vocabulary practice.

GRAMMAR FOR WRITING

1 Read the sentences and answer the questions.

a. Boyan Slat proposes cleaning up the garbage already in the ocean **whereas** Eriksen's proposal deals with stopping garbage from entering the ocean.

b. Plastic bag bans may be one way to reduce ocean pollution. **In the same way**, plastic pollution may also be reduced by asking people to change their behavior.

c. Slat has many supporters for his Ocean Cleanup project; **in contrast**, some people are very critical of his work.

1. Sentence *a* has two clauses. What are the clauses?

2. What is the difference in punctuation between sentences *b* and *c*?

3. Look at the boldfaced words. Which words introduce ideas that are similar?

4. Which words introduce ideas that are different?

Subordinators and Transitions of Comparisons and Contrasts

Comparisons and Contrasts

Comparisons point out ideas that are similar. **Contrasts** point out ideas that are different.

Subordinators

Subordinators are words that are used to compare or contrast the ideas in two clauses. They join an independent clause to a dependent clause being compared or contrasted. Examples of subordinators include *while, whereas, just as, as,* and *in the same way that*. These words introduce dependent clauses, which are not complete thoughts. The independent clause usually describes the point that is being emphasized or is more important.

- Put a comma after a dependent clause that introduces a sentence.

    Whereas Eriksen's proposal deals with stopping garbage from entering the ocean, Boyan Slat proposes cleaning up the garbage already in the ocean.

- Do not use a comma when the dependent clause follows the independent clause.

    Boyan Slat proposes cleaning up the garbage already in the ocean whereas Eriksen's proposal deals with stopping garbage from entering the ocean.

Comparison subordinators include:	Contrast subordinators include:
just as	whereas
as	while
in the same way that	

Transitions

Transitions show the connection between two independent clauses (two sentences).

Comparison transitions include:	Contrast transitions include:
similarly	in contrast
in the same way	on the other hand
likewise	however

Two independent clauses can be combined in one sentence by using a semicolon between clauses and a comma after the transition:

I love Boyan Slat's proposal**; however,** I am worried about its feasibility.

The two independent clauses can also be written as separate sentences. In this case, replace the semicolon with a period, but keep the comma after the transition:

I love Boyan Slat's proposal. **However,** I am worried about its feasibility.

Compare and contrast subordinators and transitions are used in compare-and-contrast essays, as well as problem-solution essays where different solutions are being evaluated.

2 **Read the pairs of sentences. Decide if they are comparing or contrasting information. Then use the correct transition and combine the pairs of sentences to make comparisons and contrasts.**

1. These two sentences ＿＿＿ compare (*just as*) or ＿X＿ contrast (*whereas*).

   Boyan Slat, the CEO of Ocean Cleanup, is an engineering school drop-out.

   Marcus Eriksen, founder of the 5 Gyres Institute, has a PhD in Science Education.

   Boyan Slat, the CEO of Ocean Cleanup, is an engineering school drop-out whereas Marcus
   Eriksen, founder of the 5 Gyres Institute, has a PhD in Science Education.

2. These two sentences ＿＿＿ compare (*likewise*) or ＿＿＿ contrast (*however*).

   Eriksen wants to significantly reduce the amount of garbage in the ocean.

   Slat hopes to clean up the ocean in the near future.

   _____

   _____

   _____

3. These two sentences ＿＿＿ compare (*in the same way*) or ＿＿＿ contrast (*on the other hand*).

   A lot of garbage is starting to wash up on the beaches of Hawaii.

   Garbage from the North Sea is polluting beaches in Scandinavia.

   _____

   _____

   _____

4. These two sentences ＿＿＿ compare (*in the same way*) or ＿＿＿ contrast (*while*).

   Eriksen's project deals only with stopping trash from reaching the sea.

   Slat's Ocean Cleanup project is chiefly concerned with garbage that is already in the ocean.

   _____

   _____

   _____

5. These two sentences ＿＿＿ compare (*likewise*) or ＿＿＿ contrast (*on the other hand*).

   Some scientists estimate the total amount of plastics in the ocean today is 165 million tons.

   Other scientists believe the number may be much larger due to the possibility of more microplastics being found at greater depths.

   _____

   _____

   _____

6. These two sentences _____ compare (*similarly*) or _____ contrast (*however*).

Plastic in the ocean breaks down into microplastic, but never disappears.

Organic matter such as food will eventually disintegrate or be consumed.

_____

_____

_____

7. These two sentences _____ compare (*just as*) or _____ contrast (*whereas*).

Slat's Ocean Cleanup Project will require substantial funding to succeed.

Eriksen's proposal needs a lot of money to achieve the results he wants.

_____

_____

_____

3 Read the paragraphs. Decide if the writer is comparing or contrasting. Choose the correct transitions or subordinators of comparison or contrast.

1.   Cape Town, South Africa, had been suffering from water scarcity for many years. Late in 2017, the government announced that the city was about to reach *Day Zero*, the day when reservoirs would be so low that the government would be forced to turn off the water reaching people's homes. To avoid this disastrous scenario, the government placed severe limits on the amount of water a person could use. (*While, Just as*) _____ for years people had been asked to try to conserve water, now water usage was restricted to 50 liters (13 gallons) per person per day. (*Likewise, In contrast*) _____ , in California, the average water usage per person per day is 321 liters, or 85 gallons.) Presently, people are still able to get water out of their taps; (*similarly, on the other hand*) _____ , if *Day Zero* had arrived, citizens would have been forced to go to communal water collection points for water. Before water restrictions, people were able to use as much water as they wanted. (*Likewise, However*) _____ , now special meters have been installed at homes to monitor water use.

(*Just as, Likewise*) _____ other cities and towns have had to make major changes to avoid crises, Cape Town residents have been forced to think of ways to conserve and reuse their water. Some people recycle dirty, or gray, washing machine water. (*In contrast, Similarly*) _____ , they now take showers standing in buckets and reuse gray water. (*In the same way, Whereas*) _____ , they save water by limiting the number of times they flush their toilets. As one government official said, "It was not a pretty solution, but it was not a pretty problem." Now that *Day Zero* has been averted, residents say they will never take water for granted again.

2.   Our planet has several ocean gyres accumulating plastic pollution. One of the smaller garbage patches can be found in the Mediterranean Sea. Plastic makes up the majority of

continued on next page

the garbage in the Mediterranean; (*however, similarly*) _____ , it is also the majority of the garbage found in the Great Pacific Garbage Patch (GPGP). Scientists estimate that there are 250 billion pieces of plastic in the Mediterranean. (*Likewise, In contrast*) _____ , according to a study published in 2018 by Ocean Cleanup, there are 1.8 trillion pieces of plastic in the GPGP. The weight of the garbage found in the Mediterranean is estimated to be between 1,000 and 3,000 tons. (*On the other hand, Similarly*) _____ , the estimate for the amount in the GPGP is 80,000 tons of garbage. Microplastic has been found in the stomachs of Mediterranean marine life. (*However, In the same way*) _____ , it is has been found in between five and ten percent of the fish living in the GPGP. How does it get in the fish? The smallest fish eat the microplastic thinking it is plankton. Larger fish then eat the smaller fish and the plastic they had consumed. (*Likewise, On the other hand*) _____ , we humans get plastic in our bodies by eating the larger fish.

🔎 Go to the **Pearson Practice English App** or **MyEnglishLab** for more grammar practice. Check what you learned in **MyEnglishLab**.

FINAL WRITING TASK: A Problem-Solution Essay 🔍 APPLY

In this unit, you read about ocean pollution, specifically the dangers of plastics in our waters, and some solutions that scientists and activists are working on. Discuss the different solutions and their strengths and weaknesses.

What solution(s) seem feasible and doable to you?

You are going to ***write a problem-solution essay describing the problem of ocean pollution and comparing and contrasting the possible solutions.*** In addition to the information in this unit, do research to find out about other solutions.

For an alternative writing topic, see page 205.

PREPARE TO WRITE: Organizing Your Information Using a Tree Map

1 Using a tree map helps to organize ideas that are related to a central theme, in this case a problem. In your notebook, create a tree map like the one below with a statement of the problem and possible solutions.

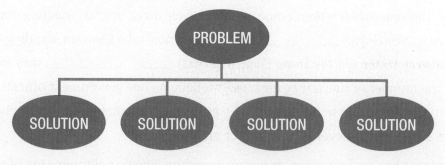

2 Choose one solution that you believe is the best. This will be the last solution you discuss in your essay.

Writing a Problem-Solution Essay

A **problem-solution** essay addresses and analyzes a problem or a challenge and then describes and discusses several solutions. In the first part of the essay, the problem is described and in the second part, the solutions are discussed, compared, and contrasted.

1. **Introduce the problem or challenge.** Capture the reader's attention by using a hook, such as a question or an impressive statistic. Present the thesis.

2. **Explain the problem.** Explain the problem, whom it affects, and the causes of the problem.

3. **Identify several solutions.** Compare and contrast the solutions and then choose the best one. Include statistics, facts, and details for all the solutions. Identify which solution is best in your opinion and state and explain this one last.

4. **Conclude your essay.** Wrap it up. Revisit your thesis, the importance of the problem, and why the solution you chose is the best. You may also want to add a quote for an interesting ending or ask the reader a question.

1 **Read the problem-solution essay about potential solutions to water scarcity.**

Water Scarcity: Big and Small Solutions

Water is one of our most valuable resources, but like many natural resources, it is becoming scarce. The World Health Organization reports that globally three out of ten people do not have access to safe, clean water at home and 2.7 billion people find water scarce for at least one month a year. Water scarcity is caused by various issues, including drought, pollution, overuse, and sometimes from conflicts such as war and dictatorial governments. Many of us who don't face water shortages often take this resource for granted; we do not understand or appreciate the vast amount of water we use and depend on daily. For example, in her book, *Replenish*, Sandra Postel, author and former director of the Global Water Policy Project, states that it takes 1,250 liters (330 gallons) of water just to make a simple cheese pizza. Most of it, she states, goes into growing the feed for the cows that we milk for cheese and growing the tomatoes. And your morning cup of coffee? Well, it takes about 129 liters (34 gallons) of water just to grow the coffee beans. Finding solutions to water scarcity, while at the same time conserving the water we have, should be our highest priority.

Some innovative ideas are being implemented worldwide to deal with water scarcity. One solution being carried out in rural India is to use solar power to make dirty water clean. Solar-powered pumps filter undrinkable water and make it useable. However, this solution is complex and costly, and villagers must buy the clean water in order to pay for the cost of the solar power technology. Another solution is the use of Fog Catchers. Fog Catchers are large nets or screens that are set up across a mountainside; they catch the morning fog which then drips into collection trays. In contrast to the previous solution, the water is free, but it is limited in quantity and would not supply enough water for a larger village or for irrigation. The Water Seer is another possible solution. The Water Seer is a large device that turns air into water. Wind turbines collect air above ground and push the air down into the ground where it condenses and turns into water. Similar to the Fog Catcher, it is not complex or costly. However, the amount of water produced is limited, and the device won't work in very dry places, nor will it work without wind. Finally, and unlike any other solution, some scientists in Belgium have created a solar-powered machine that turns urine into drinkable water!

continued on next page

While all of these solutions are promising and address the problem, they may not produce enough water to make them viable. In addition, their implementation would require massive amounts of money and resources. Therefore, the most sustainable and practical solutions are the ones that call for changes that we can make on a daily basis. These include taking shorter showers or even skipping a shower, turning off the water while washing hands and brushing teeth, running the dishwasher only when full, and reusing your pasta water for watering plants or flushing the toilet. Educating ourselves and the people around us about water usage and ways we can conserve water in our communities are essential steps. We could also donate our time or money, if possible, to causes that promote water conservation and water education.

The water we use is precious. Scientists say that by 2025, one-third of the world will be affected by water shortages, and it will only get worse after that. Preserving our water for our present and future generations should be our greatest priority. As caretakers of our world, we each have a responsibility to conserve this resource.

2 Complete the essay organizer with information from the essay in Exercise 1.

1. Introduction: Analyze the Problem What is the problem? How did it happen? Why is it a problem? Whom does it affect?	Water is becoming scarce.	
2. Compare and Contrast Solutions What are the solutions being proposed? Who is proposing them? What are the details? Evaluation What are pros and cons?	**Solution 1 (Possible)** Use solar power to make dirty water clean	**Evaluation**
	Solution 2 (Possible)	**Evaluation**
	Solution 3 (Possible)	**Evaluation**
	Solution 4 (Possible)	**Evaluation**
3. Best Solution	**Solution**	**Evaluation**
4. Conclusion Restate the thesis and why the solution chosen is best. End with a statement or question that restates the thesis statement.		

3 Create an essay organizer with information for your problem-solution essay about plastic pollution in the ocean and possible solutions. Use the organizer from Exercise 2 as a model.

4 Use your notes from Prepare to Write on page 200 and your essay organizer to plan your essay.

- Make sure your introductory paragraph has a thesis.

- Write paragraphs that discuss solutions, including comparing and contrasting.

- Write a strong concluding paragraph.

REVISE: Writing Conclusions

1 Read the sentences. Which sentences would you include in a conclusion? Why?

Ocean pollution continues to be a serious problem. Governments, organizations, and individuals need to work together to come up with workable solutions before our oceans are permanently damaged.

Ocean pollution continues to be a serious problem. People do not know how they can help, so we do not know what the future holds.

Conclusions

The **conclusion** to an essay is the writer's final opportunity to impress an opinion or idea on the reader. Most commonly, the conclusion also restates the thesis of the essay. A strongly written conclusion will stay with the reader and give the reader something to think about long after they finish reading. There are several techniques for writing strong conclusions.

1. Call for Action

This technique asks the reader to consider doing something, such as changing a behavior, donating to a cause, writing to a politician, taking a stance, or volunteering.

2. Make A Prediction

This technique asks the reader to consider a future situation and the implications or consequences if a situation continues.

3. Pose a Provocative Question

This technique asks the reader a question that requires deep thinking and reflecting. The writer does not answer the question. Rather, it is up to the reader to answer the question.

4. Use an Expert Quote

This technique asks readers to think about a quote from an expert as a way to support their conclusion and create a strong final impression.

2 Read the four conclusions. Underline the restated thesis statements. Then label each conclusion with the letter of the technique used.

Conclusion 1   Technique: _____

The water we use is precious. Scientists say that by 2025, one-third of the world will be affected by water shortages, and it will only get worse after that. Preserving our water for our present and future generations should be our greatest priority. What would your world look like without water? What will you do today to preserve and protect what we have left?

Conclusion 2   Technique: _____

The water we use is precious. Scientists say that by 2025, one-third of the world will be affected by water shortages, and it will only get worse after that. Preserving our water for our present and future generations should be our greatest priority. As caretakers of our world, we each have a responsibility to conserve this resource.

Conclusion 3   Technique: _____

The water we use is precious. Scientists say that by 2025, one-third of the world will be affected by water shortages, and it will only get worse after that. Preserving our water for our present and future generations should be our greatest priority. As the great marine biologist, essayist, and writer Sylvia Earle says, ""The single non-negotiable thing life requires is water."

Conclusion 4   Technique: _____

The water we use is precious. Scientists say that by 2025, one-third of the world will be affected by water shortages, and it will only get worse after that. Preserving our water for our present and future generations should be our greatest priority. If we do not make strong efforts to recognize and acknowledge water shortages now, our overuse and short sightedness will come back to haunt us. Imagine your world without water. It is unimaginable.

3 Revise your conclusion using two of the techniques listed. Identify the technique used.

Technique: _____

_____

_____

_____

_____

_____

Technique: _____

_____

_____

_____

_____

_____

4 Now go back to the first draft of your essay.

- Choose one of your conclusions and use it in your essay. Think about why you chose that conclusion and make sure it restates the thesis of the essay.

- Try to use the grammar and some of the vocabulary from the unit.

⬆ Go to **MyEnglishLab** for more skill practice.

EDIT: Writing the Final Draft

APPLY Write the final draft of your essay and submit it to your teacher. Carefully edit it for grammatical and mechanical errors, such as spelling, capitalization, and punctuation. Consider how to apply the vocabulary, grammar, and writing skills from the unit. Use the checklist to help you.

FINAL DRAFT CHECKLIST

☐ Does the essay state the problem and its implications clearly?

☐ Do the body paragraphs present the pros and cons of the possible solutions?

☐ Does the essay present the best solution and reasons why it is the best?

☐ Does the essay have a strong conclusion that leaves the reader with a lasting impression?

☐ Does the essay include compare and contrast subordinators and transitions?

☐ Do you use the vocabulary from the unit?

ALTERNATIVE WRITING TOPIC

APPLY This unit has presented a number of solutions to the problem of plastics polluting our waters. What are some steps you and your community have taken (or can take) to reduce the amount of plastic in our water sources? Write about what you have seen or would like to see happen and the results that would hopefully occur. Use the grammar and vocabulary from the unit.

CHECK WHAT YOU'VE LEARNED

Check (✔) the outcomes you've met and vocabulary you've learned. Put an X next to the skills and vocabulary you still need to practice.

Learning Outcomes

☐ Infer the author's point of view and possible bias

☐ Taking notes on pros and cons

☐ Creating headings based on main ideas

☐ Use transitions and subordinators

☐ Write conclusions

☐ Write a problem-solution essay

Vocabulary

☐ accumulate AWL
☐ ambitious
☐ ban (n.)
☐ consume AWL
☐ debris
☐ detect AWL
☐ discard
☐ entail
☐ entrap
☐ estimate (v.) AWL

☐ feasible
☐ hypothesize AWL
☐ pervasive
☐ portray
☐ prevention
☐ propose
☐ quantify
☐ robust
☐ toxic
☐ viability

➤ Go to **MyEnglishLab** to watch a video about water conservation in college dormitories, access the Unit Project, and take the Unit 7 Achievement Test.

LEARNING OUTCOMES

> Infer an author's appeal to authority
> Take three-column notes to show time sequence
> Identify referents for the pronoun *it*

> Use subordinators and prepositional phrases
> Use transitions
> Write a cause-and-effect essay

 Go to **MyEnglishLab** to check what you know.

Managing Your Smartphone

1 FOCUS ON THE TOPIC

1. What do people typically use their smartphones for?

2. *Nomophobia* is the fear of being without your smartphone. *Phantom vibration syndrome* is an associated problem in which people think they feel or hear their phone vibrate and check it expecting to find a message or a call—but the phone did not vibrate. Why might someone have these syndromes? What does this indicate?

READING ONE | Smartphone-Induced Problems in the Twenty-First Century

VOCABULARY

Reading One is an article about smartphone dependency. Read the letter a woman wrote to an advice columnist about her husband's phone usage. Choose the correct definition for each boldfaced word or phrase.

1. a. aversion
   b. strong need or impulse
   c. understanding

2. a. normal
   b. boring
   c. uncontrollable

3. a. fix
   b. make something happen
   c. stop

4. a. strong desire
   b. message
   c. distraction

5. a. happy
   b. aware
   c. unclear

6. a. taking money from a bank
   b. bad feelings when you stop doing something
   c. learning

7. a. decision
   b. reliance
   c. technology

8. a. inability to work normally
   b. disease
   c. mood

ASK HELPFUL HANNAH

Dear Helpful Hannah,

I've got a problem with my husband, Sam. On a recent ski vacation to Colorado, I realized that his relationship with his phone might be unhealthy. He has a constant **(1) urge** to check for messages; he checks his phone every five minutes! He's absolutely **(2) compulsive** about it. He can't stop checking even at inappropriate times, like when we are eating in a restaurant and I am talking to him! It is almost as if being bored for even the shortest amount of time can **(3) trigger** a need for him to check his phone, even when he knows he shouldn't. The **(4) temptation** to see who is contacting him is just too great. When I ask him to please put down the phone and stop ignoring me, he says, "In a minute," but still checks to see if there is an important text or if someone has posted something new on social media. I don't think he is even **(5) conscious** that he is being rude! If we go somewhere and I ask him to leave the phone at home, he suffers from **(6) withdrawal** symptoms. I just keep thinking that maybe this **(7) dependency** on his phone has become more than an everyday problem.

I recently read an article about "nomophobia." It's a real illness people can suffer from: the fear of being without your phone! I am worried that Sam may be suffering from this type of **(8) dysfunctional** behavior. Why? Because he experiences a great deal of **(9) anxiety** if he doesn't have his phone with him, even for a short time. It is so bad that he sometimes brings it into the bathroom with him.

9. a. worry

   b. relaxation

   c. experience

10. a. benefit from

    b. learn to use better

    c. gradually stop doing

11. a. increasing

    b. decreasing

    c. finishing

12. a. tools or machines

    b. plans

    c. methods

While we were in Colorado, we talked a little about his "problem," and he agreed to try to slowly (10) **wean** himself **away from** the phone. But, so far, I don't think the amount of time he spends using his phone each day is really (11) **diminishing**. He's got to do something, or I am going to throw his phone away while he is sleeping!

Who would have thought that little (12) **devices** like these could be such a blessing and yet such a curse!

— *Sick and Tired Sadie*

Go to the **Pearson Practice English App** or **MyEnglishLab** for more vocabulary practice.

PREVIEW

You are going to read an article about smartphone addiction from a journal on technology and society. Answer the questions and keep your ideas in mind as you read the article.

1. What behaviors have you noticed about people and their smartphones?

2. Why do people enjoy their smartphones so much?

3. Are there any negative consequences of owning a smartphone? Explain.

READ

Read Dr. Kelly Sanabria's article on the next page. Create a chart like the one below to take notes.

TAKE NOTES

Main Ideas	Details
Smartphone (SP) use more widespread than ever	Considered necessity by many for: • online banking • photos • health • all areas of life

Go to **MyEnglishLab** to view example notes.

Smartphone-Induced Problems in the Twenty-First Century

Dr. Kelly Sanabria

1   Smartphones are now more widespread than ever, and our reliance on them shows no sign of **diminishing**. The days when these **devices** were considered mere accessories are a distant memory. Instead, for most people smartphones are necessities, and we depend on them for many everyday tasks: online banking, photography, health, you name it. In the words of consumer products analyst Mohammed Alzarie, "There is scarcely a single area of existence that has not been affected by the rise of this technology. And the more sophisticated smartphones become, the harder it is to imagine our lives without them."

2   What effect do smartphones have on society? Should we be worried about smartphone addiction? This debate is far from new, but in 2018 it was rekindled[1] in an astonishing way. Jen Adams Beason, an elementary school teacher in the United States, had asked her students a simple question: what invention do you wish had never been created? In response to this seemingly simple prompt, nearly twenty percent of Ms. Beason's class described their dislike of smartphones. One student's work was especially unsettling. "I hate my mom's phone and I wish she never had one," the child wrote.

3   Appalled by her students' perceptions, Ms. Beason turned to social media. She wrote a post urging parents to spend less time on their phones and to pay more attention to their kids. She included a drawing from one of her students, which featured a smiling phone alongside an enormous sad face. People around the world were alarmed by the students' perspective. Within a week, her post was shared nearly 300,000 times, and even garnered[2] the attention of international news media. Thanks to Ms. Beason's students, a heartfelt discussion about smartphone use was once again on the table.

4   Researchers Brandon T. McDaniel and Jenny Radesky coined the term "technoference" to describe the phenomenon that Ms. Beason had observed. In the journal Child Development, they argued that, "Heavy parent digital technology use has been associated with suboptimal[3] parent-child interactions." Another educator, Abbey Fauntleroy, heard from all of her students that their parents spent more time on social media than they did talking to them.

5   Child psychologist Amelia Deering was dismayed by the experiences of Ms. Beason and Ms. Fauntleroy. However, she was not surprised. "In recent years I have observed **compulsive** smartphone use in dozens of families," she said. "Most often, the desire to access social media is what **triggers** this worrying behavior." Ms. Deering's colleague, John Peat, PhD., was also troubled. He said, "There are parents who are able to balance their responsibilities to their children with their use of technology." However, he went on to make the point that, "Ms. Beason's assignment has cast a harsh light on childrearing in the digital age."

---

[1] **rekindled:** started again, reawakened
[2] **garnered:** got, gained
[3] **suboptimal:** less than optimal, not the best possible

continued on next page

6 Even apart from this context, it is hard to argue with the notion that smartphones seem to control our lives. A Harvard Business School study found that 70 percent of managers check their smartphones within an hour of getting up, while 56 percent do so less than one hour before going to sleep. Even more astonishingly, 51 percent of these professionals look at their smartphones continually while they are on vacation. Still, Ms. Beason's experience demonstrated the true power of this technology. In most cultures the bonds that exist between family members are considered some of the strongest that people are capable of making. These ties also constitute the basic building blocks of society. This brings up an important question that we all need to address: if a pocket-sized device is capable of undermining these relationships, should people be concerned about other effects of this technology?

"US adults spend an estimated 4 hours and 15 minutes on their phones each day..."

7 A large body of evidence suggests that we should indeed be worried. Many researchers are reluctant to use the term "addiction" when speaking about smartphones—this word, after all, has a strict clinical definition—but there is widespread consensus that **dependency** is an issue. Most people could easily think of times when the **urge** was so strong that they used their smartphones even though, at that moment, it was inappropriate to do so. "The **temptation** to check one's phone is often just too much to resist," says Professor Erin Morrow of the University of Oregon. "The fact that many people use them while driving, even to surf the web and text, suggests, in my view, that phones are deemed more valuable than personal safety. By doing so, these people are endangering not only themselves but others, as well. Frankly, I see the topic as a mental health issue."

8 The concept of smartphone dependency is backed up by data. US adults spend an estimated 4 hours and 15 minutes on their phones each day, while in the UK adults spend an average of 65.3 hours per month using this technology. Similar trends have been observed in other countries. The phenomenon of "phantom vibration syndrome" is further evidence of dependency. The condition, in which people think that their phones are ringing even when they are not, may affect up to 90 percent of people. While not necessarily dangerous, this does suggest that our phones hold tremendous power over our brains, as thoughts about them always seem to be present in our minds.

9 A survey by the organization YouGov supports this information. YouGov determined that over half of the adult population experiences feelings of **anxiety** when they cannot access their phones. An even larger proportion of people become stressed, show **withdrawal** symptoms, such as anger, frustration, or the inability to concentrate, or display otherwise **dysfunctional** behavior. YouGov came up with the name "nomophobia," short for "no-mobile-phone *phobia*," to describe the negative emotions that being without smartphones can provoke.

10 A related concept is that of "absent presence." Lisa Kleinman, a researcher at the University of Texas, developed this term to describe how smartphones prompt people to exit real-world social situations in favor of virtual ones. Checking your phone while you are out with friends, on a date, in a meeting, or while someone is speaking directly to you are all examples of this problem. Dr. Kleinman asks, "How can we effectively communicate with those physically around us, when either by our own volition[4] we begin to use technology or, we disengage unexpectedly?" Her research further supports the idea, so heartbreakingly observed by Ms. Beason, Ms. Fauntleroy, and others, that—at least in part as a result of technology—the bonds which unite our communities are breaking down.

---

[4] **volition:** choice, decision

continued on next page

11 Worldwide, roughly two-thirds of people own a mobile phone. Most of these mobile phones are smartphones. Both mobile phone ownership and smartphone use specifically are projected to continue increasing. By some estimates, there may be 5 billion active phone users within the next decade. In light of these numbers, it is likely that smartphone-related problems will become even more commonplace. **Weaning** ourselves **away from** this technology is clearly something many people need to consider. How can we begin to do this?

12 One way to reduce phone use is to simply buy an alarm clock. Research suggests that in some countries, more than two-thirds of people rely on their phones to wake them up in the morning. This practice has been linked to issues such as restless sleep and insomnia, because it is hard for people to resist checking their phones throughout the night. Buying an alarm clock enables people to leave their phones in a different room, which in turn helps to achieve peaceful, uninterrupted sleep.

13 Another common strategy is to download a tracking app to monitor the number of times you check your phone within a given period. The average person checks his or her phone nearly fifty times per day, although for younger people, that figure rises to more than seventy. From these numbers, it is clear that smartphones represent a constant interruption of our daily routines. By using a tracking app, people can see exactly how much time they spend on their phones, which is usually much more than they realize. By learning this number, users can more easily set goals and track progress to reduce their phone use.

14 Removing potentially distracting apps from your home screen is also a method you may want to try. That way, you won't be tempted to quickly jump from one app to another. Better still is to put these apps into a folder on your second page. Another technique is to turn off as many alerts and notifications as possible. This will reduce the number of times that your smartphones dings, thereby reducing your urge to check it.

15 A final tactic is to simply turn your phone off. If you are eating a meal with friends or family, consider turning your phone off before the meal begins so you can give your companions your full attention. This requires discipline, and you will have to be strict about not using your phone in situations where you do not truly need it. However, you will likely become conscious of the situations and emotions that make you want to check your device. You might realize that you fall back on your smartphone when you feel bored or insecure. This awareness will change the way you think about your phone. Every time you pick it up, you should be making a **conscious** decision to do so. You should not be using your phone simply out of habit.

> **"...more than two-thirds of people rely on their phones to wake them up in the morning."**

16 If we take these steps, future generations will have the chance to look back on the early twenty-first century and feel grateful. Communities will enjoy greater quality of life and will no longer suffer from "technoference," "phantom vibration syndrome," and "nomophobia." Individual smartphone users will benefit from reduced anxiety and stress, and harmful withdrawal symptoms will be long forgotten. And most important of all, situations like those that arose in Ms. Beason and Ms. Fauntleroy's classrooms will be a thing of the past.

17 A world where we continue to choose technology over meaningful interpersonal communication is not a viable option. In order to achieve the more desirable of these visions, we have to understand that the choice is ours, and ours alone, to make.

MAIN IDEAS

Check the four statements that represent the main ideas of Reading One.

☐ 1. People use smartphones while driving despite the danger it may cause.

☐ 2. The urge to access social media can trigger compulsive smartphone use.

☐ 3. Smartphones have negative effects for society.

☐ 4. There are a number of ways to reduce smartphone use.

☐ 5. "Nomophobia" and "phantom vibration syndrome" are serious problems.

☐ 6. People use smartphones for online banking and taking photos.

☐ 7. Smartphone use is widespread and considered a necessity by many people.

☐ 8. Parents don't pay attention to kids because of smartphones.

☐ 9. There are many symptoms of smartphone dependency.

☐ 10. Many researchers are reluctant to use the term "addiction" when speaking about smartphone use.

DETAILS

1 Choose the two correct answers to complete each statement.

1. Ms. Beason's post on social media

   a. was shared nearly 300,000 times.

   b. was ignored by the international news media.

   c. included a drawing by one of her students.

2. In discussions about Ms. Beason's post,

   a. parents promised to change their behavior so their children would be happier.

   b. it became apparent that many other teachers had noticed this problem.

   c. one teacher noted that all her students said their parents spend more time on social media than with them.

3. A Harvard Business School study of managers' smartphone use found

   a. 51 percent continuously check their phone even when on vacation.

   b. 70 percent check their phone within an hour of getting up.

   c. 56 percent get one hour less sleep a night because of their phone.

4. When discussing smartphone use, researchers

   a. feel it is acceptable to use your phone for emergencies while driving.

   b. generally agree that dependency is a serious issue.

   c. are hesitant to use the word "addiction" to describe smartphone use.

5. Smartphone dependency is backed up by data such as

    a. in the United Kingdom, adults spend more than two hours a day on their phone.

    b. many people use their phone while driving, which is unsafe.

    c. in the United States, adults spend more than four hours a day on their phone.

6. A YouGov survey also indicates smartphone dependency. It found more than half of the adult population

    a. feel anxiety when they can't access their phone.

    b. exhibit dysfunctional behavior if they don't have their phone.

    c. exhibit withdrawal symptoms after one hour without their phone

7. Lisa Kleinman's term "absent presence" refers to checking your smartphone in inappropriate situations such as when you are

    a. worried about your children.

    b. on a date.

    c. in a meeting.

8. The reading discusses a number of strategies for reducing smartphone use; for example,

    a. buying an alarm clock.

    b. leaving your phone at home when you go out.

    c. removing distracting apps from your home screen.

9. Further strategies discussed in the reading include

    a. using a tracking app to monitor the number of times you use your smartphone.

    b. turning off notifications.

    c. turning down the brightness of the phone, making it less inviting to use.

10. According to the reading reducing smartphone use will

    a. lower your monthly phone bill.

    b. reduce anxiety and stress.

    c. help you stop suffering from "nomophobia," "absent presence," and "technoference."

2 **Look at your notes and at your answers in Preview. How did they help you understand the article?**

MAKE INFERENCES 🔍

Inferring an Author's Appeal to Authority

To help make their ideas more believable, authors often refer to experts who support their point of view. Experts add importance and validity to the author's position. The author may quote an expert directly or either paraphrase or summarize the expert's ideas. Statistics provide further factual information that helps support an author's point of view.

Look at the example and read the explanation.

In Reading One, Dr. Sanabria uses statistics and quotations from many experts that support her ideas about smartphones.

Look at paragraph 1. In paragraph 1, she includes a quotation from consumer products analyst Mohammed Alzarie. Why does Sanabria do this? What idea is she trying to support?

> Smartphones are now more widespread than ever, and our reliance on them shows no sign of diminishing. The days when these devices were considered mere accessories are a distant memory. Instead, for most people smartphones are necessities, and we depend on them for many everyday tasks: online banking, photography, health, you name it. In the words of consumer products analyst Mohammed Alzarie, <u>"There is scarcely a single area of existence that has not been affected by the rise of this technology. And the more sophisticated smartphones become, the harder it is to imagine our lives without them."</u>

The quotation strengthens Sanabria's argument by supporting her idea that smartphone use is widespread and smartphones can now be considered a necessity. She shares the quotation in order to show us that she is not alone in her thinking and that other professionals also feel the same way.

1 **Read the excerpts containing statistics and quotes from experts. For each excerpt, write Sanabria's opinion that is supported by the quote or statistics and how the information strengthens Sanabria's argument.**

    1. A Harvard Business School study (*paragraph 6*):

    Even separate and apart from this context, it is hard to argue with the notion that smartphones seem to control our lives. A Harvard Business School study found that 70 percent of managers check their smartphones within an hour of getting up, while 56 percent do so less than one hour before going to sleep. Even more astonishingly, 51 percent of these professionals look at their smartphones continually while they are on vacation.

    Sanabria's opinion that is supported by the underlined statistics: _____

    _____

    How the statistics strengthen Sanabria's argument: _____

    _____

2. Professor Erin Morrow of the University of Oregon (*paragraph 7*):

A large body of evidence suggests that we should indeed be worried. Many researchers are reluctant to use the term "addiction" when speaking about smartphones—this word, after all, has a strict clinical definition—but there is widespread consensus that dependency is an issue. Most people could easily think of times when the urge was so strong that they used their smartphones even though, at that moment, it was inappropriate to do so. "The temptation to check one's phone is often just too much to resist," says Professor Erin Morrow of the University of Oregon. "The fact that many people use them while driving, even to surf the web and text, suggests, in my view, that phones are deemed more valuable than personal safety. By doing so, these people are endangering not only themselves but others, as well. Frankly, I see the topic as a mental health issue."

Sanabria's opinion that is supported by the quote: _____

_____

How the quote strengthens Sanabria's argument: _____

_____

3. YouGov (*paragraphs 8–9*):

While not necessarily dangerous, ["phantom vibration syndrome"] does suggest that our phones hold tremendous power over our brains, as thoughts of them always seem to be present in our minds.

A survey by the organization YouGov supports this information. YouGov determined that over half of the adult population experiences feelings of anxiety when they cannot access their phones. An even larger proportion of people become stressed, show withdrawal symptoms, such as anger, frustration, or the inability to concentrate, or display otherwise dysfunctional behavior. YouGov came up with the name "nomophobia," short for "no-mobile-phone phobia," to describe the negative emotions that being without smartphones can provoke.

Sanabria's opinion that is supported by the information: _____

_____

How the information strengthens Sanabria's argument: _____

_____

4. Researchers Brandon T. McDaniel and Jenny Radesky (*paragraphs 2 and 4*):

What effect do smartphones have on society? Should we be worried about smartphone addiction? This debate is far from new, but in 2018 it was rekindled in an astonishing way. . . .

Researchers Brandon T. McDaniel and Jenny Radesky coined the term "technoference" to describe the phenomenon that Ms. Beason had observed. In the journal *Child Development*, they argued that, "Heavy parent digital technology use has been associated with suboptimal parent-child interactions." Another educator, Abbey Fauntleroy, heard from all of her students that their parents spent more time on social media than they did talking to them.

Sanabria's opinion that is supported by the quote: _____

_____

How the quote strengthens Sanabria's argument: _____

_____

Work in a small group. Choose one of the questions. Discuss your ideas. Then choose one person in your group to report the ideas to the class.

USE YOUR NOTES

Use your notes to support your answers with information from the reading.

1. Which behaviors mentioned in the text have you observed in day-to-day life? How do they affect the social environment?

2. Dr. Sanabria gives advice for overcoming smartphone dependency. Do you think people can easily follow this advice? Why or why not?

▶ Go to **MyEnglishLab** to give your opinion about another question.

READING TWO | Unplugging Wired Kids: A Vacation from Technology and Social Media

PREVIEW

1 Look at the title of the reading and the picture. Write two questions that you think will be answered in this reading.

_____

_____

2 Look at the boldfaced words in the reading. Which words or phrases do you know the meanings of?

READ

1 Read the blog post about a technology-free vacation. As you read, guess the meanings of the words that are new to you. Remember to take notes on main ideas and details.

Unplugging Wired Kids:
A Vacation from Technology and Social Media
The Momoir Project

my summer vacation

1 It's day one of our vacation on Cortes, a remote island in the BC wilderness[1] and my son is **literally** lying on the couch of our rustic[2] A-frame moaning, "iPhone. iPhone. iPhone." In front of him is a wall of windows facing a glistening ocean and coming in from the open deck doors—a warm, beautiful breeze. Clearly, he sees and feels none of it. He's too deep in his electronics withdrawal.

---

[1] **wilderness:** a large natural area of land that has never been farmed or built on
[2] **rustic:** simple and old-fashioned in a way that is attractive and typical of the countryside

continued on next page

2 Back at home in Vancouver, after five minutes of listening to this kind of groveling, I'd normally **relent**. Instead of screaming "Shut up," I'd hand it over in defeat. He'd win.

3 Not here. We came here to get away from it all—our lives, technology, the constant pull of email, Facebook, video games, and the never-ending ping of the iPhone.

4 Before we left, I told my ten-year-old son the rules: We were all going electronic-free for a week. There could be a few movies on the odd[3] night, but no TV, no video games, no email. And here we are on day one and already, he can't stand it.

5 My six-year-old daughter and my husband are doing just fine. They are outside on the deck carving pieces of driftwood and singing. Meanwhile, my son is inside blinded to the opportunities in front of him, complaining that he doesn't like the beach.

6 Confounded, I walk outside to let him suffer. I walk down the grassy pathway to the beach. It's so stunning, I can barely manage to read on my blanket. I just want to stare out at the islands and the glistening ocean. The eagles soar overhead. The seals pop their heads out of the water, and there isn't another soul in sight. My son can do whatever he wants. But he's not going to ruin the quiet and beauty of this trip for me.

7 Day two. We spend the entire morning, and part of the afternoon, digging for clams and oysters and swimming in the lagoon. My son is one with his shovel, looking for the smallest clams and filling buckets with shellfish and other sea treasures. When we get back to our cabin, I give my son his book, put him in the shade on a lovely garden swing and it's almost dinner when he looks up.

8 The next few days pass in a blur of sun and sand. My husband **ensures** we do something every day to get out of the cabin and explore. One day, we all spend an afternoon swimming at the freshwater lake. Another day, my husband takes my son on a three-hour hike around the headland.

9 On day six, he's lying beside me on the beach watching the sunset. We are wrapped together in a blanket and as I watch him play with the sand in his hands, the grains slipping through his fingers, I realize how much time has slowed down for both of us. It's exactly what I wanted. Finally, after just a few days, we are able to sit quietly without **twitching**, without thinking about screens, without the constant interruptions of phone calls and email. Two hours pass, and, in that time, he happily throws rocks into the water, listens to a man play guitar down the beach, plays Frisbee in the grassy field behind us.

10 He's too young to see it, but it's clear to me. A week away from our dependence on electronics and we've slowed right down. We are breathing deeper and, literally, noticing the grains of sand. Life is good. If only we could live on vacation.

11 How do you handle the **influx** of technology in your house? How do your kids handle it? Do you ever feel the need for a vacation from technology?

---

[3] **odd:** different from what is expected

2 **Compare your notes on main ideas and details with a partner's. How can you improve your notes next time?**

🔊 Go to the **Pearson Practice English App** or **MyEnglishLab** for more vocabulary practice.

Taking Three-Column Notes to Show Time Sequence

When you use three-column notes, you are identifying the main ideas and details in a text. Three-column notes can be used to show a variety of relationships, including time sequence. List dates / times in the first column and in the right columns next to each date / time write the activities / events / locations / feelings, etc. that took place. The labels on the second and third columns will vary depending on the story. This is a visual way to keep track of the sequence of events in a story.

In Reading Two, the author describes her week-long vacation with her family. She focuses on her son's transformation from phone "addiction" to his being able to relax without any technology. She describes his activities and feelings on a nearly day-by-day basis. In a three-column notes format, the first column would list the dates, the second column would list activities, and the third would list feelings.

How did her son feel and what was he doing on day one of the vacation?

He is frustrated because he does not have his phone. He is ignoring the beautiful surroundings.

Date / Time	Son's activities	Son's feelings
day one	lying on couch begging for his phone, ignoring his surroundings	frustrated

Complete the three-column notes showing the son's activities and feelings during his vacation. Compare your completed notes with a partner's.

Date / Time	Son's activities	Son's feelings
before the vacation		
day one	lying on couch begging for his phone, ignoring his surroundings	frustrated
day two		
the next few days		
day six		

➤ Go to **MyEnglishLab** for more note-taking practice.

COMPREHENSION

1 **Complete each statement. Use your notes from Reading Two to help you. Discuss your answers with a partner.**

1. At the beginning of the vacation, the author's son couldn't enjoy himself because _____

_____.

2. This vacation was unusual because _____

_____.

3. One way the husband helped break the dependence on electronics was _____

_____.

4. The result of a week away from electronics was _____

_____.

2 **Review the boldfaced words from the reading with a partner. Use a dictionary or ask your teacher for any meanings you still do not know.**

1 Go back to Reading Two. In the last sentence of paragraph 7, underline the pronouns *we,*
I, and *he.* To which person does each pronoun refer?

Identifying Referents for the Pronoun *It*

Pronouns usually clearly refer to a previously mentioned person or thing. In this excerpt from
paragraph 5, "My six-year-old daughter and my husband are doing just fine. **They** are outside on the
deck carving pieces of drift wood and singing," *they* clearly refers to "my daughter and my husband."

The referent for the pronoun *it* is sometimes not as clear. *It* may refer to an idea, not a concrete
person or thing.

In paragraph 1 the author writes:

> In front of him is a wall of windows facing a glistening ocean and coming in from the open
> deck doors—a warm, beautiful breeze. Clearly, he sees and feels none of **it**.

What does *it* refer to?

It = the beautiful environment: the glistening ocean and the beautiful weather.

At times, pronouns can also refer to information that follows the pronoun. In paragraph 3, the
author writes:

> We came here to get away from **it** all—our lives, technology, the constant pull of email,
> Facebook, video games, and the never-ending ping of the iPhone.

What does *it* refer to in this passage?

it = their everyday lives including all aspects of technology: email, social media, video games,
and phones.

2 Read the excerpts from Reading Two. Explain in your own words what the boldfaced
pronouns refer to.

1. "We were all going electronic-free for a week. There could be a few movies on the odd night,
   but no TV, no video games, no email. And here we are on day one and already, he can't stand
   it." (*paragraph 4*)

   Explanation: _____

   _____

2. "I realize how much time has slowed down for both of us. **It**'s exactly what I wanted."
   (*paragraph 9*)

   Explanation: _____

   _____

3. "He's too young to see **it**, but **it**'s clear to me. A week away from our dependence on
   electronics and we've slowed right down." (*paragraph 10*)

   Explanation: _____

   _____

Go to **MyEnglishLab** for more skill practice.

CONNECT THE READINGS 🔍

ORGANIZE

Reading One and Reading Two address the effects (problems) caused by our growing dependence on phones and other electronic devices. In Reading One, Dr. Sanabria includes the opinions of experts regarding dependency issues. In Reading Two, the writer uses her son as an example of somebody's experiencing the negative effects that overreliance on phones and other electronic devices may cause. Both readings offer solutions for how to manage phone dependency.

USE YOUR NOTES

Review your notes from Reading One and Two. Use the information in your notes to complete the chart.

Complete the graphic organizer by categorizing the items as either effects (problems) or solutions. Write the letters of the items in the graphic organizer below. According to the readings, each problem has specific solutions.

a. Compulsive phone checking

b. Don't let checking phone become a habit

c. ~~Download a tracking app~~

d. Turn off notifications and alerts

e. Spend less time on social media

f. Don't keep phone where you sleep

g. Move some apps off home page

h. ~~Go electronics free for a set period of time~~

i. ~~Buy an alarm clock~~

j. Don't use phone while driving

k. ~~Causing family breakdown~~

l. Make it a conscious decision to check your phone

m. ~~Turn phone off before meals~~

n. ~~Set goals to check your phone less each day~~

o. Restless sleep and insomnia

p. Keep busy with non-electronic activities

q. Put some apps in folders

r. Using phone at inappropriate times

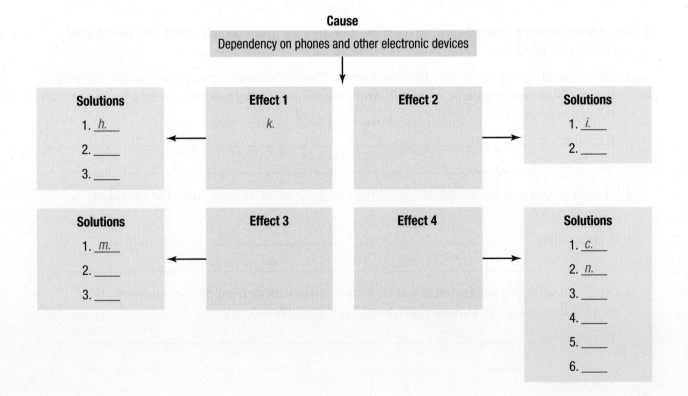

Cause

Dependency on phones and other electronic devices

Solutions	Effect 1	Effect 2	Solutions
1. _h._	k.		1. _i._
2. ____			2. ____
3. ____			

Solutions	Effect 3	Effect 4	Solutions
1. _m._			1. _c._
2. ____			2. _n._
3. ____			3. ____
			4. ____
			5. ____
			6. ____

SYNTHESIZE

Go back to page 208 and reread Sick and Tired Sadie's letter describing her husband's smartphone dependency. Using information from Organize, complete the advice columnist's response to Sadie explaining the effects of his dependency and how she can help her husband manage it. Decide whether the blanks are an effect (problem) or a solution. Then complete the letter using the effects and solutions you identified in Organize.

Dear Sick and Tired Sadie,

    I applaud you for recognizing that your husband has a problem. The cause of your husband's problem is smartphone dependency, and he certainly is not alone.

    Smartphone addiction causes a variety of problems such as _____, insomnia, _____, and compulsive phone checking, to name a few. Fortunately, there are strategies that he can use to counteract the negative effects of his smartphone.

    First of all, if he has restless sleep or _____, you could tell him to _____ _____. In fact, he should also _____ _____.

    Another effect of smartphone addiction is the urge to compulsively check one's phone. One reason for this might be that he feels constantly distracted by the apps on his phone. If this is the case, there a few things he could do. First, _____ _____ _____. He could also _____ _____.

    Nevertheless, apps can also be useful for solving this problem. If you feel that he is checking his phone too often, there are other steps he can take to alleviate this problem. For example, _____ _____.

    By using this kind of app, he could see exactly how much time he spends with his phone and set goals to diminish his use.

    You might also want to suggest he turn off _____ as this will reduce the number of times his phone dings so he won't feel the urge to check it as often.

    Lisa Kleinman has identified a concept known as "absent presence," which refers to smartphone users favoring the virtual world over real-life social situations. In other words, using the phone _____. To avoid this problem, when your husband is with friends, _____.

He needs to become aware of when and how often he uses his phone. Each time he uses his phone, it should be a _____ and not just something he does out of habit or boredom.

    If your husband is able to implement these strategies, he (and you) will see a big change. The effects will be that he will feel more relaxed and his relationship with friends, family, and co-workers may also improve. I hope this advice helps, and I wish you and your husband good luck overcoming this problem.

– Helpful Hannah

◆ Go to MyEnglishLab to check what you learned.

Managing Your Smartphone   **223**

VOCABULARY

REVIEW

Complete the sentences with the words in the boxes.

diminish	relent	trigger	wean (someone) away from

1. For some people, boredom often can _____ the need to check their phone to see if they have new email or news updates.

2. I am worried that the time my daughter spends on her phone will _____ her interest in sports.

3. Although it is difficult, these employees report that they have been able to slowly _____ themselves _____ using their phones compulsively.

4. Despite the fact that I did not believe my son needed a smartphone, his constant begging for one caused me to _____ and buy him one.

anxiety	dependency	devices	twitching	urge

5. For many students, sitting in class for too long can trigger a very strong _____ to check their phone as soon as class is over.

6. In the past, people kept connected through their computers, but most people now use other _____ , such as tablets and smartphones, to stay in touch at all times.

7. Many people say they would experience "a great deal of _____" if they lost their phone and couldn't replace it for a week.

8. Scientists are studying whether smartphone _____ can really be considered an addiction.

9. Some signs of heavy smartphone usage can be mental—loss of concentration, inability to focus on your surroundings—and others can be physical, such as _____ and headaches from eyestrain.

compulsive	conscious	dysfunctional	influx	literally	temptation

10. Although extreme smartphone usage may not actually be an addiction, it results in a lot of _____ behavior, some of which may cause long-term damage.

11. In order to cut down on your phone dependency, you need to be able to resist the _____ to constantly check it for updates and e-mail.

12. You might not be _____ of it, but your constant phone checking behavior affects your concentration at school and work.

13. In the case of an emergency, having a phone can _____ save your life.

14. _____ use of electronic devices can lead to physical ailments, such as tendonitis, carpal tunnel syndrome, and eye strain.

15. The constant _____ of new information is one of the reasons that people compulsively check their phones.

EXPAND

Look at the boldfaced words and phrases. They have similar meanings but different degrees of intensity. Circle the word or phrase in each sentence that has a *stronger* meaning.

1. Many people feel the **urge / compulsion** to check their phones up to thirty-five times a day.

2. When I misplace my phone, I **search / look** for it until I find it.

3. His phone usage could be considered a(n) **addiction / dependency**.

4. For some people, being in class can **cause / trigger** a need to check their phone for news updates.

5. Because my wife is constantly checking her phone, I feel as if she is **ignoring me / not listening to me**.

6. Last night during dinner, my brother was **repeatedly / frequently** checking his email on his phone.

7. My sister was on the phone so much on our vacation, that I felt she was **blinded to / not aware of** how beautiful our surroundings were.

8. After I expressed my concerns to her, she made a **commitment / decision** to wean herself away from her phone.

9. The smartphone, more than any other gadget, **steals / takes** from us the opportunity to maintain our attention.

10. Because my phone is constantly dinging with alerts and notifications, it is hard for me to engage in **thought / contemplation** and reflection.

11. I **dislike / can't stand** when people interrupt a conversation to answer their phone.

12. If you know you are not strong enough to resist the temptation of constantly checking your email, you should probably **shun / avoid** people who constantly text you.

CREATE

APPLY **Answer the questions as the people listed. Use the words given. Change the word form if necessary.**

1.	compulsion	influx	trigger	urge

To a manager in the study by Harvard Business School (Reading One):

Why are you constantly checking your phone from the moment you wake up until you go to bed, even when you are on vacation?

_____

_____

_____

2.	ensure	conscious	diminishing	wean away from

To the parent of the student in Ms. Beason's class who hates her mom's phone (Reading One):

How are you trying to manage your phone usage, and what effect is it having on your child and your life?

_____

_____

_____

3.	dependency	dysfunction	temptation	withdrawal

To Professor Erin Morrow of University of Oregon (Reading One):

Do you consider extreme smartphone usage a true addiction? Explain.

_____

_____

_____

4.	anxiety	urge	dependency	diminishing	ensure

To child psychologist Amelia Deering (Reading One):

Why do you think it is important for parents to try to wean themselves away from excessive smartphone use?

_____

_____

_____

5.	can't stand	device	relent	repeatedly	twitching

To the ten-year-old boy who went electronics-free for a week (Reading Two):

At the start of the week, what did you think of your mother's idea of going without electronics? How did the way you felt change as the week progressed?

_____

_____

_____

🖱 Go to the **Pearson Practice English App** or **MyEnglishLab** for more vocabulary practice.

GRAMMAR FOR WRITING

1 Read the sentences and answer the questions.

a. <u>Because you can receive a continuous stream of messages and alerts on a smartphone</u>, you are able to stay up-to-date on news anytime and anyplace.

b. My son couldn't enjoy the natural beauty all around him <u>due to the fact that he was suffering from electronics withdrawal.</u>

c. <u>As a consequence of texting while driving</u>, police are seeing an increase in accidents.

1. How many clauses are there in each sentence?

2. Are the underlined clauses of each sentence introducing a cause or an effect?

3. How is the punctuation different in sentence *b* from sentences *a* and *c*?

Subordinators and Prepositional Phrases That Express Cause

1. Certain words act as signals to show cause-and-effect relationships. Sentences describing a cause-and-effect relationship have two clauses. The **cause clause** explains why something happened. The **effect clause** explains the result of what happened.

Cause: Because more and more people have smartphones today,

Effect: people have more and more interruptions in their lives.

2. Subordinators and prepositional phrases show the relationship between the two clauses. They introduce the cause.

Introducing the Cause	
SUBORDINATORS	**PREPOSITIONAL PHRASES**
since	due to the fact that + (clause)
because	because of the fact that + (clause)
as	due to + (noun)
	because of + (noun)
	as a consequence of + (noun)
	as a result of + (noun)

continued on next page

3. **Punctuation When Stating Causes with Subordinators and Prepositional Phrases**

- The **cause clause** is introduced by *because, since, as, due to the fact that* or *because of the fact that*. When the cause is at the beginning of the sentence, use a comma at the end of that clause.

Because you can receive a continuous stream of messages and alerts on a smartphone, you are able to stay up-to-date on news anytime and anyplace.

- When the cause is at the end of the sentence, do not use a comma.

You are able to stay up-to-date on news anytime and anyplace **because you can receive a continuous stream of messages and alerts on a smartphone**.

4. **Prepositional Phrases**

Due to the fact that and *because of the fact that* are followed by a clause (subject + verb)	*Due to, because of, as a consequence of,* and *as a result of* are followed by a noun or a noun phrase

Due to the fact that <u>many people</u> <u>are using</u>
             subject   verb
 their smartphones while they are driving, there
 	
 has been an increase in automobile accidents.
	Due to <u>smartphone usage while driving</u>,
	              noun phrase
	 there has been an increase in automobile
	
	 accidents.

2 **Complete the paragraphs using subordinators and prepositional phrases of cause-and-effect.**

People using a phone while driving has become more and more of a problem.

_____ many drivers can't stop texting even when driving, more accidents are
     1.

occurring. Drivers are a lot more careless than in the past _____ their phone
                                                     2.

usage. Using your phone while driving can also lead to fines or even losing your license

_____ it is illegal in many states and countries. Recent studies have shown that
     3.

talking on the phone while driving reduces brain activity by 37 percent. It's no wonder there

have been more accidents _____ this reduced brain activity.
                                      4.

Pedestrians using their phones can also have and cause problems. People who are texting

while they walk take almost two seconds longer to cross at an intersection. _____
                                                                           5.

this increased time in the crosswalk, they are more likely to be hit, especially by distracted

drivers. When using a phone, pedestrians are also four times more likely to ignore traffic signals.

_____ pedestrians are not paying attention, drivers must be extra careful.
     6.

3 Write *C* (cause) or *E* (effect) for each set of sentences. Then combine the sentences. Be sure to use commas correctly.

1. _C_ My brothers are constantly checking their phones.

   _E_ They often tune me out when I am speaking to them.

   (due to the fact) _Due to the fact that my brothers are constantly checking their phones, they_

   often tune me out when I am speaking to them.

2. ____ Many people choose to buy a smartphone instead of a laptop.

   ____ Smartphones are small, relatively cheap, and easy to use.

   (since) _____

   _____

3. ____ Over 50 percent of people check their phone continuously during vacation.

   ____ Vacations may not be as relaxing as in the past.

   (Because of the fact that) _____

   _____

4. ____ I feel very anxious and disconnected from the world.

   ____ My phone has been broken for a week.

   (as) _____

   _____

5. ____ Smartphones constantly interrupt and distract people.

   ____ It can take longer to do simple tasks.

   (because) _____

   _____

6. ____ Using a phone in during an exam is prohibited.

   ____ You will receive a failing grade if you do.

   (as a consequence of) _____

   _____

7. ____ Rehabilitation facilities are now available to treat this problem.

   ____ Nomophobia, the fear of being without your mobile device, is now recognized as a serious problem.

   (due to) _____

   _____

8. ____ Some college students spend more time on their phones than in class and studying.

   ____ They are getting lower grades and retaining less information.

   (due to the fact that) _____

   _____

➤ Go to the **Pearson Practice English App** or **MyEnglishLab** for more grammar practice. Check what you learned in **MyEnglishLab**.

In this unit, you read about the negative consequences of smartphone dependency, as well as the positive consequences of managing smartphone use.

You are going to *write a cause-and-effect essay focusing on the effects that another popular technology—such as tablets, e-readers, MP3 players, or GPS—has had on its users and on society.*

For an alternative writing topic, see page 239.

PREPARE TO WRITE: Using a Flowchart

A **flowchart** shows how a series of actions, events, or parts of a system are related. A flowchart is especially useful when mapping out a series of causes and effects. Look at the flowchart showing the effects of smartphones. Which effects are positive? Which are negative? Some of the effects cause another effect and, in some cases, a further effect, like a chain.

1 In your opinion, are these effects positive, negative, or both? Mark each box with (+), (–), or (+ –). Then discuss with a partner. Did you agree?

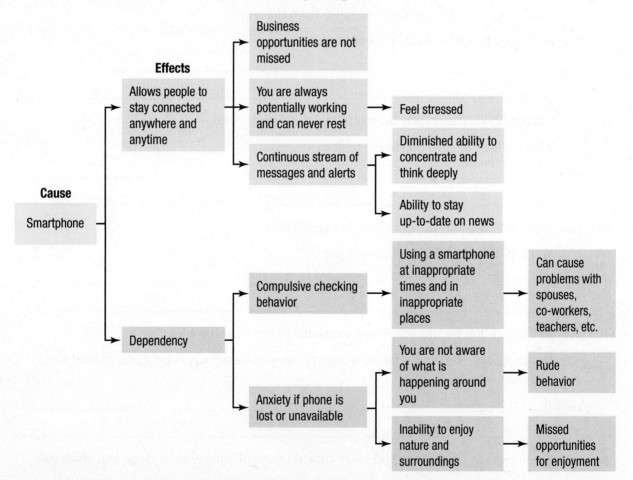

2 Describe a solution for any negative effects that you have identified in the above flowchart.

3 Create a flowchart of the effects of a technology you would like to discuss in your essay. Mark the effects as positive, negative, or both. For any negative effects that you have identified in your flowchart, suggest a solution.

WRITE

Writing a Cause-and-Effect Essay

A **cause-and-effect essay** discusses the causes (reasons) for something and the effects (results). There are many ways to organize causes and effects and show how they are related. A cause may have only one effect or multiple effects.

A **simple** cause and effect:

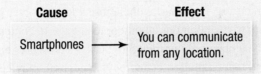

One cause with **multiple effects**:

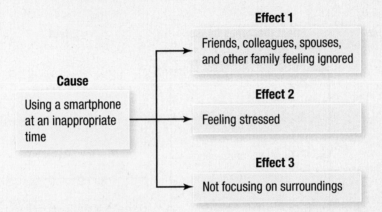

A cause leads to an effect, which in turn can become a cause for a new effect. This is called a **causal chain**.

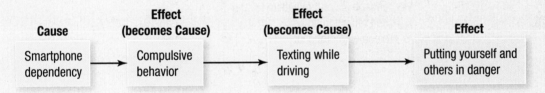

If your essay has a causal chain, describe all steps of the chain so the reader can fully understand how the causes and effects relate. Do not jump directly from the initial cause to the final effect.

Incorrect

Because of smartphone dependency, you are putting yourself and others in danger.

Correct

Smartphone dependency may lead to compulsive behavior. This behavior may include using your smartphone at inappropriate times. For example, some people feel compelled to text all the time, even when driving. This behavior may put you and others in danger.

1 Read the excerpt from an article about some of the effects smartphones are having on society. Then complete the cause-and-effect chart.

People keep their smartphones near them "from the moment they wake up until the moment they go to bed," and throughout that time the devices provide an almost continuous stream of messages and alerts, as well as easy access to myriad compelling information sources.

"By design," [author Nicholas Carr] says, "it's an environment of almost constant interruptions and distractions. The smartphone, more than any other gadget, steals from us the opportunity to maintain our attention, to engage in contemplation and reflection, or even to be alone with our thoughts." Carr, who writes extensively in *The Shallows* about the way that computer technology, in general, may be diminishing our ability to concentrate and think deeply, does not have a smartphone.

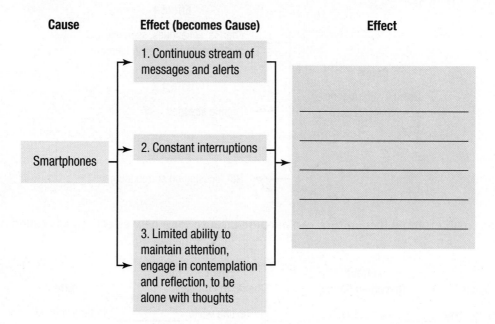

2 Answer the questions with a partner.

1. Look at the flowchart from Prepare to Write, Exercise 1, on page 230. What are some examples of multiple effects of the technology that you chose?

2. Can you find an example of a causal chain within the flowchart?

3. Look at your flowchart from Prepare to Write, Exercise 3, on page 230. Are there examples of multiple effects and causal chains? Look at a partner's flowchart. Can you find examples of multiple effects and causal chains?

3 An outline can help you to organize a cause-and-effect essay. Look at the outline of paragraphs 1–8 in Reading Two. Note that the author sometimes introduces a cause first and then writes about the effect. At other times, the author starts with the effect and then states the cause. In addition, a cause can have multiple effects.

CAUSE	I. Writer wants her family to enjoy an electronic-free vacation.
EFFECT	A. They go to a remote island in the wilderness of British Columbia, Canada.
CAUSE	1. Writer's son is suffering smartphone withdrawal.
EFFECT	a. Son cannot enjoy the beauty of their surroundings.
CAUSE	2. Husband and daughter are doing fine because they have found things to do that don't rely on electronics.
EFFECT	a. They are suffering no withdrawal symptoms.
CAUSE	3. Time passes.
EFFECT (BECOMES CAUSE)	a. Son seems to have forgotten about smartphone.
MULTIPLE EFFECTS (1–3)	1. He spends an enjoyable day at the beach. 2. He reads in the garden. 3. He stays active swimming and hiking.

4 Complete the cause-and-effect outline for Reading One (paragraphs 12–17). Use the information in the box.

> download a tracking app to monitor phone use
>
> choose people over devices
>
> reduced anxiety and stress
>
> situations like those the teachers found are a thing of the past
>
> blogs give advice on reducing technology use
>
> communities will enjoy greater quality of life
>
> harmful withdrawal symptoms are gone
>
> all of our lives will be better
>
> remove apps from your home screen

CAUSE
    I. Dr. Sanabria wants to explore ways to wean ourselves from technology.

EFFECT
(BECOMES CAUSE)
       A. _____

MULTIPLE EFFECTS
(1–3)
          1. buy an alarm clock

          2. _____

          3. _____

MULTIPLE CAUSES
(A–E)
    II. By taking steps now, we will help future generations.

       A. _____

       B. no more "technoference", "phantom vibration syndrome," and "nomophobia"

       C. _____

       D. _____

       E. _____

MULTIPLE EFFECTS
(a–c)
          1. Overall effects

            a. choose real life over virtual life

            b. _____

            c. _____

5 Make an outline about the effects the technology you have chosen has had on its users and on society. Think about how you will organize and order the causes and effects from your flowchart. Make sure to include background information, a thesis statement, and a conclusion. Your conclusion could be a prediction, a solution, a question, or a summary of key points. Share your outline with a partner and discuss changes, if necessary.

6 Look at the information in Prepare to Write on page 230, your flowchart, and your outline. Now write the first draft of your cause-and-effect essay.

- Review the background information and thesis statement. Your essay will discuss the effects a particular technology (cause) has had on the user and society. (Note that you will not write about the causes leading up to the creation of the technology.)

- Make sure your body paragraphs include correct subordinators and prepositional phrases to express cause and effect.

- Choose the conclusion type that will best describe the effects on which you have focused.

REVISE: Using Transitions

1 Read the sentences. Which sentence introduces a cause first? Which one introduces an effect first?

a. As a consequence of relying on smartphones for driving directions, we have lost our ability to read maps.

b. We have lost our ability to read maps as a consequence of relying on smartphones.

Transitions

Certain words act as signals in sentences to show cause-and-effect relationships. In addition to subordinators and prepositional phrases that you studied in Grammar for Writing, page 227, transitions are a way to show this relationship. Transitions introduce the effect and are used in the second of two related sentences.

Cause-and-effect relationships signaled by a transition can be written as one sentence with the clauses separated by a semicolon and a comma following the transition word or phrase. This relationship can also be written as two sentences. Although the transition generally introduces the second (effect) sentence, it can be placed in several positions.

Cause: More and more people have smartphones today.

Effect: people have more and more interruptions in their lives.

As one sentence:

More and more people have smartphones today; as a result, people have more and more interruptions in their lives.

As two sentences:

1. More and more people have smartphones today. As a result, people have more and more interruptions in their lives.

2. More and more people have smartphones today. People, as a result, have more and more interruptions in their lives.

Transitions show the relationship between the two ideas.

Introducing the Effect with Transitions

as a result
consequently
so
for this reason
therefore
thus
as a consequence

Stating Effects with Transitions

When using transitions, the effect is always stated after the cause.

continued on next page

Punctuation When Using Transitions

The **effect** is introduced by words such as *consequently, as a result, for this reason, therefore,* and *thus*. Cause and effect can be combined into one sentence by using a semicolon and a comma.

> You can receive a continuous stream of messages and alerts on a smartphone; **consequently, you are able to stay up-to-date on news anytime and anyplace.**

They can also be two separate sentences.

> You can receive a continuous stream of messages and alerts on a smartphone.
>
> **As a result, you are able to stay up-to-date on news anytime and anyplace.**

Be careful. A sentence with *so* uses only a comma.

> You can receive a continuous stream of messages and alerts on a smartphone, **so you are able to stay up-to-date on news anytime and anyplace.**

2 **Use transitions to complete the paragraph based on the outline in Write, Exercise 3, page 233. Try to use a variety of different transitions.**

The writer of the *Unplugging* article wanted her family to enjoy an electronic-free vacation;

_____ , she took them to a remote island in the wilderness of British Columbia.

On the first day of the vacation, her son was suffering from acute smartphone withdrawal;

_____ , he couldn't enjoy the beauty of their surroundings. On the other hand,

her husband and daughter were doing fine. They had found things to do that didn't rely on

electronics, _____ they suffered no withdrawal symptoms. As time passed,

her son forgot about his smartphone. _____ , he was able to have a good

time at the beach and enjoy reading. He was no longer thinking only about his smartphone.

_____ , he was also able to have fun hiking and swimming.

3 **Write C (cause) or E (effect) for each set of sentences. Then combine the sentences two ways using transitions. Use commas and semicolons correctly.**

1. _C_ Employees at usemyphone.com started taking predictable time off.

   _E_ There was increased efficiency and collaboration among employees at usemyphone.com.

   (as a result) *Employees at usemyphone.com started taking predictable time off; as a result, there was increased efficiency and collaboration among employees.*

   (for this reason) *Employees at usemyphone.com started taking predictable time off. For this reason, there was increased efficiency and collaboration among employees.*

2. _____ It is easy to stay in contact with people even when they are not at home.

_____ Many people have smartphones.

(so) _____

_____

_____

(therefore) _____

_____

_____

3. _____ People cannot concentrate or think deeply.

_____ Smartphones create an environment of constant interruptions and distractions.

(consequently)_____

_____

_____

(thus) _____

_____

_____

4. _____ There are approximately 40,000 medical apps available today for smartphones and tablets.

_____ It is like having a health expert at your fingertips.

(as a consequence) _____

_____

_____

(thus) _____

_____

_____

5. _____ Smartphone apps can remotely turn on and off the heat in your home when you are out.

   _____ Homeowners can save money and help to cut down on the use of fossil fuels.

   (as a result) _____

   _____

   _____

   (so) _____

   _____

   _____

6. _____ The number of hardcover and paperback books being sold has declined.

   _____ Many people use tablets and e-readers for most of their reading.

   (for this reason) _____

   _____

   _____

   (consequently) _____

   _____

   _____

4 Now go back to the first draft of your essay.

- Add cause and effect transitions as needed.

- Try to use the grammar and some of the vocabulary from the unit.

🔘 **Go to MyEnglishLab for more skill practice.**

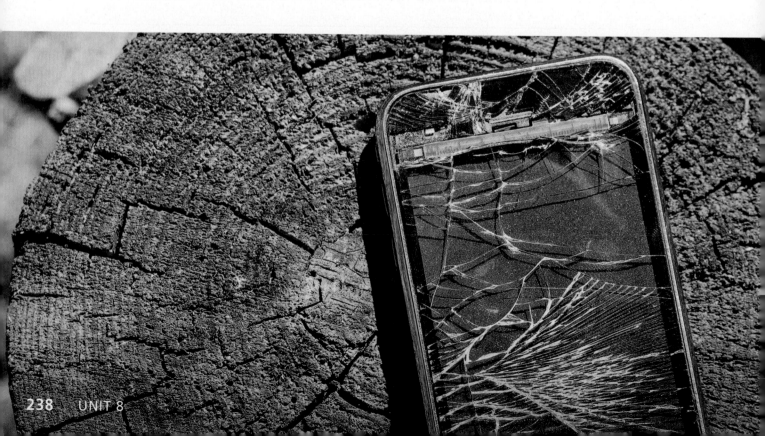

EDIT: Writing the Final Draft

APPLY Write the final draft of your essay and submit it to your teacher. Carefully edit it for grammatical and mechanical errors, such as spelling, capitalization, and punctuation. Consider how to apply the vocabulary, grammar, and writing skills from the unit. Use the checklist to help you.

FINAL DRAFT CHECKLIST

☐ Does the essay have a clear topic and controlling idea?

☐ Does the essay follow your outline?

☐ Does the essay have effective support and details or examples?

☐ Does the essay have appropriate cause-and-effect sentences?

☐ Does the essay have an effective or thought-provoking conclusion?

☐ Does the essay have effective cause-and-effect transitions?

☐ Do you use vocabulary from the unit?

ALTERNATIVE WRITING TOPIC

APPLY Computer technologies have both advantages and disadvantages for their users and for society in general. What do you think are the three biggest advantages and the three biggest disadvantages? Explain. Use the grammar and vocabulary from the unit.

CHECK WHAT YOU'VE LEARNED

Check (✔) the outcomes you've met and vocabulary you've learned. Put an X next to the skills and vocabulary you still need to practice.

Learning Outcomes

☐ **Infer an author's appeal to authority**

☐ **Take three-column notes to show time sequence**

☐ **Identify referents for the pronoun *it***

☐ **Use subordinators and prepositional phrases**

☐ **Use transitions**

☐ **Write a cause-and-effect essay**

Vocabulary

☐ anxiety

☐ compulsive

☐ conscious

☐ dependency

☐ device AWL

☐ diminish AWL

☐ dysfunction

☐ ensure AWL

☐ influx

☐ literally

☐ relent

☐ temptation

☐ trigger (*v.*) AWL

☐ twitch

☐ urge (*n.*)

☐ withdrawal

Multi-word Units

☐ **wean (someone) away from**

🔊 Go to **MyEnglishLab** to watch a video about video games, access the Unit Project, and take the Unit 8 Achievement Test.

EXPAND VOCABULARY

UNIT 4

Vocabulary

action

active

concept `AWL`

cognitive

neural

novel

numerous

percent `AWL`

predict

psychologist `AWL`

UNIT 5

Vocabulary

ancient

constant `AWL`

ideal

limited

loveless

personal

practical

remaining

shimmering

youthful

UNIT 6

Multi-word Units

called up

clear out

come up

dry up

end up

figure out

fixed up

found out

go back

keep on

let down

pick up

sitting around

think back

UNIT 8

Vocabulary	**Multi-word Units**
addiction	blinded to
avoid	can't stand
commitment `AWL`	
contemplation	
ignore `AWL`	
frequently	
repeatedly	
search	
shun	
steals	

ACADEMIC WORD LIST VOCABULARY AWL

Words with an * are target vocabulary in the unit. The remainder of the words appear in context in the reading texts.

abandon* (v.)
abstract
academic
access (v.)
accessibility
accumulate*
achieve*
achievement
acquire*
administration
adult (adj.)
adult (n.)
advocate* (n.)
affect (v.)
alter
alternative*
analyst
analyze
apparent
apparently*
approach* (n.)
area
aspect*
assembly
assignment
assume
assurance
attachment
attain
attitude
attribute (n.)
author (n.)
available
awareness
benefit (v.)
benefit* (n.)
bonds (n.)
brief (adj.)

capability
capable
category*
challenge* (n.)
challenging (adj.)
chapter
chart (v.)
chemical (n.)
circumstance
classic
colleague
comment (v.)
commit
commitment*
communicate
communication
community
compensate*
computer
concentrate
concept*
conclude
conclusion
conduct
confirm
consensus*
consist (v.)
constant* (adj.)
constant (n.)
constantly
constitute
consult* (v.)
consume*
consumer
contact (n.)
context
contrary
contribute

controversy*
conventional*
coordination
coordinator
corporation
create
creative
culture
data
debate (n.)
decade
define
definitely
definition
demonstrate
depressed (adj.)
depression
despite
detect*
device*
devote*
devotion
diminish*
display (v.)
diverse
dominate
draft (v.)
economic
economics (n.)
editor
element
emerging* (adj.)
emphasis
emphatic*
enable
enormous
ensure*
environment*

environmental
estimate (*n.*)
estimate* (*v.*)
eventually
evidence
evolutionary
evolve
exclude
exhibit (*v.*)
expert (*adj.*)
expert (*n.*)
expertise*
expose
exposure
feature (*v.*)
fee
file
final
finally
financial
flexible*
focus (*v.*)
formula
founder
framework
fundamental
funding (*n.*)
furthermore
generation
global
globe
goal
grade (*n.*)
grant (*n.*)
highlight (*n.*)
hypothesize*
identify
ignore*
image*
imagery

immigrant
impact* (*n.*)
implement
inappropriate
incident
indistinct
individual (*adj.*)
individual (*n.*)
inevitably*
insecure
inspect
institute
institution
integral
intelligence
intelligent
intelligently
intensity
interact
interaction*
interpret*
invariably
investigate
investigation
investment
invisible
involve
issue (*n.*)
item
job
journal (*n.*)
layer (*n.*)
lecture
legal
legally
link* (*v.*)
locate
mechanism
media
medical

mental
method
military
minimum
monitor (*v.*)
motivate
motivation
negative
network (*n.*)
norm (*adj.*)
normal
normally
notion
obvious*
ongoing
option
output
overall
panel (*n.*)
participate
partner (*n.*)
passive
perceive
percent*
percentage
perception*
period
persistence
perspective
phenomenon
philosopher
physical
plus (*prep.*)
policy
portion
pose (*v.*)
positive
potential (*adj.*)
potential* (*n.*)
potentially

predict

predictable*

preliminary

presumptuous*

previous

previously

primarily

prime

prior

process (n.)

process (v.)

professional (n.)

prohibitive

project (n.)

project (v.)

proportion

psychologically

psychologist*

psychology

publication

publish

purchase (v.)

pursue

radically*

react

reaction

reconstructed (adj.)

recover

recovery

region

regional

relevance

reliable*

reliance

reluctant

rely

remove

require

required (adj.)

requirement

research (n.)

researcher

reside

resident

respond

response

restore

retain*

reveal

revolutionize*

role

schedule (n.)

schedule (v.)

scheme (n.)

security

seek

sequencing (n.)

shift (n.)

similar

similarly

source (n.)

source (v.)

specifically

sphere

strategy

stress (n.)

stressed (adj.)

structure (n.)

summarize

survey (n.)

survival

survive

suspend

tape (v.)

target (n.)

task (n.)

team

technical

technically

technique

technological

technology

tense (n.)

text (n.)

theme

theory

thereby

topic

trace (n.)

transform*

trend (n.)

trigger* (v.)

ultimately*

unconventional

underestimating

unique*

virtual

vision

visual (adj.)

visualise

volunteer (n.)

volunteer (v.)

widespread

GRAMMAR BOOK REFERENCES

NorthStar: Reading and Writing Level 4, Fifth Edition	*Focus on Grammar, Level 4*, Fifth Edition	*Azar's Understanding and Using English Grammar*, Fifth Edition
Unit 1 Past Perfect	**Unit 4** Past Perfect and Past Perfect Progressive	**Chapter 2** Past Perfect: 2-8
Unit 2 Gerunds and Infinitives	**Unit 9** Gerunds and Infinitives	**Chapter 14** Gerunds and Infinitives Part 1: 14-1, 14-2, 14-3, 14-4, 14-5, 14-6, 14-7, 14-8, 14-9, 14-10, 14-11,14-12 **Chapter 15** Gerunds and Infinitives Part 2: 15-1, 15-2, 15-3, 15-4, 15-5, 15-6, 15-7, 15-8, 15-9, 15-10
Unit 3 Past Unreal Conditionals	**Unit 23** Past Unreal Conditional Sentences	**Chapter 20** Unreal in the Past: 20-4
Unit 4 Adjective Clauses	**Unit 12** Adjective Clauses with Subject Relative Pronouns **Unit 13** Adjective Clauses with Object Relative Pronouns	**Chapter 13** Adjective Clauses: 13-1, 13-2, 13-3, 13-4, 13-5, 13-6, 13-7, 13-8, 13-9, 13-10, 13-11
Unit 5 Simple Past, Present Perfect, Present Perfect Progressive	**Unit 3** Simple Past, Present Perfect, Present Perfect Progressive	**Chapter 1** Simple Past Tense: 1-4 **Chapter 2** Present Perfect vs. Simple Past: 2-6 Present Perfect Progressive: 2-7
Unit 6 Concessions		**Chapter 13** Showing Direct Contrast: *While*: 17-5 Adverb Clauses of Condition: 17-8, 17-9, 17-10, 17-11

NorthStar: Reading and Writing Level 4, Fifth Edition	*Focus on Grammar, Level 4, Fifth Edition*	*Azar's Understanding and Using English Grammar, Fifth Edition*
Unit 7 Transitions and Subordinators to Compare and Contrast		**Chapter 13** Expressing Contrast: Using *Even Though*: 17-4 Showing Direct Contrast: While: 17-5 **Chapter 19** Showing Contrast: 19-7 Showing Direct Contrast: 19-8
Unit 8 Subordinators and Prepositional Phrases that Express Cause		**Chapter 19** Using *Because Of* and *Due To*: 19-2 Cause and Effect: Using *Therefore, Consequently,* and *So*: 19-3 Other Ways of Expressing Cause and Effect: *Such...That* and *So...That*: 19-5

CREDITS

Unit 1
Pages 2–3: Ollyy/Shutterstock; 4 (background): Thesomeday123/Shutterstock; 7: Geraint Lewis/ Alamy Stock Photo; 14: Marka/Alamy Stock Photo; 16–17: Triff/Shutterstock.

Unit 2
Page 32–33: Photocreo Michal Bednarek/Shutterstock; 34: Perry/Shutterstock; 36: Bob London/Alamy Stock Photo; 37: Goir/Shutterstock; 42 (Marla Runyan): Michael Steele/Getty Images; 42–43 (background: clouds, sky): GraphiTect/Shutterstock; 42–43 (background: running track): Topimages/Shutterstock; 54: Oranzy Photography/ Shutterstock.

Unit 3
Page 60–61: Fotohunter/Shutterstock; 64 (background): Adam Gault/OJO Images Ltd/Alamy Stock Photo; 70 (bottom): Vladimir Gjorgiev/Shutterstock.

Unit 4
Page 86–87: The Old Major/Shutterstock; 91: Africa Studio/Shutterstock; 96 (chimpanzee): Anup Shah/The Image Bank/Getty Images; 96–97 (background): Berezka_ Klo/Shutterstock; 97 (bees): Bettapoggi/Shutterstock; 103: Maciej Olszewski/Shutterstock; 110: Africa Studio/ Shutterstock.

Unit 5
Pages 116–117: Simona Pilolla 2/Shutterstock; 120–123 (background: paper texture): Andrius_Saz/Shutterstock; 120–123 (background: floral motif): HiSunnySky/ Shutterstock; 121 (Blue Grotto): Boris Karpinski/ Alamy Stock Photo; 122 (wedding rings): Danko Mykola/ Shutterstock; 127: Creative Family/Shutterstock.

Unit 6
Pages 144–145: M_Agency/Shutterstock; 149: Robert Kneschke/Shutterstock; 154: Denise Hager, Catchlight Visual Services/Alamy Stock Photo.

Unit 7
Pages 176–177: Fotos593/Shutterstock; 180 (Titan Tiger fish): Paulo Oliveira/Alamy Stock Photo; 180–182(background): Mr.Anaked/Shutterstock; 183: Katy Flaty/Shutterstock; 187–188 (background: ocean): Johnny Giese/Shutterstock; 187 (boom trapping garbage): Nightman1965/ Shutterstock; 188 (environmental activists): Ritchie B Tong /EPA/Shutterstock; 192–193: Photoraidz/Shutterstock.

Unit 8
Pages 206–207: Ollyy/Shutterstock; 210: Snapic Photo Production/ Shutterstock; 211: Cobalt88/Shutterstock; 212: Amenic181/Shutterstock; 217: Gladskikh Tatiana/ Shutterstock; 218: Abscent/Shutterstock; 220: Altanaka/ Shutterstock; 238: Inspired_by_the_light/Shutterstock.

ILLUSTRATION CREDITS

ElectraGraphics

NOTES

NOTES

NOTES

NOTES

NOTES

NOTES

NOTES